A Poetics of Translation

A Poetics of Translation
Between Chinese and English Literature

David Jasper
Geng Youzhuang
Wang Hai

Editors

BAYLOR UNIVERSITY PRESS

Cover Design by Hannah Feldmeier
Cover Art from *The Chinese Classics: With a Translation, Critical and Exegetical Notes, Prolegomena, and Copious Indexes*, by James Legge, D.D. (Hong Kong: At The Author's; London: Trübner, 60, Paternoster Row, 1800).

Library of Congress Cataloging-in-Publication Data

Names: Jasper, David, editor. | Geng, Youzhuang, editor. | Wang, Hai, 1977– editor.
Title: A poetics of translation : between Chinese and English literature / David Jasper, Geng Youzhuang , Wang Hai, editors.
Description: Waco : Baylor University Press, 2016. | Includes bibliographical references and index.
Identifiers: LCCN 2015026596 | ISBN 9781481304184 (hardback : alk. paper)
Subjects: LCSH: Translating and interpreting—Social aspects. | Chinese literature—History and criticism. | English literature—History and criticism. | Chinese literature—Translations into English. | English literature—Translations into Chinese. | East and West. | Written communication in literature.
Classification: LCC P306.8.C6 P64 2016 | DDC 418/.020951—dc23
LC record available at http://lccn.loc.gov/2015026596

Printed in the United States of America on acid-free paper with a minimum of 30 percent post-consumer waste recycled content.

CONTENTS

PART II
STUDIES IN TRANSLATION: CHINA AND THE MISSIONARIES

PART III
TRANSLATION AS DISLOCATION

INTRODUCTION

This book of essays is the result of academic conversations between scholars in China and the West relating to issues in translation. These essays have their beginnings in a series of conferences hosted by Renmin University of China in Beijing. "Issues in translation" refers not only to the linguistic challenges of translating from Chinese into English or English into Chinese but also to the wider questions of cultural translation at a time when China is in a period of rapid change and the world is having to adjust in response; and scholars within the humanities are required to learn very quickly to live within the exchange of ideas often with few precedents to guide or advise them. Of necessity, some of the thinking in these essays is therefore experimental and tentative, as in the case of Wang Hai's work on the idea of *wu wei* (lit. "doing nothing") and radical passivity in the reflection of Western thinkers like Maurice Blanchot. We do not apologize for this spirit of experimentation and for the variety that marks these essays. "Translation" is a widely used and disputed term, and it always has been. The deliberately wide range of essays indicate that translation can aspire to being a precise and highly technical science, or it can be broad and visionary—and each has its place. We can therefore include the highly scholarly work of James Legge, or the poetic vision of

Ezra Pound; both exercise the cross-cultural discipline of observation and of being observed.

Western literature, from the mysterious figure of Marco Polo to the "deliberate fictions"[1] of Daniel Defoe and Mark Twain, has constructed portraits of China born of dreamy parody or sheer prejudice. It was, perhaps, the philosopher Leibniz in the seventeenth century who, though he never set foot in China, studied and wrote extensively on China, using his correspondence with a number of Jesuits living in China and his sense of the similarity between his own mathematical and religious pursuit of the harmony of matter, the power of reason, and his understanding of Chinese thought. In his most important work on the subject, *Novissima Sinica* (*Latest News from China*) (1699), Leibniz promoted the "practical philosophy" of Chinese life and the sound moral sense of the "natural religion" of Confucianism.[2] In his later writings, Leibniz turned the issue around to a degree, acknowledging that the West might teach philosophical insights to China, not least in the matter of textual interpretation. What is remarkable is how close Leibniz, using the traditions of the Jesuits and Matteo Ricci, is to portraying the painstaking and highly scholarly "translations" of James Legge, missionary and Oxford professor, one hundred fifty years later.

Nor, as Jonathan Spence has clearly indicated,[3] is the imaginative genius of literature to be dismissed in our quest for mutual understanding between cultures East and West. Although but a few pages long, Jorge Luis Borges' dense, metaphorical, and multilayered story "The Garden of Forking Paths" is almost impossible to summarize. Suspended between Shandong Province in China, a house in England, and the Germany of the First World War, the story's narrator is Dr. Yu Tsun, a "former professor of English at the *Hochschule* in Tsingtao," and, it would appear, a German secret agent. The key figure is the Englishman Stephen Albert who "had been a missionary in Tientsin 'before aspiring to become a Sinologist.'"[4] In other words, Albert (who is described by Yu Tsun as "no less great than Goethe") is a kind of fictional James Legge, an interpreter of classical Chinese texts and of labyrinths, one of which he appears to inhabit. There are stories within stories—just as Eric Ziolkowski explores in his essay on the great literature of China (*The Journey to the West*) and the West (*Hamlet* and *Don Quixote*)[5]—and a great-grandfather, Ts'ui Pên, who aspires "to write a novel that might be even more populous than the *Hung Lu Meng*."[6] That is Borges' reference to the great eighteenth-century Chinese novel *The Dream of Red Mansions*, set within the riddling space of a garden.

Borges' literature, even with its dreams and fantasies, cannot be dismissed from our scholarly deliberations. Translation is also about observing and being observed, about creating and being created in the minds of others. As Christian missionaries like Legge were drawn by the mysteries of the Chinese texts they labored to translate and interpret, so truth becomes wider, more relative, more difficult than their theology had seemed to have room for.

And yet the contributors to this book are all scholars with a background in either literary studies or religion. Although most of the essays are based in readings of literary texts, this is not exclusively the case. Andrew Hass, in the final essay in the book, begins his discussion in the context of a recent exhibition by contemporary Chinese artists in the Metropolitan Museum of Art in New York and is concerned with graphic differences in script between China and the West. In the work of these artists (who have left China), Chinese characters become unreadable as texts but are now shown as works of art in strange acts of self-translation.[7] And as the characters become unreadable, we enter the realm of the mystical and the pursuit of a "pure language," not so far removed from the obsession of the eighteenth century with the recovery of the original language of humanity, the so-called language of Adam—an obsession in which Chinese, set apart from the Indo-European roots of language, played its part.

All the essays in this book reflect in some way the final impossibility of the task of translation—always, at best, approximate, often reflecting much more about the cultures from which we come than those to which we reach out, for whatever purpose. And yet there are universals, it would seem, though often mysterious and elusive, in human creativity and human thought.

The book is divided into three sections. The first, "Readings in the East and West," contains three essays by David Lyle Jeffrey, Eric Ziolkowski, and John T. P. Lai, all concerned with comparative readings of texts from East and West, and their merging in translation. Jeffrey—who introduces the key figure of the missionary scholar James Legge, the first professor of Chinese language and literature in Oxford—addresses the importance of poetics and the importance of intuition, even in one so often rather prosaic as Legge, in the pursuit of the ancient Chinese sense of the religious and "transcendence." Legge was well aware of the relationship between poetry and law (both natural and revealed) in the Psalms as well as in the classical Chinese odes interpreted by Kong-zi.[8] In his conclusion, Jeffrey expands the understanding of translation to that of the exchange of consciousness between East and West.

Eric Ziolkowski's essay, the only literary exercise that is not directly related in some way to the Bible and scripture, is a comparative reading of three great works of literature from three different cultures—England, Spain, and China. Each one of them—*Hamlet*, *Don Quixote*, and *The Journey to the West* (surely one of the greatest "novels" ever written)—provides examples of the "tale within the tale" and of narratives nestling within narratives as literature enfolds upon itself, and echoes between texts are heard across vast distances of space and time. In the great "novels" of China, *The Journey to the West* or *The Dream of Red Mansions*, fiction dramatizes its own fictionality, as in Proust or Italo Calvino, until the world becomes text and reading becomes universal (a theme taken up by Elisabeth Jay in her essay). For most scholars and readers in the West, the great works of Chinese literature (we have not given any attention to contemporary Chinese literature as it appears in endless streams of translations in Western bookstores) are still largely unknown outside very narrow circles of experts; it is our hope that this condition can be addressed and a readership for books like *The Journey to the West* or *Dream of Red Mansions* can be encouraged outside the small coterie of scholars of comparative literature, so that they take, for Western readers, their proper place alongside Dostoevsky, Dante, Shakespeare, and Aeschylus. Chinese literature and language will then be perceived quite differently from the manner in which it was perceived in the late nineteenth century, when Legge was described as a "professor of an exotically irrelevant language."[9] Until the nineteenth century in England, perceptions of China rarely extended beyond the fantasies of "chinoiserie,"[10] and even the often formidable linguistic scholarship of missionaries in China, as is made clear in the essays of John T. P. Lai and B. H. McLean (in the second section of this book), rarely took the reading of Chinese texts much further than the distortions of evangelization and Christian teaching.

As late as 1913, Timothy Richard published his "translation" of *The Journey to the West* as a Christian allegory to be compared to *The Pilgrim's Progress*. As the new subject of "sinology" began to become more evident in England with the establishment of university professorships in London, Oxford, and Cambridge, the interpretation of Chinese texts, as described by Elisabeth Jay, remained too often rooted in a preoccupation with the cultural concerns of Victorian England rather than with China itself.[11] The second section of the book consists of five essays by Trevor Hart, Zhao Jing, B. H. McLean, Elisabeth Jay, and David Jasper, all of which concentrate on the translation and interpretation of Chinese texts by European missionaries working in China in the nineteenth century. As David Jasper's essay makes clear, this often involved vigorous debate between these early Western scholars as the new field of sinology developed.

The third section of the book, titled "Translation as Dislocation," draws upon the work of Chinese scholars (with the exception of Andrew Hass) and the West as perceived through Chinese eyes. For in China, also, as Yang Huilin's paper clearly indicates, there was a move to read and translate Western literature that goes back at least to the early years of the nineteenth century. Chinese interest in Shakespeare begins not, indeed, with a translation of the plays themselves but with a translation of Charles Lamb's *Tales from Shakespeare*, though this was followed by a number of translations of the plays by both Chinese and Western translators including the American missionary Laura M. White. In some ways, Yang's essay indicates the perhaps final impossibility of translating *The Merchant of Venice* and its rootedness in Western theological conflicts into Chinese. And yet we are called to speak in the language of literature across the gaps that divide us, and as Yang puts it, "Comparative studies should go further to understand the contexts of the varied understandings."

Yang ends his essay with a reference to John Dryden on "English dramatic poetry," and it is with Dryden that Yang's colleague at Renmin University, Geng Youzhuang, begins his essay. Geng reminds us that translation of great poetry is not simply a matter of philological and linguistic expertise but often a return to the elusive genius of "poetics." It is hearing the echoes in poetry that only the true poet—even one originally wholly innocent of the language from which the poetry originally speaks—can respond to the poetic. Is this another universal principle in literature? Ezra Pound knew no Chinese at all when he first translated ancient Chinese poems, yet as he put it, "Silence captured me." The evaluation of Pound's "translations" from the Chinese must draw upon an element of the subjective, yet it cannot be without significance that one Chinese scholar, looking back with approval to the judgment of T. S. Eliot, has called Pound "the inventor of Chinese poetry for our time."[12] If this is arguably the case, then it serves to indicate that the elusive quality of resonance is somehow central to the translation of language and culture—a theme that supports also Wang Hai's essay on Maurice Blanchot and the concept of *wu wei.*

Very different from the poetic work of Pound was the experience upon which the essays by Trevor Hart, Elisabeth Jay, B. H. McLean, John Lai, Zhao Jing, David Jasper, as well as David Lyle Jeffrey in this volume ultimately draw—that of the Western Protestant missionary enterprise in China from the early nineteenth century, and the meeting of the classical literature of China with the texts of the Bible and its antique poetry. It is evidence of the largely negligible place of the serious scholarly study of Chinese language and culture in Europe, and especially in England, that it was not until the later years of the nineteenth century that professorships in Chinese were established in the two ancient English universities of Oxford and Cambridge. James Legge, at Oxford, had been a missionary in Hong Kong for thirty years before his academic promotion, a calling that is reflected in his massive and learned translations of the Chinese classics into English. It is to the scholarly work of Christian missionaries and one early sinologist with whom Legge unwillingly found himself in conflict, Herbert Giles, a former diplomat in China and professor of Chinese at Cambridge, that many of the essays in this volume are dedicated. From the work of Walter Medhurst early in the nineteenth century to Timothy Richard much later, attention to the Chinese language and its literature in such works as *The Journey to the West* was part of the task of the Christian evangelist. It was only in the work of Legge and Giles (as shown in the essays of Jeffrey, Hart, Zhao, Jay, and Jasper) that the true foundations were wrought of the study of comparative religion and literary culture and that perceptions of Chinese literature and language and their cultural and historical contexts were gradually changed in the earlier years of the twentieth century.

As scholars we do not necessarily claim special originality. The work of many others such as Chloë Starr precedes us, while the field of Sino-Christian theology, as well as the study of the ancient Chinese religious traditions, is now flourishing in China and, indeed, further afield. None of us among the Western scholars can claim to be professional sinologists—but that may be a strength as much as a weakness. For the task of the scholar is as much as anything to listen and to be attentive, seeking to make meaning where the signs are hard or even almost impossible to read and hear. It is also to be sensitive to the insights of the imagination in both the literary and the visual arts, listening to the "resonances" within and between cultures. Perhaps as important as anything, the meetings from which these papers have grown have been opportunities to develop new forms of collegiality among scholars, so that the meeting of East and West in a rapidly developing world and global culture is not simply in economic or political terms but offers the beginning of new forms of friendship within the field of the humanities such as only universities, when they are at their best, can offer. As one of our colleagues at Renmin University of China once put it, we can only open doors through which others who come after us might pass. It is our hope that this book will open doors and windows between East and West, and that, among our readers, a few will feel drawn to follow where we have tried to lead.

David Jasper, Geng Youzhuang, and Wang Hai

Part I

READINGS IN THE EAST AND WEST

1

POETIC DESIRE AND THE LAWS OF HEAVEN

James Legge's Shi-jing *and the Translation of Consciousness*

David Lyle Jeffrey

In his gracious introduction to Arthur Waley's 1937 translation of *Shi-jing* (诗经, *The Book of Songs*), Stephen Owen remarks that this ancient collection of "odes" remains to its culture "both poetry and scripture."[1] Though it appears in connection with Waley's work, this judgment was first formed for English readers by Waley's predecessor, James Legge, in his landmark edition and translation of 1871,[2] and it instances a reverence which has become basic to Western readings of these poems ever since.[3] In Legge's translation (and rich exegetical and philological notes), it becomes almost possible to imagine the reverence with which Kong-zi himself received and preserved the ancient odes. The degree to which Legge's magisterial work makes this illusion conceivable, I will argue here, is a function of his imaginative philological intuition and empathetic desire to achieve personal participation in the spiritual ethos of the ancient culture in which the songs were sung. To achieve this required of him much more than a technical semiotics and a pursuit of linguistic equivalence.

It will be evident from my title that I have taken my theme from the ancient "The Great Preface" to the *Odes*, which Legge printed and translated in his edition, especially as the preface itself articulates a theory of poetry. I want to suggest that Legge, in his response to that text as a translator, understood the preface as a cryptic theory of poetic diction, analogous in some respects to such theories in the West, but embodying a conception of poetic language both similar and dissimilar to the European examples by which he and his fellow missionary translators had been trained. His deep desire to understand the dissimilarity, I suggest, is what sets his work apart. It also doubtless confused and alarmed those among his colleagues, both missionary and academic, who lacked his level of achievement in the language, his philological intuitions, and perhaps also the intensity of his affections for China.

Poetic Diction

According to Owen Barfield, in his famous book on the subject:

> When words are selected and arranged in such a way that their meaning either arouses, or is obviously intended to arouse, aesthetic imagination, the result may be described as *poetic diction*. Imagination is recognizable as aesthetic, when it produces pleasure merely by its proper activity. Meaning includes the whole content of a word, or of a group of words arranged in a particular order, other than the actual sounds of which they are composed.

Barfield goes on to say, disarmingly, that he means by poetry "a realm of human experience in which such an expressions as 'prophets old' may, and probably will, 'mean' something quite different from 'old prophets.'"[4] Though Barfield wrote a century after Legge, the view of poetic diction he expresses is congruent with definitions with which Legge would have been familiar (e.g., those of Horace in his *Ars Poetica*, referred to by both).

But that is only part of the story. Barfield is, of course, defining the general character of poetic diction within Indo-European literature cultures as he also knows them, and yet it will be evident that his remarks about word order and arrangement require to be understood and applied somewhat differently when applied to synthetic languages (Latin, German), transitional languages (early modern English), or analytic and isolating languages, the premier example of which is Chinese. Barfield's characterization invites comparison with the definitions given in "The Great Preface," a document not only from a different linguistic context but that, even if we follow Choo He (and Legge himself) in suspecting

"The Great Preface" to be largely a Han dynasty work, probably reflects a Sino-Tibetan conception of poetic language centuries older.

"The Great Preface" begins by grounding poetic diction in the practice of concentrated meditation:

> 1. Poetry is the product of earnest thought. Thought [cherished] in the mind becomes earnest, exhibited in words, it becomes poetry.[5]

We may presumably take the ancient author to be excluding both normatively discursive speech and the prose of chronicles and records of the court such as those that Kong-zi also preserved and Legge translated. Barfield excluded prose on the same basis. What follows here, however, is an intensifier, for strong emotion is identified as organic to ancient Chinese poetry:

> 2. The feelings move inwardly, and are embodied in words. When words are insufficient for them, recourse is had to sighs and exclamations. When sighs and exclamations are insufficient . . . recourse is had to the prolonged utterances of song. When those prolonged utterances of song are insufficient . . . unconsciously the hands begin to move and the feet to dance.[6]

This is not quite an analogue to Wordsworth's "spontaneous overflow of powerful emotions recollected in tranquility"[7] but a notion of more immediate and even charismatic relation between emotional impulse and expression such as Legge would readily have identified with another non-European poetry, especially as one finds it in the Hebrew Psalms, poems he knew intimately in Hebrew as well as in Latin and the English of the King James Version (KJV). In the Hebrew Psalms, this relationship between intensity of emotion and subsequent poetic expression is regularly articulated. For example:

יָגַעְתִּי—בְּאַנְחָתִי
אַשְׂחֶה בְכָל-לַיְלָה מִטָּתִי
בְּדִמְעָתִי עַרְשִׂי אַמְסֶה

I am weary with my groaning;
all the night make I my bed to swim;
I water my couch with my tears.

(Ps 6:6 KJV; cf. Ps 42:1-5)[8]

בְּשׁוּב יְהוָה אֶת־שִׁיבַת צִיּוֹן
הָיִינוּ כְּחֹלְמִים׃
אָז יִמָּלֵא שְׂחוֹק פִּינוּ
וּלְשׁוֹנֵנוּ רִנָּה

When the LORD turned again the captivity of Zion,
we were like them that dream.
Then was our mouth filled with laughter,
And our tongue with singing.

(Ps 126:1-2 KJV)

Often, contemplative psalms (such as Ps 53) will erupt into an exclamatory poem following (e.g., Ps 54), or the alteration will occur rapidly within one poem (e.g., Ps 40). Meditation that turns to praise and exaltation is characteristic of the Hebrew Psalter: "thou hast turned for me my mourning into dancing," says the poet (Ps 30:11). David is famous for his charismatic dance before the Ark of the Covenant (2 Sam 6:14), and there is reason to believe that some of the songs of Israel were performed with accompanying dance. Thus, Hebrew poetry that Legge knew well would have provided him some associative perspective for "The Great Preface" on these points concerning poetic composition and performance.

But "The Great Preface" proceeds to characterize a relationship between the music and internal harmony and style of poems for which there is only allusive parallel in the dedications and performance directions of the Psalter:

> The feelings go forth in sounds. When those sounds are artistically combined, we have what is called musical pieces. The style of such pieces in an age of good order is quiet, going on to be joyful;—the government is then a harmony. Their style in an age of disorder is resentful, going on to the expression of anger; the government is then a discord. Their style, when a state is going to ruin, is mournful, with the expression of retrospective thought; the people are then in distress.[9]

Here our ancient author makes a direct connection between the character and perhaps genre (as well as mood) of poetic diction, and the overall social well-being and harmony out of which the poets write. It will be evident that a presupposition of communal consciousness as effectively the source of poetic voice is strikingly different from modern notions of poetic voice, so much more inherently individualistic. What the author seems to be saying is that the writing of poetry and the diction peculiar to it will be profoundly reflective of the collective experience of harmony or disharmony in the state. He does not say, though I think the *Odes* themselves richly illustrate it, that the thought that deepens and is concentrated into words in many of the odes expresses a profound desire for such social harmony and sublimates the expression of personal desire accordingly. Even when the voice or persona of the poem is represented as that of an individual and the experience as intense, it is nonetheless a representative voice, and the poem is metonymic. In this too we may apply to many of the ancient Chinese odes what Robert Alter has said about poetry in Hebrew: "There are . . . many biblical poems in which any implied events, even metaphoric ones, are secondary while what is primary is a predicament, an image or a thematic idea that is amplified from verset to verset and from line to line."[10]

Finally, according to canon 5 of "The Great Preface," poetry in the *Odes* is not merely a key to the state of health and harmony of the people (as certainly it is in the Psalms), but ancient Chinese kings were said to employ poetry as a means of exemplifying healthy marital relations and such filial piety as could, at the level of family, undergird health in the wider society. Poetry is a bearer of social wisdom. This, too, is a topos in the Psalms, even where the poem's microcosm of society is a harem, as in Psalm 45, *eructavit cor meum*, an example that finds its parallel in the *Odes*.[11] It will be recognized that the theme of filial obedience and marital harmony is likewise a major theme in another book of Hebrew poetic discourse, namely the Proverbs. This, too, is a book of the Hebrew Bible that Legge would probably have memorized in his youth, since it was a practice to do so in the Scottish Congregational churches in which he grew up.

The fourth canon of "The Great Preface" would have struck anyone with a British education as quite compatible with their own views of how to train young minds for civil service: "[T]o set forth the successes and failures [of government] to move Heaven and Earth, and to excite spiritual Beings to action, there is no readier instrument than poetry." Barfield, a British lawyer, provides parallel insight to this and a similar passage in the *Lun Yu* of Confucius when he says that "just as the study of the law [in the Middle Ages in Europe] was a valuable exercise for other purposes besides the law, so today the study of poetry and the poetic element in all meaningful language is a valuable exercise for other purposes than the practice or better enjoyment of poetry."[12] For Barfield this is an application of his dictum that "only by imagination . . . can the world be known";[13] he was schooled in an era when the preferred training for the British civil service was still a degree in classics, not only for the sake of grounding language learning, but for training the mind to perceive in older cultures their inherent social decorum. In similar fashion, for Kong-zi and other early appreciators of the classical Chinese odes, it is evident that poetry was an instruction in the adaptation of human emotions and desires to a decorum in which order in the state could reflect more perfectly a universal or cosmic harmony, order in the heavens. This relation of poetry and law (natural and revealed) is likewise to be found everywhere in the Psalms, as Legge knew well, beginning with the very first lines of Psalm 1:

אַשְׁרֵי־הָאִישׁ אֲשֶׁר ׀ לֹא הָלַךְ בַּעֲצַת רְשָׁעִים
וּבְדֶרֶךְ חַטָּאִים לֹא עָמָד
וּבְמוֹשַׁב לֵצִים לֹא יָשָׁב׃
כִּי אִם בְּתוֹרַת יְהוָה חֶפְצוֹ
וּבְתוֹרָתוֹ יֶהְגֶּה יוֹמָם וָלָיְלָה׃

> Blessed is the man that walketh not in the counsel of the ungodly,
> nor standeth in the way of sinners,
> nor sitteth in the seat of the scornful.
> But his delight is in the law of the Lord,
> and in his law doth he meditate day and night.
>
> (Ps 1:1-2 KJV)

Legge was certainly aware that the Hebrew Psalms were composed more or less in the same era as the Chinese classical odes, and it is evident from his published work that he had speculated about this matter of their comparable antiquity.

Legge as Translator

Both James Legge and Owen Barfield, whom I have introduced by way of casting some light on Legge's formidable task as a translator of poetry, formed their theories in dialogue with Max Müller, the great comparatist of religion, who was Legge's contemporary and sometime colleague. Müller had maintained the view that Chinese and Western literary cultures were essentially incompatible, their poetry incommensurable.[14] Müller published this opinion in 1892, more than twenty years after Legge's translation of the *Odes*. Müller's sense that analogous translation would not work with Chinese texts in the way they did with European texts was, as almost everyone now acknowledges, well founded. Yet his belief that Eastern Sacred Books must be "judged from within"[15] may actually have been more fully appreciated by Legge, who had come to see that a qualitative appropriation of sense was much to be preferred to a word-for-word attempt at rendering a supposed "equivalent in English"—indeed, that such a traditional approach could effectively destroy the very meaning it sought to convey:

> Therefore, those who explain the Odes, may not insist on one term so as to do violence to a sentence, nor on a sentence so as to do violence to a general scope [*zhi*, meaning "will, determination, intention, purpose"]. They must try with their thought to meet that scope, and then we shall apprehend it.[16]

What does Legge mean by "scope"? As we shall see, a great deal.

It will be apparent to any multilingual person that between any two languages we can have apparently analogous translation with divergent indicative value being the unintended result. Thus the famous dictum about the impossibility of translating any kind of poetry accountably to the original: *traductore, tradittore*. The French equivalent of this curse is only slightly more optimistic: in Canada we say *traduction vers l'anglais*, implying that the translation never quite gets there. (Interestingly, French *traduction* produces in English "traduce," which means to tell a lie.) Legge was under no illusions regarding this general predicament, yet his confidence in meaningful translation was much greater than the cynicism of these clichés. His optimism may have owed in part to his Scottish nonconformist heritage, in which close attention to scriptural texts in teaching and sermonizing depended upon exegetical practices and competent use of the original biblical languages, Hebrew and Greek, as well as commentary in Latin. On this point Norman Girardot, in his landmark study of Legge, remarks admiringly that "Legge's incredibly diligent and prolonged effort in acquiring a familiarity with the Chinese commentarial tradition in the manner both of a native scholar and of an evangelical biblical exegete gives his English translations a special fidelity and commentarial authority."[17] For Legge, approaching the study of Chinese texts in the context of a disciplined approach to their traditional commentary was but to extend a long-established practice. His tireless memorization of the Bible and diligent pursuit of commentaries in various European languages, in addition to his several hours of daily study of Chinese with a competent native speaker, seem to have worked together to produce in him a sensitivity both to ethos and to verbal nuance few foreigners could match. It also helped to ensure that the special qualities of "scope" peculiar to ancient Chinese poetry was being continuously refracted through his understanding of the transmission and translation of the biblical texts he persistently worked and reworked over the entire course of his life.[18] He was aware, accordingly, of the impact of sound change as well as the evolution of meaning in words that characterize all language and that in Chinese no less than any other language problematize attempts to translate and interpret written texts long removed from their point of composition.

In fact, Chinese poses greater problems in regard to the relation of sound and sense than perhaps any other great language. As S. Robert Ramsey has remarked, in a European language such as English one can fairly readily reconstruct, especially in poetry because of the rhyming words (his example is the prologue of the *Canterbury Tales*), the sound values of an earlier epoch in the language. By comparison, the classical poems of China are mute. The modern reader does not hear a Tang verse the way it sounded when it was written. Instead,

> [the reader] customarily reads the characters with Mandarin (or perhaps Fukinese, Cantonese or Shanghainese) pronunciations, and in so doing treats the poem as if it had been written in a modern Chinese dialect. This removes it more than a thousand years from the time of the poet.[19]

Legge was keenly aware of this; the *shoo* (書, book) character he describes as a double, "pencil-speaking," and, he notes, it "is often used as a general designation for the written characters of the language."[20] Yet the pronunciation of even so universal a term is not uniform. That the characters yielded very different sounds in Fukien (Hokkien), Cantonese, and Mandarin was early on a challenge to him; as he studied the *Odes* and became aware that some characters stood in a one-to-one relation to an object or action, while others served "to give the sound without any indication of the component parts,"[21] his appreciation of the difficulty of accurate translation sharply increased. Though there are lexical patterns, such as the way in which most characters are formed by union of a radical and a phonetic element,[22] there were evident elements of sound-change that left developments in morphology almost untraceable. Linguistic specialists agree that ancient Chinese (ca. 1750–256 BC) had some inflections, with personal pronouns declined for case; one of the noun endings seems to have been *r*, now lost, interesting in relation to terms for "song" or "poem," for when we compare the general old Semitic and Hebrew *shir*, "song," with Chinese *shi*, a word that may once have had a final *r* and sounded very similar, we may be looking at a possible loanword.[23] Legge seems to have recognized that the ancient Chinese seems to have had heavy breathing or strong aspiration as a means of differentiating consonants, a parallel to old Hebrew.[24] Linguists now tend to think that, originally, ancient Chinese had no tones; Legge sees the evidence but opines that there may have been at least some tones by the time of the *Odes*.[25] An irrefragable evidence of sound-change for Legge is the failure in any modern dialect of otherwise predictable, regular ancient rhymes.[26]

More to the point of a translator's challenge, however, is the evidence of changes in meaning. Throughout Legge's copious and invaluable philological notes, one sees how change may have occurred in the meaning of various characters in a way obscure to ancient commentators and Legge alike. This can reduce the ancient commentators to speculation or to a creative adequation based on the normative meaning of that character in their own contemporary speech. Legge tries to adjudicate, often admirably, between historically separated definitions, but the problem of meaning change is sufficiently great that he occasionally pronounces a line (or more) simply untranslatable.[27] He also sees that an evolution in the range of meaning associated with a given character is traceable in the attempts, in different eras, to translate it. For example, in a note to *Woo e*, number 9 in the Odes of T'ang, he writes,

> 燠=煖 "warm;" but Choo makes it 久 "long-lasting;"—in consequence, that is, of the thickness of the robes, and their good quality. Others give the character the meaning of 安 "tranquil," "secure."[28]

It will be evident that, as in European languages, there is an evolution of meaning here related to the metaphorical possibilities in the term; metaphors easily become ossified, and their original sense fades. Occassionally, as in this example, there is a perceptible evolution from external physical sensation to internal psychological feeling. One of the indications of the direction of this evolution, and that it represents effectively an evolution of consciousness, is the development noticed also by Kalgren, namely that where in ancient Chinese there was a tendency to single character representation of nouns and verbs, there gradually emerged a doubling, perhaps so as to indicate the internalization of meaning. One of Kalgren's examples is the shift from *kien* (見, see) to *k'an kien* (看見, look-see), but a more indicative one for our purposes is the shift from *I* (意, meaning) to *i-si* (意思, meaning-thought). Lexically this is a movement from external definition to internal contemplation, the latter term of which, as we have seen, "The Great Preface" makes intrinsic to poetry and poetic diction.[29]

It may be helpful to recall an example from European languages to take the measure of this point on more familiar territory: all who deal with the Greek text of John's gospel realize that the writer's choice to employ the Greek term λόγος to refer to the incarnation was to situate his reader's appreciation of the appearance of the Jewish Messiah within the context of Hellenic philosophical thought. But this has not been unproblematic for translators and theologians alike: *logos* in the Greek of the pre-Socratic philosophers (e.g., Epicharmus of Syracuse) is a kind of divine prototype or ideal form of the cosmic intelligence. It has something of a derivative force of "reason" in Aristotle, without the transcendent reference. By the later Stoics it has come to mean something like "active life principle," a usage clearly in the background of John's use of Ἐν ἀρχῇ ἦν ὁ λόγος to refer to Jesus as the incarnation of the creating and sustaining wisdom instantiated in the cosmos itself. But once John's phrase is translated into Latin and other later European languages, this meaning evidently undergoes further development. Despite that his knowledge of Hebrew included an awareness of the fundamental bivalence in which *davar* (דְבָרֶ) can mean both "word" and "work," or "event," Jerome's *in principium erat verbum* preserves less of either the Hebrew register or the accumulated force of the Greek *logos*. When later European languages diverge further, separating *le verbe incarné* from *mot* and *parole*, or in Luther's German, opting for *im Anfang war das Wort*, a fissure widens between nominalistic reference and the idea of a transcendent principle. While in the KJV λόγος is translated "Word" somewhat less problematically in 1611 than it might be today, in Robert Morrison's translation it is rendered as *yán* (言, the spoken word). Here the misprision is genuinely misleading, for rather than the original Johannine sense, it interpolates the "biblical consciousness" common among free-church evangelicals. Legge would certainly have recognized the reflex, apparent also in Robert Morrison's dictionary, by which translators intent on translating a work like the Bible tend to look for analytic or dynamic equivalence for terms as they know them in vernacular contemporary translation and usage.[30] Legge's project of translation *from* Chinese to English of classic texts from Chinese antiquity was conceptually of greater scope, seeking a diachronic rather than merely synchronic understanding.

To Girardot's biography as well as that of Lauren Pfister, we are indebted for many telling clues to Legge's early philological self-discipline, so helpful for later work. He spent part of his adolescence translating George Buchanan's (1506–1582) "Latin rendition of the Psalms and his (Latin) history of Scotland" into English, then back into Latin and comparing it with the original.[31] This daunting sort of practice was encouraged by some of the most rigorous Scottish classicists of his day, and it persisted well into the next century. F. F. Bruce, the notable New Testament scholar, following his successful tenure as a professor of classical Greek and Latin in Glasgow, and holder of the Rylands Chair of Biblical Criticism and Exegesis at the University of Manchester, once answered a question about how he defined the term "theologian." Bruce replied, only in part facetiously, "A theologian, sir, is someone who can take the Septuagint Greek text of the Hebrew Scriptures, and without any aid beyond his own command of both languages, turn it back into something very like the original Hebrew and then, without appreciable error, return it to the Greek of the Septuagint."[32] Legge would, I think, have enjoyed the joke, identified with the standard, and concurred in its status as foundational to "theology."

Girardot adds to his assessment of Legge's virtues as a translator that he personally identified with Confucius; like Kong-zi, he both loved the ancient texts and sought to be their faithful "transmitter, not a transformer."[33] Such self-effacement, a Christian as well as Confucian virtue, allowed him "to communicate in a carefully chosen and richly annotated, if not always syntactically graceful or stylistically beautiful English, the authentic transformative power of some ancient Chinese books."[34] This is very high praise indeed, recalling the accolades accorded by many to the translation by the KJV translators of the Hebrew Old Testament, especially its poetry.[35]

Legge's presuppositions as a translator clearly helped him rise to an unusually high level. To begin with, he considered, in just the fashion upon which Stephen Owen has remarked, the ancient Chinese texts as Chinese "scripture."[36] He thought of the ancient Five Classics in Chinese literature and the later Four Books as functioning for their culture in a fashion not dissimilar to the Books of Moses and the Gospels. Like many other Protestant translators, including translators of the Bible, he believed that despite the occasional vagaries of imperfect translation, a keen attention to the spirit of the texts would allow them to be understood perspicuously enough as to their essential meaning. The key to discovering this spirit, or ethos of poetry in another tongue—and especially from another time—was in deep immersion in the original language itself, then, as Zhu Xi had said, finding "the meaning of the poems in the poems themselves."[37] This recollects Müller's notion that the translator/interpreter of ancient oriental texts must locate what was *symbolically hidden in the original terms*, not going out too far on the limb of presumed religious analogy. To be sure, Legge did go out pretty far on that limb anthropologically, finding analogies between Hebrew rituals of sacrifice and worship suggested in the Psalms and those in the *Odes*, even to the degree of his famous emotional extravagance (one may think of it as a Scottish Congregationalist's equivalent of David dancing nearly naked before the ark), when in 1873 he ascended the steps of the Temple of Heaven in Beijing and there, with his shoes removed and hand-in-hand with his companions, he sang the doxology (presumably in the version he knew best, namely that of the Scottish Psalter).[38] But perhaps in just such self-abandon he expressed most clearly the quality of identification by which, in his habituation to a rigorous *askesis* of philological discipline in translating other ancient texts, he was enabled to grasp something of the essential spirit of ancient Chinese poetry in a way no Westerner before him seems to have managed.

In a fashion reminiscent of that ascribed by Deborah Shuger to the translators and exegetes of the Hebrew Bible in the Renaissance,[39] Legge seems to have made significant advances by initially focusing less on the authors or even individual poems but rather, through them, trying to understand their overall cultural milieu. Thus, though we can discern important aspects of his translation stylistically that owe to his reading of biblical wisdom books (Proverbs, Ecclesiastes, Song of Solomon,[40] Isaiah, and the Psalms)—all works characterized by Hebrew poetic diction—we see beyond this an affinity for their ancient ethos. When we consider both ethos and poetic diction together—and inasmuch as the poetic diction of the KJV is frequently echoed in the phrasing of Legge's translation, the affinity seems almost natural—we can hardly avoid the impression of similarities. It will be clear that some of the odes offer parallels in phrasing. Thus:

皇矣上帝, *Huang yi Shang di*
临下有赫。 *lin hia yu ho*

Great is God,
Beholding the lower world in majesty.

(Da Ya, Book 1.VII; Legge, *Odes*, 448;
cf. Karlgren, *Odes*, 194; cf. Isa 66:1)

彼君子兮,
不素餐兮! *pu su ts'an hi*

He would not eat the bread of idleness!

(Odes of Wei VI, 伐檀; Legge, *Odes*, 169;
cf. Karlgren, *Odes*, 70–71; cf. Prov 31:27)

Or, in the manner of Ecclesiastes concerning the accumulation of worldly possessions,

宛其死矣,
他人是愉。

You will drop off in death,
And another person will enjoy them.

(Odes of Tang II, 山有枢; Legge, *Odes*, 176; cf. Eccl 2:18)

There are other instances in which Legge seems aware of the possibility of such analogy yet works scrupulously to avoid a false parallel, lest he subvert his original.[41]

> 好是正直。
> 神之听之,
> 介尔景福。
>
> Loving the correct and upright,
> So shall the Spirits hearken to you,
> And give you large measures of bright happiness.

(HsiaoYa, Book 6.III, 小明; Legge, *Odes*, 366;
cf. Karlgren, *Odes*, 160; cf. Ps 45:7; Prov 10:29)

He might well here have translated *shen* (神) as "God," but in this case chose otherwise (the Spirits).

Anyone who, like Legge, has attempted to translate them will have noted that in the Hebrew Psalms there are different names for God, principally Jahweh and Elohim, the former of which is singular and the latter plural. Additionally we find the ambiguous *Adonai* (Lord) and *melech* (king), either of which may refer to the deity or to human persons, such as the political king, and occasionally, as in Messianic psalms, the ambiguity is regarded by interpreters both Jewish and Christian as pointing to a deliberate double sense. In others, such as Psalm 45, "My heart is indicting a good matter . . . concerning the king," we have a marriage poem strikingly similar to those found in the classical *Odes*[42] in which the name for God, Elohim, is applied ambiguously to the king in question (45:6) as well as to God himself (45:7). Legge came to think that "since its earliest formation, *Ti* [*di*] has properly been the personal name of heaven, while *Tien* has had much of the force of the name Jahve, as explained by God himself to Moses."[43]

A reader of Arthur Waley's translations will notice that the diction of the Psalter in both the Book of Common Prayer (Coverdale) and the KJV translations have their place in his 1937 version. One example, from his translation of the same lines from Hsiao Ya as in Legge above, must here suffice to represent a larger pattern:

God loves the upright and straight.
The spirits, they are listening,
And will give you blessings for evermore.

(Waley, no. 207, p. 197; cf. Prov 10:29; 28:20)

King Wen is a prince before God, who "ascends and descends, / On God's left hand, on his right" (Waley, no. 235, p. 227), yet he "toiled to serve God on high" and "received many blessings" (Waley, no. 236, p. 229), and when God converses with King Wen, he speaks in a fashion reminiscent of God to King David:

God said to King Wen,
"I am moved by your bright power.
Your high renown has not made you put on proud airs,
Your greatness has not made you change former ways,
You do not try to be clever or knowing,
But follow God's precepts."

(Waley, no. 241, p. 238; cf. 1 Kgs 3:10-15)

In fact, if anyone can be said to be in thrall to KJV diction qua diction, it is probably Waley, even to the point of his using it to solve problems in difficult passages (e.g., "He has become my protector, my light," and "in whom all blessings meet," in no. 173). Legge, though aware of metrical parallels with the Hebrew Psalms (e.g., between Ode I.3.1 and the Psalms of Ascent)[44] is more restrained in making verbal parallels to English biblical diction. He is keenly attentive to deeper compatibilities of diction and grammar, such as the way in which a phrase in regard to King Wen's gifts of judgment has the force of the *hiphil* in Hebrew.[45] He seems to have been striving for something perhaps deeper, more fundamental than verbal parallels.[46]

Participation and Understanding

Between the notion (or goal) of technical linguistic mastery and cultural, a great gulf is fixed. No one, I think, will deny that cultural understanding requires a tremendously deep and detailed engagement with the language and forms of expression present in the culture one seeks to understand. But technical mastery of a semiotic system is not, by itself, sufficient for the kind of understanding Legge pursued. Here is what he said:

> In the study of a Chinese book there is not so much an interpretation of the characters employed by the writer as a participation in his thoughts; there is the seeing of mind to mind.[47]

This is to raise the purpose in translation far above the reliable communication of information. Legge sought transformation, not only for the Chinese, but transformation in himself. In order that he might "speak *from* the heart," he wrote, he must be able to "speak *to* the heart," what Girardot calls "a mutually educative process of moral transformation," a kind of "sanctification" (likewise Girardot's term) for both.[48] This attitude, reflecting a will to profound participation in the thought of the other, as Girardot dryly remarks, "was not generally characteristic of missionaries at the time."[49] A more charitable way of putting this might be to say that for many of his contemporaries the hard work of translation was utilitarian labor, while for Legge it was a joyous dedication of life, transcending matters of mere signification in a quest for the intrinsic good of right relationship with a people he had come to love for their own sake. What we are speaking of at this juncture is desire—even poetic desire—in the translator.

Certainly, this desire also included Legge's wish to make the gospel available to his Chinese interlocutors of the present. In this he agreed wholeheartedly with the goals of his fellow missionaries. But his further wish to share from his own patrimony or "Golden Treasury" did not lead him, either linguistically or anthropologically, to assume that prior to the coming of Western missionaries the Chinese had no access in their own Golden Treasury to an understanding of the divine or of "the Laws of Heaven." In his prolegomena, "The Manners of the Ancient Chinese," he exhibits this conviction plainly.

> Many missionaries have thought, and it has been recently repeated, that the Chinese have never had but a very uncertain belief in a Supreme Being. This opinion is founded on the circumstance that the expression *T'ëen* [*tien*], Heaven, is found employed by Chinese moralists more often than the expression *Shang-te*, the Supreme Lord. The quotations I have just made show us the ideas of the ancient Chinese

> in a more favorable light. *Shang-te* is represented by the Shoo-king as a Being perfectly just, who hates no one.[50]

He further observes of "the China of the Book of Poetry" in the prolegomena to his great edition,

> The Book of Poetry abundantly confirms the conclusion drawn from the Shoo-king that the ancient Chinese had some considerable knowledge of God. The names given to him are *Te*, which we commonly translate *emperor* or *ruler*, and *Shang Te*, the *Supreme Ruler*. My own opinion, as I have expressly endeavored to vindicate it in various publications on the term to be employed in translating the Hebrew *Elohim* and Greek *Theos*, is that *Te* [*Di*] corresponds exactly to them, and should be rendered in English by *God*.[51]

In contradistinction to some of his contemporaries from the London Missionary Society, Legge could see in the evidence of ancient Chinese literature neither an absence of moral order nor the lack of a theistic perspective. Already in 1861, in his discussion of Mengzi, he allows that the "heathen" man in China may be a "gentile without the law" but for all that "is still a law to himself."[52] He is quoting here the apostle Paul (Rom 2:14), as he makes it clear that he finds Confucian literature expressive of the natural law.[53] This is not to say, as Girardot unfortunately implies, that he was comparing the Chinese to the Jews in their access to a special revelation. It is to say, that like the poet in Psalm 19, Legge finds in the starry skies above a refraction of God's glory that has gone out into all the earth and that "there is no speech nor language" in which such natural revelation fails to tell its story. In the pagan poem of the sun-god (Ps 19:4a-6), though certainly less precisely than in the Torah (the special revelation adduced after verse 7), the psalmist clearly finds another echo of the divine glory. To think like the psalmist in this way was not, for Legge, more than to think with his fellow Aberdonian from Huntly, George MacDonald, that *mythopoesis*, wherever it occurs, points to some transcendent reality; and much like Paul in Acts 17, Legge further thinks a sense of that reality in Chinese terms provides a basis for conversation between himself and his "gentile" hearers. Sadly, this conviction would lead him into sharp conflict with his fellow missionaries, especially in what came to be known as the "terms controversy." This episode has been much rehearsed; a brief outline will serve the purpose of this essay.

Much in this debate confirms the maxim that history repeats itself; most immediately, the "terms" controversy among Protestant missionaries of the late nineteenth century reiterates the "rites" controversy among Catholic missionaries of the late sixteenth and early seventeenth centuries. In the earlier squabble, the Jesuits following Matteo Ricci had made extensive use of Chinese texts, in their case allowing them in many ways to be seen as a kind of moral equivalent of Christian doctrine. When the Franciscans arrived, they were aghast at what they viewed as syncretism verging on apostasy among the Jesuits, and their embassy to Rome was able to persuade Pope Clement XI to abolish the entire Jesuit mission in 1704. The Franciscans "won" their battle for a more abstract term for reference to God (excluding *tien* 天 and *shang te* 上帝 [now usually transliterated as *shang di*] and substituting *tianzhu*, "Lord of heaven"), but when in their triumph they urged Clement to forbid worship in Confucian temples and also ancestor rites, it was too much for the emperor, who then simply banned Christianity altogether.[54]

The "terms" controversy of the 1870s and 1880s was founded upon a similar scruple on the part of some among the evangelical missionaries. They believed *shang di* and *di* especially to be terms of idolatry, blasphemous when used in reference to the biblical God.[55] They held a conference on the topic in 1877 and with serious misgivings included Legge, easily the most prestigious scholar among them. Legge, firmly on the side of *shang di* and *tien*, believed that their exclusive alternative, *shen* (spirit, spirits), was too weak, given ancient Chinese culture as he understood it, to represent the God of the Bible.[56] For their part, his fellow missionaries were of the opinion that he had, in his love for China, become syncretistic, abandoning his Christian theological principles for a comparative religionist reductionism akin to that of Max Müller.

Translating the Ineffable

Assessing religious controversies as to substance is notoriously difficult, not least because so much of what may seem threatening to parties on one side or another remains below the surface of more visible symptoms and symbols. In this case, the *visibilia* were as highly profiled as possible, namely the choice of an appropriate Chinese term by which to designate God in the new Chinese Bible and in subsequent Christian literature in China. The preference of Legge for *di*, *shang di*, and in some cases *tien*, precisely *because* these terms were understood by his colleagues to be ancient Chinese names for God, was rejected as a kind of blasphemy when applied to the Christian Scriptures. The majority of London Missionary Society members wanted the less precise term *shen* (神), meaning in its original context "spirit" or "spirits," as well as "gods," perhaps out of a conviction that it had less taint of association with ancient as well as more recent "heathen" practices. But behind and beneath this objection was more than the semiotic dispute. The majority of the society had its basic linguistic training in England from an essentially positivist perspective, one which believed in the possibility of achieving in good translation a kind of equivalency. Theologically, they were literalist readers of the Bible; they had a limited experience of poetry. They were also men of the New Testament primarily, scholars whose ancient language of preference was naturally Greek.

Yet, as Rev. J. S. Roberts put it in his remarkable essay for the 1877 Shanghai conference, they were far from unaware that the sovereign objective of analytic equivalency was much more difficult to achieve when translating *from* Chinese. Going the other way, from Greek to Chinese (much as had been the case for the Benedictines when translating from Latin into Anglo-Saxon), there were no equivalents in the host language for certain abstract theological terms such as "justification," "sanctification," "grace," and "faith." Their tendency to seek equivalence, moreover, sometimes defaulted to material equivalence, with unfortunate consequences for theological understanding.[57] If those factors were not enough, there was the challenge that one Chinese term might well, in different contexts, mean something so distinctly other as to seem to require an entirely different word. Clearly, the presupposition of translators trained on Indo-European examplars that "translation . . . is essentially analogical" was being put to the test. Roberts' solution—namely to translate the object (*res*) that a word signifies rather than the verbal sign (*signum*) itself,[58] though rational enough as an expedient—raised as many difficulties as it intended to solve.

Roberts' essay was an informed and intelligent address to such general problems of translating from Chinese into English. But it is clear that he had been asked to deflect the expressed convictions of Legge concerning acceptable names for God and to bolster the case for a more culturally neutral and notably abstract term, namely *shen* as employed earlier by Robert Morrison in the Union Bible. Roberts explicitly bypasses consideration of the etymological history of this term and stresses that the translator's task is rather to identify its "present, practical application" so as "to discover its *exact* equivalent in other tongues." He asserts that there are two analogues present in each of Hebrew, Greek, and English: (a) ruach, *pneuma*, spirit and (b) elohim, *theos*, gods. In other words, concerning names for God an unambiguous analogous term in Chinese exists, and for Roberts, Morrison in his translation had found it. This argument clearly gratified Legge's opponents.

But Roberts did not stop at this point. He acknowledged that "with every fresh historic revelation of God in some new phase, a new name expressive of that phase is added in the Scripture." He also noted the problem of equivocal expression, a universal linguistic phenomena, and suggested that in such cases the Chinese version of the Bible should be left ambiguous, so as not to close off legitimate possibilities of meaning.[59] Further, citing Williamson's preface to his Mandarin dictionary, he called into question the analogical presuppositions with which he began, at least to the degree that words and phrases in any language have "one or more inherent fixed, and limited meanings, which are capable of logical definition, and of expression in other descriptive terms of the same language."[60] What follows from this candid problematization of equivalence sufficiently indicates that the missionaries who opposed Legge on the "term question" were not, as sometimes they have been represented, unsophisticated or unaware of the peculiar properties of Chinese. We observe this not only in Roberts' acknowledgment of the prevalence of term nonequivalents but in his recognition that in Chinese "the paucity of its time particles, and connectives expressive of relation and logical inter-dependence, when compared with Western tongues" creates a different mode of speech. Roberts associates this with the "conciseness and subtlety" of Chinese, which often suggests rather than renders explicitly; what he does not say, even when mentioning the relative absence of expressed auxiliary verbs (e.g., "to be," "to have") in Chinese by comparison with Western languages, is that taken together with the way abstract terms in English "are often most idiomatically expressed by Chinese concretes,"[61] these features of Chinese cumulatively make for a distinctive—and un-Western—modus of relationship between a speaker's consciousness and the external world. Among Roberts' respondents, Rev. J. Edkins alone seems to have noticed the way in which this textured diachrony in Chinese, evidenced reflexively in the frequency with which Chinese speakers and writers recur to "old obsolete forms of speech" with pleasure, creates, if not temporal dislocation, then a de-emphasis on the insistent present so visible in Western orientations to meaning and usage.[62] One wishes to know more about this: Is it comparable to the recursion of English poets from Spenser to Richard Wilbur and preachers innumerable, for effect, to citation in archaic translation (e.g., of the KJV) or affectation of such speech in certain rhetorical contexts? Ironically, of all the members of the society, the best Chinese philologist and sinologist, the one most keenly aware of all of these features—and more—was not to be represented in the published proceedings, even in a comment, since by then he had been effectively censured. Moreover, Legge's experiments in translating and retranslating the *Odes* were beginning to reveal an ear for nuance and voice that could have contributed much more to the topic of the conference had opportunity presented itself; he discovered, for example, the shift back and forth between present familiar and an archaic formal voice essential to the style of the songs and so

> purposefully changed the register of the English voice to reflect the ranges of formality and informality in the original. For imperial prayers to *shang-di* and to ancestors, and in one ode expressing filial piety toward older parents, he rendered the passages into the pronouns of the King James English ["thee," "thou"] to carry over the sense of reverence.[63]

It will be clear that an effort of this kind readily transcends the establishment of semiotic equivalence alone; Legge was trying to register spiritual sense. Legge's paper was eventually published separately as a pamphlet.[64] There is surprisingly little in it about the *shang di* controversy per se. Legge is much more concerned with what he regards as insensitivity on the part of some missionaries to the admirable qualities of Chinese culture and literature taken on their own terms and considered more deeply.[65] He makes it clear that in his view, the task of translating and of proclaiming the Christian gospel more cogently in China required a prior understanding of Chinese literature, one capacious enough to appreciate ethos and unique modes of discourse that might enable a better appreciation of how, in Pauline terms, one might appropriate the lesson of the "altar to the unknown God" (Acts 17:16-34) in the Chinese context. This is a reiteration of what he had said a dozen years earlier in his prolegomena to his edition and translation of the Chinese classics: "China, separated from the rest of the world, and without the light of revelation, has played its part, and brought forth its lessons, which will not, I trust, be long without their fitting expression."[66] Here we see into the heart of the matter: most missionary translators' dominant focus was on achieving "equivalency," analogous translation of synchronous usage, translating a Greek text into Chinese of the nineteenth century. Legge had long become interested in translation that was going in precisely the opposite direction, from Chinese into English, and, sensing the chasm between the Enlightenment mentality of his contemporaries and Confucian thought, in probing its diachronic texture for deeper cultural understanding. He wanted not merely to listen but to "hear" from deep within the texture of ancient Chinese poetic diction its own religious aspiration and affections and—as he might come to understand that ancient, far off music—to know and love better the Chinese people whose heritage this was, and thus to grasp in a deeper way the identity of the people he had come to serve.[67] In all of this there is no evidence of a diminishment in his own evangelical convictions concerning the gospel or of the importance of communicating it in China.[68] Legge simply thought his colleagues, however well intentioned, were going about their evangelical effort in the wrong way.

Learning to Think Another's Thoughts

Since, as we have seen, there were no substantive doctrinal differences between Legge and his fellow missionaries, something less perspicuous but not less urgent was at stake, and it is not entirely captured by their divergence over what name or names to use for translating the biblical names for God. Lauren Pfister identifies the missionaries' aversion to Legge's sinological approach with their fear that making any kind of alliance with the Chinese cultural system "was to advocate a dismantling of basic Christian convictions in theology and ethics."[69] This religious reason, which we might think of as a fear of relativism, was further reinforced by a strategic political reason, namely apprehension that to use classical and Confucian texts as a point of departure was in effect to subordinate the missionaries' work to the oversight of "imperial monopoly," since high government officials were the primary locus for the practice of Chinese religious rituals.[70] Both reasons reflect a fear that becoming "too Chinese" would result in a marginalizing of their original evangelical effort.

Such apprehensions point to a major anthropological variance with Legge, namely that while most of the missionaries thought of their work in terms of a transformation of individual consciousness on the modern European model, Legge, perhaps especially because of his extended intimacy with ancient Chinese literature, had come to think more in terms of the collective consciousness of the Chinese people as an evolution of meanings from ancient to modern times. Although he does not articulate the linguistic dimension of his notion in the way that Owen Barfield was later to do, I think some of Barfield's thought in these matters may help us to grasp what, at the intuitive level, Legge was learning from his patient study, not only of Confucian texts but also of the ancient classical odes that were in many ways their conceptual foundation. In this regard, it is of no small significance that Legge's most formative experiences with the Christian Scriptures were not with the New Testament in Greek but with poetic texts of the Hebrew Bible, in Hebrew.

For Barfield, as for Levy-Bruhl, there is a kind of ancient poetry in which the dissociation of objects and words was not, as with us moderns, distinct.[71] Instead, there was an internalized participation, which "begins by being an activity . . . essentially a communal or social activity."[72] Such activities resist abstraction; "their existence does not derive from the individual"[73] but, like language itself, from unconscious intersubjective agreement. For Barfield, in ancient cultures,

> the essence of *original* participation is that there stands behind the phenomena, *and on the other side of them from me*, a represented which is of the same nature as me. Whether it is called "mana" or by the names of many gods and demons, or God the Father, or the spirit world, it is of the same nature as the perceiving self, inasmuch as it is not mechanical, but psychic and voluntary.[74]

This is certainly a species of consciousness but not, in our modern sense, self-consciousness. When we, as moderns far removed from the state of participation, think of anything, we are aware (especially since Descartes) of "the self that does the thinking." We think to distinguish and are detached in that sense from that which we are thinking about. Ours is what Barfield calls "alpha-thinking," and it excludes participation by its very nature. In a telling sentence, Barfield observes:

> The history of alpha-thinking accordingly includes the history of science . . . and reaches its culmination in a system of thought which only interests itself in phenomena to the extent that they can be grasped as independent of consciousness.[75]

Linguistics, of which translation and translation theory is a subfield, is just such a science. The externalization our alpha-thinking entails makes it difficult, perhaps nearly impossible, to see into a language that appears to involve a high degree of immanently instantiated participation, precisely because in such a diction the concrete particularity of speech inhabits a universe from which neither self-consciousness (in our sense) nor abstractions of distance have become, as they are for us, objective. This is partly what we imply in our own condescending term, "pre-scientific."

Paradoxically, Barfield suggests, what we moderns "see" is largely determined by our preexistent beliefs.[76] That is, the phenomenologists have something right; we tend to see what we have been taught to see, whether it is "there" or not. Barfield does not try to claim that the withdrawal from participation that alpha-thinking has brought about is without its advantages—our science and our sense of individual identity owe to it. To put it in a way pertinent to this essay, the Westminster Catechism would not be conceivable without alpha-thinking, and there is a kind of conception of the relationship of divine transcendence to mortal existence that takes much comfort in such objectifications. The Westminster Catechism was essentially the preexistent structuring of belief that motivated many of Legge's colleagues in their pursuit—often to excellence—of the alpha-science of linguistics and translation.

That granted, apprehending an ancient poetry in which the reflexes of original participation still shape the poem is now possible only through a kind of imaginative leap, a leap beyond our normative linguistic conventions and our worldview categories. Barfield thinks that this use of the imagination had its last flourishing in the Western Middle Ages, in which poets and theologians alike wrote out of a conviction that

> God's own knowledge was alike the cause of all things and identical with his substance, and man participated in the being of God. Indeed, it was only by virtue of that participation that he could claim to have any being.[77]

Closer to ourselves, Legge's fellow townsman George MacDonald, in his view that *mythopoesis* was in modern times more than ever essential to personal recovery of universal religious participation, was surely on a similar track of thought.

I do not claim for James Legge a theory of poetic diction so theoretically grounded as that of Barfield. What I do suggest is that he noted many of the same distinctions between a language of participation and linguistic models of scientific equivalency and that he saw that a translation of consciousness involved imaginative transpositions not merely of perspectives East and West but of Then and Now. His colleagues seem genuinely to have feared that in his attempt to enter into the very world of the classical odes, he was on the brink of idolatry. A more sympathetic observer might well conclude that, from Legge's perspective, the risk of idolatry lay quite in the opposite direction. Thinking about the ancient odes as inhabiting a universe of discourse more like that of the poems of the Hebrew Scriptures than like the analytic Greek of the Pauline Epistles, and desiring to know the soul of the Chinese people through their own aspirations to harmony with the ways of heaven, he was content to try to get the Chinese scriptures right in their own terms before asserting the terms of the Christian Scriptures in what could easily be a misleading "Chinese version."

2

THE TALE WITHIN A TALE AS UNIVERSAL THEME

A Comparative Reading of Hamlet, Don Quixote, *and* The Journey to the West *(*Xiyouji*)*

Eric Ziolkowski

When Genetic Relations Are Lacking

I wish to begin by quoting a statement made just over fifty years ago by the French writer and advocate for the field of comparative literature, Étiemble:

> In China, between the 5th and the 18th centuries, starting from the hagiographic themes of Buddhism preached in the spoken language to convert masses, a whole literature of realist and magical short stories was created, the *siao chouo*, which, uniting, working on, and influencing one another, produced little by little the great Chinese novels (*Hong-leou mong*, *Kin-p'ing-mei*, etc.) which flourished at the time when, in Europe, bringing together the picaresque of Spain, the libertinage of the *Decameron*, the beauty of the *Novelas ejemplares*, there appeared *Gil Blas*, *Tom Jones*, *Moll Flanders*, and a score of other novels whose technique, tone and spirit shockingly resemble what, sheltered from any Western influence, was being elaborated in China. Certainly, over there as in the West, the vogue of the novel seems to coincide with the flowering of a bourgeois or merchant class; but who would claim that the European novel, like the Chinese novel, sprang from Buddhist preaching?

> And how is it that Chinese novelists give to their masterpieces the very forms adopted by the 18th century European novelists? A systematic study of the novels produced by those civilizations most alien to ours . . . would perhaps bring to light and make obvious, on the one hand, the permanent elements of the genre of the "romance," those elements without which there can be no novel, and on the other hand, those constituent parts of the genre which result, more or less arbitrarily, from historical circumstances. Here is a case where the study of genres is not founded upon *relations of fact* [*rapports de fait*] of an historical order. Will we say, then, that this is not legitimate?[1]

Étiemble, in yearning to discern a transculturally present, formal, structural level of the novel as a genre, a level where "the permanent elements of the genre of the 'romance' " transcend "*relations of fact* of an historical order," put his finger on what Claudio Guillén a decade later identified as "a central *desideratum* of comparative studies," namely, "the consideration of poetic theory with regard to both Eastern and Western writing—to civilizations between which no genetic relations have existed,"[2] a project that the late Anthony C. Yu, concurring with Guillén several years later, found to be in "urgent need for greater methodological precision."[3]

In view of these considerations, in this essay I wish to broach a basic question within the framework of several "genetically" unrelated texts, not all of which are even of the same genre: Might not literature, or, to press the question down to an even more fundamental level, might not the art of storytelling have ingrained within its very nature, regardless of the civilization or group within which it develops, an irrepressible need at some point to call attention to itself by replicating within itself the very narrative act it is engaging in as storytelling or, indeed, as literature? In offering a cognitive, evolutionary, "naturalistic account of art and fiction," Bryan Boyd submits that "we have evolved to engage in art and in storytelling because of the survival advantages they offer our species"—for example, "prepar[ing] minds for open-ended learning and creativity; . . . improv[ing] our social cognition and our thinking beyond the here and now[;] . . . invit[ing] and hold[ing] our attention strongly enough to engage and reengage our minds, altering synaptic strengths . . . by exposing us to the supernormally intense patterns of art."[4] If all this is true, might it not be only natural that the promotion of human self-understanding, another of storytelling's chief functions according to Boyd,[5] would seek expression in literature precisely through a self-reflective display of storytelling's own narrative workings—that is, through the narrating not only of a tale within a tale, but of a tale that somehow mimics or recapitulates the broader tale within which it occurs?

I wish to entertain this question by considering a specific, shared aspect of three pivotal literary classics, one of them Chinese, the other two European, and all of them dating remarkably from within two decades of each other. The first is one of China's Four Great Classical Novels, the full hundred-chapter version of *The Journey to the West* (*Xiyouji*, lit. *The Record of the Westward Journey*),[6] published in 1592, often albeit controversially ascribed to Wu Cheng-en (ca. 1500–1582).[7] The second is William Shakespeare's tragic drama *Hamlet*, composed putatively in the years 1599–1601, entered in the Stationers' Register on July 26, 1602, and published in two different quartos over the next two years. The third is Miguel de Cervantes' satirical novel *The Ingenious Gentleman Don Quixote of La Mancha* (*El ingenioso hidalgo don Quijote de la Mancha*), whose two parts appeared successively in 1605 and 1615, the second part coming a year after a spurious sequel to part 1 had been published by an unknown author under the pseudonym Alonso Fernández de Avellaneda (1614). It should be noted that *The Journey to the West*, *Hamlet*, and the *Quixote*, though composed so closely together in time, most likely came into existence in complete cultural isolation from each other. *The Journey to the West* was not only written before *Hamlet* and the *Quixote*, but whoever its author was could not have known of Shakespeare or Cervantes, neither of whom in turn knew of *The Journey to the West* or its author. Cervantes almost certainly never heard of Shakespeare, and there is no sure evidence that Shakespeare ever knew of Cervantes. Although it is possible that the Bard of Avon read Thomas Shelton's 1612 English translation of the *Quixote*,[8] his doing so would have been irrelevant to his composing of *Hamlet* a decade earlier—as would be the striking coincidence that the two men's deaths occurred but a day apart: Cervantes' on April 22, 1616, and Shakespeare's, the next day, April 23.

Borges' Discomfort

What might lead us to consider these three works in relation to each other, aside from the striking temporal proximity of their compositions?

Let us consider a prefatory observation Anthony Yu made in his book on *Hongloumeng* or *The Story of the Stone* (also known as *Dream of the Red Chamber* or *Dream of Red Mansions*), that Qing masterpiece that appeared in 1791, almost exactly two centuries after *The Journey to the West*'s hundred-chapter version. As a text that emphasizes its own literary nature and being, and explores and dramatizes its own fictionality (in Yu's words) "by structuring literally the origin, genesis, production, and reception of the tale into the plot of the tale itself," *The Story of the Stone* indulges a theme and technique that, while constituting "a rare—perhaps even unique—achievement in the history of Chinese literature," are in fact "commonplace in Western literatures," as exemplified by *Hamlet* and the *Quixote*; and before them, the *Odyssey*; and after them, James Joyce's *Ulysses* and Wallace Stevens' *The Auroras of Autumn*.[9] This insight might prompt us to take special note of an occurrence in *The Journey to the West* that not only seems to anticipate that same theme and technique of self-referential fictionality Yu identified but also finds remarkable analogies in *Hamlet* and the *Quixote*, a point ignored by C. T. Hsia when he characterizes *The Journey to the West* and the *Quixote* as "two works of comparable importance in the respective developments of Chinese and European fiction."[10] Specifically, I have in mind the device or effect, found in heraldry, for which André Gide coined the term *mise en abyme*, literally "placing in [an] abyss," to refer to a kind of self-reflexive devise by which a work of art or literature allows its own subject to be found embedded on a smaller scale within itself. "In a work of art," explained Gide in an 1893 entry in his journal, "I rather like that one finds transposed, on the scale of the characters, the very same subject of that work," a device he compares to "the method of a coat of arms, which consists of placing in the first [escutcheon], a second 'in abyss.'"[11] As stated by Lucien Dällenbach, who popularized the term among literary scholars in the late 1970s, the *mise en abyme* is "a means by which the work turns back on itself, and appears to be a kind of *reflexion*."[12]

Let us consider the tactic the Monkey King, Sun Wukong, employs when, at the climax of *The Journey to the West*'s so-called Hamlet episode (chs. 37–39),[13] he confronts the disguised Daoist demon who murdered the ruler of Black Rooster Kingdom, usurped the throne, stole the queen, and forbade the prince and legitimate heir (that is, the dead ruler's son by the queen) to see her ever again. Monkey came to the rescue after the dead king's ghost approached Monkey's master, the monk

Xuanzang or Tripitaka, through a dream for help, much as the ghost of Hamlet's kingly father approached the prince, urging him to avenge his own murder by his brother, Hamlet's uncle Claudius, who had married the ghost's widow, Hamlet's mother, and assumed Hamlet's father's throne. Monkey reads aloud to the demon king's face, in the presence of the dead ruler's ghost, the prince, Tripitaka, and the latter's other two disciples, as well as the demon's marshals, a deposition that recounts the story of the demon's crime—and that in turn elicits from the demon a response every bit as guilt-revealing as Claudius' response to Hamlet's play within a play representing Claudius' crime (see ch. 39).[14]

As uncanny as are the various acknowledged parallels between the plots of *Hamlet* and *The Journey to the West*'s Black Rooster Kingdom episode, what warrants our attention here is the shared phenomenon of a tale within a tale: that is, of *Hamlet*'s re-presenting an approximation of its own story within itself, through Hamlet's "play," as the characters themselves look on; and of the re-narration, within *The Journey to the West*, of one of the novel's own episodes, through Monkey's deposition to the demon king in the presence of other characters. A comparable phenomenon occurs in the *Quixote*, whose protagonists themselves become readers and discussants of the *Quixote*, as they, in the novel's second part, have read part 1 and now converse about it. Jorge Luis Borges, once commenting on this Cervantine contrivance, opined that the effectiveness of its counterpart in *Hamlet* is lessened by the imperfect correlation between the principal play and the secondary one. (Perhaps no one has ever been more qualified to comment on this phenomenon than Borges, being himself the author of the famous short story that takes it to the extreme, "Pierre Menard, autor del *Quijote*" [1939, "Pierre Menard, Author of the *Quixote*"], about a French critic who becomes so obsessed with trying to construe the *Quixote* that he rewrites the novel verbatim in its entirety.).[15] As Borges pointed out, however, not only does an artifice analogous to and more astonishing than Cervantes' come into play toward the end of Vālmīki's epic poem, the *Rāmāyana*, where the hero Rāma hears the *Rāmāyana* sung to him by his own sons in the presence of Vālmīki, by whom they have been taught it,[16] but chance (*el azar*) also worked out something similar in *A Thousand and One Nights*, known also as the *Arabian Nights*. There, on one particular night, identified by Borges only as "night DCII [*la noche* DCII]," the sultan hears his own story told by the sultana: "He hears the beginning of the story, which embraces all the other stories as well as—monstrously—itself. Does the reader perceive the unlimited possibilities of that interpolation, the curious danger—that the Sultana may persist and the Sultan, transfixed, will hear forever the truncated story of *A Thousand and One Nights*, now infinite and circular?"[17]

Borges, avowedly discomfited by these phenomena, likened them to the idea formulated by the American philosopher Josiah Royce (1855–1916) that an absolutely exact map of England, if located within England, would have to contain, as part of itself, a proportionate, tiny, though exact representation of itself, and that this representation in turn would have to contain as part of itself a proportionate, infinitesimal, though exact representation of itself, and so on ad infinitum. Such thoughts of a map within a map or of stories within stories make us uneasy, Borges concluded, because they "suggest that if the characters in a story can be readers or spectators, then we, their readers or spectators, can be fictitious."[18] This conclusion, we might note, seems ironic if not logically inconsistent in view of Borges' well-established image as a proto-postmodernist: if, as Nathan Scott put it, "[l]iterary fictions . . . [in postmodern times], are and ought to be 'self-reflexive,' their chief interest lying in the degree of radicality with which they subvert any expectation of their making reference to a reality extrinsic to their own internal grammar of myth and metaphor,"[19] then we, as readers or spectators outside of the text, could hardly be "fictitious" (in the same way that everyone and everything within the text is "fictitious"), given that absolute break between what is intrinsic to the text, and all that is extrinsic in relation to it—including us. Either Borges was not truly a postmodernist (at least in the way Scott construed the term), or his avowed uneasiness in the face of stories within stories seems discrepant.

History, or the World, as Book

Although Borges does not mention the Shakespearean insight that all the world's a stage and all the men and women merely players,[20] he closes by alluding to Thomas Carlyle's observation "in 1833" that the history of the world constitutes "an infinite sacred book [*un infinito libro sagrado*]" written, read, and interpreted by all human beings, in which they themselves are inscribed.[21] This idea, which Carlyle invoked often, and in different forms,[22] anticipates the American process theologian Charles Hartshorne's (1897–2000) notion that every human life amounts to a "book" that, upon its completion (at the individual's death), will achieve an immortality of sorts through God's omniscience of its "pages."[23] This notion, minus the notion of "God's omniscience," finds loose, genetically unrelated albeit provocative Chinese analogues in *The Journey to the West*, specifically in the images of the ledger-registry of births and deaths, kept in King Yama's Underworld, from which the Monkey King erases his own name, and the names of all the other monkeys, with the result that thenceforth "many mountain monkeys . . . did not grow old" (ch. 3); and in the later mention of "the Long-Life Book" in which "[Monkey's] name divine, forever recorded . . . / And kept from falling into saṃsāra, will long be known" (ch. 4).[24] But where did Carlyle's idea of world history as a sacred book come from? Staunch Germanophile that he was, he could have derived it from German Idealists such as Schelling, who posited human history as "a play" (*Schauspiel*) in which the deity "reveals and discloses himself successively,"[25] and Hegel, who set forth a similar notion in his *Lectures on the Philosophy of History* (*Vorlesungen über die Philosophie der Geschichte*, delivered in Berlin, 1821, 1824, 1827, and 1831; published posthumously, 1837), deploying theatrical terminology routinely to describe the Spirit's concrete self-manifestation "[o]n the stage [*auf dem Theater*] . . . [of] Universal History."[26] At the same time, given the deep-seated substratum of Calvinism in Carlyle's thinking, together with his Romantic sense of a "natural supernaturalism" pervading the world,[27] Carlyle's notion of world history as an infinite sacred book may also reflect the influence of Calvin's own conception of the cosmos as "a dazzling theater [*theatrum*]."[28]

This idea of history or the world as a divine theater is further akin to a host of other notions from both within and outside of the European Christian tradition: for example, John Donne's idea of each of our individual lives as a sentence already inscribed in a book by God;[29] or the idea, found as early as in the Qur'ān 11:6, of the world as a book composed and read by God: "No creature is there crawling on the earth, but its provision rests on God; / He knows its lodging place / and its repository. *All / is in a Manifest Book*."[30] Indeed, notwithstanding the qur'ānic construal of pre-Islamic times as the "time[s] of ignorance,"[31] the idea of the world as text appears not only to predate the Qur'ān (e.g., in Augustine's characterization of the created universe as the "book of nature [*librum naturae*]" authored by God),[32] but to be practically as old as is written literature itself. David Damrosch points out that the cuneiform symbols of the ancient Mesopotamians, derived from natural objects, corresponded to the lines and patterns that astrologers traced in the sky and that diviners sought in terrestrial sources.[33] For the Mesopotamians, as the late French Assyriologist Jean Bottéro observed, "the whole of creation was presented as an immense page of divine scripture. When everything was normal and routine, with nothing special to attract the attention, the divine 'writers' therefore had nothing to point out to human beings, their readers. If they had to pass on some particular decision that had been taken, they would arrange to produce some unusual, singular, or monstrous phenomenon."[34] As Damrosch further notes, the fact that the Assyrians themselves had already drawn this comparison of creation to a text is revealed in a hymn to the sun god Shamash, extolling his ability to "read" the world by his own radiance:

> . . . lofty judge, creator of the above and below,
> you scan all lands in your light like a graven sign.
> [You w]ho never weary of divination,
> you render daily verdicts for heaven and earth.[35]

Other Stories within Stories

Of course, the concept of the world as text and that of a text within a text, though surely related to one another, are not identical, even though Borges discusses them together. When he wrote on this subject, Borges by no means mentioned all instances of the story within a story; he only scratched the surface. Among the most noteworthy examples about which he was silent are several that are undoubtedly the very earliest on record, as they are found in arguably the world's first written work of secular literature: the ancient Babylonian and Assyrian *Epic of Gilgamesh*.[36] One of these examples occurs in the initial encounter of the poem's eponymous hero with Šiduri, the "ale-wife . . . by the seashore."[37] Although this scene is most famous, justly, for Šiduri's speech discouraging Gilgamesh from persisting in his arduous, futile quest of immortality, and encouraging him to return home and find satisfaction in quotidian pleasures,[38] Šiduri's request that he identify himself[39] elicited from him a brief recitation of his unequaled feats of preternatural heroism, performed with his beloved companion Enkidu, who then died as a consequence.

[Gilgameš spoke to] her, [to the ale]-wife:
"[*My friend Enkidu and I,* . . . . . .] . . .
[We it was who joined forces and climbed the mountain] country,
[seized the Bull of Heaven and killed the Bull of Heaven,]
[destroyed Ḫumbaba, who lived in the] Cedar [Forest,]
[killed] lions [in the mountain *passes.*]"
[. . . .]
[. . . my friend Enkidu, whom I love so deeply,]
[who with me went through every danger:]
[*the doom of mankind* overtook him,]
[. . . .]
[I grew fearful of death and so roam the wild.][40]

Here, in this narrative résumé of his exploits with his friend Enkidu and their tragic aftermath, Gilgamesh has in effect retold in a hyper-condensed form the story of the *Epic of Gilgamesh* that we have already read, and of which he is and remains the hero, even as he now recites his own story. What is more, this is neither the first nor the last time that Gilgamesh recounts his own adventures: he did so earlier, in his lament of Enkidu's death,[41] and he will do so again, when he encounters, successively, the boatman Ur-šanabi (Urshanabi) and the immortalized survivor of the great flood, Ūta-napišti (Utnapishtim).[42] Although he thus narrated repeatedly his own story within his own story, Gilgamesh has yet to be recognized as the earliest recorded reciter of self-referential tales within a tale. He is, nonetheless, a precursor, if not the prototype, of various other seminal Western examples of this phenomenon, none of them mentioned by Borges. For example, the prophet Nathan tells King David the parable about David's own sin (2 Sam 12:1-15). Homer's Odysseus hears both his own dispute with Achilles and his own chief role in the sacking of Troy, sung of by the Phaeacian bard Demodocus, before singing to the Phaeacians the song of his own subsequent adventures.[43] And Beowulf hears his own triumph over Grendel paralleled with Sigemund's dragon slaying in a poem chanted by an anonymous minstrel.[44]

But even if those reading the Hebrew prophetic Scripture, the Homeric epic, or the medieval Anglo-Saxon poem might perforce wind up wondering à la Borges whether they themselves are real or fictitious, no Western conceptualization or inscription of this quandary has ever matched the succinctness, clarity, or sheer memorableness of Zhuangzi's butterfly dream and his consequent uncertainty over whether he was the dreamer or the dreamed. Indeed, such Western literary analogues as

Calderón de la Barca's play *La vida es sueño* (1635, *Life Is a Dream*), Voltaire's tale *Le blanc et le noir* (1764, *The White and the Black*), and Franz Grillparzer's "dramatisches Märchen" (dramatic folktale) *Der Traum ein Leben* (composed 1831, performed 1834, published 1839; *Life, a Dream*) may come across as extended, unwitting variations on Zhuangzi's oneiric conundrum, which one of Nabokov's narrators will also seem to echo in addressing the reader about the deceptive experience of one's seeming to wake up: "Actually, though, this is a false awakening, being merely the next layer of your dream, as if you were rising up from stratum to stratum but never reaching the surface. . . . Yet who knows? Is this reality, *the* final reality, or just a new deceptive dream?"[45] In the Chinese context, Zhuangzi's conundrum brings to a head assumptions about the illusory nature of reality that, as Yu found reflected in *The Story of the Stone*,[46] are common to Daoists and Buddhists alike. Borges himself, who apparently cultivated an informed interest in Chinese history and culture,[47] on various occasions other than the aforementioned one invoked the example of Zhuangzi's butterfly dream in the course of arguing against the notion of time, and cited him also to illustrate "infinite *regressus*,"[48] a concept directly related to the Cervantine and Shakespearean phenomena of stories within stories.

Literary Incarnation and the Story of Transmitting Scriptures

I do not know whether Borges ever read any of the Western-language translations of *The Journey to the West* or *The Story of the Stone* that were available prior to his death in 1986. If he did so, in either text he would have encountered a narrative that lays as much stress as the *Quixote* does upon its own textual, narrative nature. Of the many authorities aside from Borges who have commented on this phenomenon in Cervantes' novel, three will suffice to be cited here. Carlos Fuentes found the *Quixote*'s "essence" to be a five-level "critique of reading that projects itself from the book toward the outer world, . . . and for the first time in literature, a critique of creation contained within the created work itself."[49] John J. Allen reminds us that Cervantes' novel "entails the story of readers reading, or misreading, and of writers writing, or failing to write."[50] Not only, as mentioned above, have most of the main characters in part 2 read part 1, but, as Allen elaborates, almost all the leading personages in both parts are readers of chivalry books or some other genre of fiction. Don Quixote goes insane at the start from too much reading and in the end is sorry he lacks time to read another genre of literature. The author patently wrote the novel in reaction to his own reading. Don Quixote and his village priest both aspire to write. The criminal Ginés de Pasamonte claims to be in the middle of writing a book. Don Quixote's "humanist" guide to the Cave of Montesinos is an author by profession. And Cide Hamete Benengeli, the Arab from whose manuscript the *Quixote* purports to have been rendered into Castilian by a Moorish translator, is so prone toward literary productivity that he suggests he must restrain himself from writing more than he already does in part 2. Allen adds, "In the text, there is explicit discussion and criticism not only of narrative fiction but of drama and lyric as well. Books and manuscripts are bought and sold, handled, read aloud, acted out, annotated, translated, criticized, printed, plagiarized, burned, buried, and even kicked around by the devils of hell."[51]

Long before Fuentes and Allen, Américo Castro anticipated their observations in proposing that the "supreme novelty" of the *Quixote* lay in its inauguration of a new form of literary creation, one that

> shows us that the reality of existence consists in receiving the impact of all that can affect man from without, and in transforming these influences into outwardly manifest life processes. The illusion of a dream, devotion to a belief—in short, the ardently yearned for in any form becomes infused in the existence of him [*sic*] who dreams, believes, or longs; and thus, what was before transcendency without bearing on the process of living becomes embodied into life.[52]

The *Quixote*'s overarching theme is thus "the interdependence, the 'interrealisation' of what lies beyond man's experience and the process of incorporating that into his existence,"[53] a process Castro calls incarnation (*encarnación*). Among all the external "incitements" that become "incarnated" in the lives of the *Quixote*'s characters, the spoken, written, and printed word stands foremost. The first of the novel's two parts essentially grows out of books Don Quixote has read. Part 2 grows out of part 1, as the life of the protagonist incorporates his consciousness of having already been the subject of a book. And the Don Quixote of part 2 perpetuates himself and the literary interpretation of the fictive author, Cide Hamete Benegeli, coming across to those who meet him as both a living man and a "human-literary figure."[54] "The traditional themes of literature," Castro observes, "are now fused with the living experience of those themes; the book then becomes not only a book, but it also becomes the reader who has incorporated its poetic material into his very life."[55]

Anyone reading the opening lines of Cervantes' prologue to the *Quixote*'s first part and chapter 1 of *The Story of the Stone* in each other's light will be struck by the two texts' shared concern with the question of their own literary genesis: "Idle reader: . . . I could not contravene the order of nature; that in it everything will engender its likeness. And so, what could my sterile and badly cultivated wit engender but the tale of a dried, shriveled, capricious offspring . . . ?"[56] "Gentle reader, what, you may ask, was the origin of this book? Though the answer to this question may at first seem to border on the absurd, reflection will show that there is a good deal more in it than meets the eye."[57] In view of all that Yu revealed about the examination by the *Hongloumeng* of its own sense of its fictionality, especially as that examination is modulated by Buddhist conceptions, it seems only fitting that he should affix a quotation from the *Quixote* as the epigraph to his chapter on the *Hongloumeng*'s perception of literary fiction as a medium for disseminating desire (*qing*): "His imagination was filled up with all he read in books" (*Llenósele la fantasía de todo aquello que leía en los libros*).[58] But what about *The Journey to the West*? If this novel cannot be said to display the same sort of sense of its own fictionality as does the *Hongloumeng*, it does engage continuously and irrepressibly in rehearsing tales within a tale.

In elaborating an explanation of the *Hongloumeng*'s manifold Buddhist intimations, Yu emphasizes the fact that Buddhism "came as a religion of the books, as an invasion of a powerful, alien textual tradition into a civilization with no less powerful a textual tradition of its own."[59] This observation might facilitate our grasping the significance of certain prominent threads of self-referential fictionality running through the narrative fabric of *The Journey to the West*, whose central titular action fictionalizes an actual historic feat that was performed in service of that Buddhist scriptural "invasion": the pilgrimage by the Buddhist monk Xuanzang (596?–664) from China to India, his lengthy sojourn there, and his journey back to China, an achievement that encompassed seventeen years, all to retrieve and translate sacred scriptures to reform the Mahāyāna tradition in China. For *The Journey to the West* itself is, as a novel, a form of scripture, and as a scripture about the retrieval of scriptures, it seems all the more fitting that it should, whether or not by the author's intent, incessantly call attention to its own scriptural nature by continually enfolding within itself condensed recapitulations of its own developing narrative. In pursuing this suggestion, I cannot resist quoting a suggestion by the Daoist commentator on *The Journey to the West*, Liu I-ming (1734–1820), that would be worthy of one of Borges' more inspired moments of meditation on metafiction: "*The Journey to the West* is transmitted through the story of the transmission of the scriptures by the Tathāgata Buddha, that is all. If one can truly understand *The Journey to the West*, then the three baskets of the true scripture will be found within it. Only he who knows this can read *The Journey to the West*."[60] I shall later return to this observation.

For all its *Hamlet*-like allure, Wukong's aforementioned deposition to the demon king is by no means the only story within a story in *The Journey to the West*; indeed, whereas the play within the play, which occurs midway through *Hamlet* and is arguably the main turning point in the overall plot, finds no analogies elsewhere in that drama, Monkey's retelling of the treachery perpetrated against the ruler of Black Rooster Kingdom crystallizes a pattern of recapitulatory narratives within a narrative that runs throughout *The Journey to the West*. Consider several examples from the first seven chapters alone, which constitute what could be a self-standing novella about the birth, life, and misadventures of Wukong up through his being captured and confined beneath Five-Phases Mountain by Tathāgata Buddha (ch. 7). An early, miniature story within the broader story occurs at the end of the second chapter, when Wukong returns to Flower-Fruit Mountain after his successful journey in quest of immortality and treats all the monkeys there with a precise account of his travels, including both the itinerary and his accomplishments.[61] Later, in chapter 6, a brief summary of the various offenses Monkey perpetrated in his revolt against Heaven—his theft of the immortal peaches, the imperial wine, and Laozi's divine elixir, and his disruption of the Peach Festival (ch. 5)—as well as the ongoing cosmic war being waged against him is included in the edict issued by the Jade Emperor calling for Monkey's destruction (ch. 6).[62] Not far into chapter 7, when all other means have failed to subdue him, and the Jade Emperor appeals to the Buddha to help contain Monkey, a longer, more detailed account of the latter's history and exploits up to the present moment is recited to the Buddha (ch. 7),[63] making the Tathāgata himself a listener to the (recapitulated) story we have just read.

What I have mentioned is but a sampling of the stories within the story from chapters 1–7 that collectively establish what will persist as a deep-seated narrative pattern—and a lyrical pattern as well, as the "some seventeen hundred poems"[64] woven into the narrative fully participate in this pattern—throughout the novel's ninety-three subsequent chapters. In what remains of this essay, we must confine ourselves to some relatively brief observations to illustrate this distinctive, pervasive phenomenon in this vast novel. The pattern we have already considered in connection with Monkey in the first seven chapters recurs, from chapter 8 to the novel's end, most saliently through the autobiographical accounts offered over and over by four of the novel's five central characters: Monkey, Xuanzang, and their three fellow pilgrims to the West, the pig Zhu Bajie, also known as Zhu Wuneng or "Idiot," and the river creature Sha Wujing, also known as Sha Monk. (The fifth pilgrim, the Dragon King of the West Sea, appears mostly as a horse, ridden by Tripitaka, and so hardly speaks at all.) The pattern we are discussing is even highlighted, inadvertently, by the controversy surrounding the ninth chapter of the hundred-chapter version, which tells the story of Xuanzang's ill-fated father, Chen Guangrui, and of Xuanzang's fatherless birth and early years. If some scholars are correct that this chapter may have been added to the original novel by some late-Ming compiler,[65] one of its main purposes appears to be to provide a previously lacking *Ur*-account of the family origin, birth, and life of Xuanzang leading up to his first encounter with Guanyin in chapter 12, precisely to serve as the biographical record that is seemingly echoed in the nine[66] later places in the novel that allude to the Chen Guangrui episode, beginning with the lengthy poem that introduces Xuanzang in chapter 12, when he has been chosen as altar master of the Grand Mass of Land and Water.[67] A later allusion, short enough to quote here, occurs in chapter 37, at the beginning of the "Hamlet episode." There, upon hearing about the ghost's and the prince's plight, and remarking that it resembled what he himself had undergone from birth through young manhood, Tripitaka recapitulates in a nutshell the extensive earlier narrative (in ch. 9) of his own background and early ordeal involving his murdered father:

> Long ago my father was killed by a pirate, who also took my mother by force. After three months, she gave birth to me, and I escaped. . . .
>
> *I had neither father nor mother when I was young,*
> *And the prince at this place has lost his parents.*
>
> (*JW* 2:167)

As Anthony Yu pointed out, this pattern of introducing a protagonist through the narration of a set of biographical incidents that are then, on repeated later occasions in the novel, rehearsed or recalled in various ways also occurs in the cases of Monkey, Zhu Bajie, and Sha Wujing.[68] But even with their individual cases, together with Tripitka's, the pattern does not exhaust itself, we might add, because it can be found even more broadly operative, beyond the constant rehearsals of the individual protagonists' lives. That is, the same pattern is manifest in the repeated retellings and synopsizing of the Westward journey of all five pilgrims together, even as this journey continues to unfold. For example, in chapter 39, just before he recites his deposition to the murderer of the Black Rooster monarch, Monkey recounts to that demon, in brief, the commissioning of Tripitaka by Guanyin to embark on his Westward journey, the emperor's sanctioning of that journey, and Tripitaka's ensuing enlistment of Monkey, Zhu Bajie, and Sha Wujing as his fellow pilgrims.[69] And later, in chapter 54, in a city of women only, when asked by the city's queen why his rescript from the Tang emperor bears his name but not his disciples' names, Tripitika introduces them by summarizing the story—based on chapter 8—of how they all happened to be brought together on their joint quest for scriptures in the West:

> "My eldest disciple," answered Tripitaka, "comes from the Aolai country in the East Pūrvavideha Continent; the second disciple, from a village in Qoco in the west Apargodānīya Continent; and the third, from the River of Flowing Sand. All three of them had transgressed the decrees of Heaven. The Bodhisattva Guanshiyin, however, liberated them from their sufferings, as a result of which they were willing to make submission and hold fast the good. So that their merits might atone for their sins, they resolved to accompany me and protect me on my journey to the Western Heaven to acquire scriptures. Since they became my disciples when I was already on my way, their names therefore had not been recorded on the rescript." (ch. 54)[70]

Suffice it here to say that the incessant recurrences of this pattern we have discussed in *The Journey to the West* climax in the novel's ninety-ninth, penultimate chapter, with Guanyin's inspection, entailing the complete listing within the narrative, of the "registry" of the eighty "calamities" or "ordeals" endured by Tripitika thus far in the course of the novel[71]—beginning with his banishment (under the name Gold Cicada) from the Buddha's realm in his previous life (ch. 8) and his almost being killed after (re)birth (ch. 9), and then encompassing all his subsequent ordeals, including the several prior to his embarkation as a pilgrim (chs. 9), and the numerous subsequent ones, experienced by him mostly in the company of his fellow pilgrims (chs. 13–98).

Here we might marvel that the entire novel, excepting the preliminary Monkey novella (chs. 1–7) and the yet-to-be-read final, hundredth chapter, has just been retold within itself, albeit satirically boiled down to the synopsized form of a mock-bureaucratic "registry." But this is not all that might catch our attention. Recalling Liu I-ming's observation that "*The Journey to the West* is transmitted through the story of the transmission of the scriptures by the Tathāgata Buddha," we might be struck that the recitation of the "registry" of calamities follows almost immediately the full itemized report, given by the Buddha's disciples Ānanda and Kāśyapa to the Tathāgata near the end of the previous chapter, of the 5,048 scrolls of Sūtras and Śastras that the Buddha gave the pilgrims to transport back to China (ch. 98).[72] If this coinciding of the itemizing of the scrolls and the listing of Tripitaka's "ordeals" has the effect of drawing the story of the pilgrims' journey into a direct association with the Buddhist scriptures whose retrieval was the purpose of that journey, this association is sealed by Guanyin's disclosure, right after the itemizing of the scrolls, that the pilgrims' journey, when completed, will have encompassed the exact same "perfect canonical number" of days as the number of scrolls: 5,048 (ch. 98).[73]

This symbolic fusion of the novel's whole narrative about Xuanzang's scripture-seeking journey with the scriptures themselves was betokened all along by the name borne by the novel's scripture-seeking monastic protagonist, Xuanzang, from the end of chapter 12 onward.[74] *Tripiṭaka* (three baskets) denotes not only the containers in which Buddhists stored their scrolls but also the three main types (baskets) of teachings inscribed upon those scrolls: Sūtras, Abhidharma, and Vinaya.[75] In retrospect, we now realize, the fusion of narrative of *The*

Journey to the West with the scriptures whose attainment was the journey's goal was encapsulated early on: upon hearing the Chan Master's oral recitation of the Heart Sūtra, whose entire text was interpolated in the narrative, Tripitaka, "spiritually prepared," was able to memorize and to absorb it instantaneously upon that single hearing (ch. 18)[76]—and hence to "incarnate" it in the same way Castro observes Don Quixote to have "incarnated" books of chivalry.

The crucial difference is that, from beginning to end, it is his insanity that impels Don Quixote on his several sallies and his endless chain of illusory misadventures, whereas the sanity of Tripitaka's adventurous and often death-defying trek is never questioned, despite the monk's having been warned from the outset "that the waters [on the way to the Western Heaven] were wide and the mountains very high; . . . that the roads were crowded with tigers and leopards; . . . that the precipitous peaks were difficult to scale; and . . . that the vicious monsters were hard to subdue" (ch. 13; cf. ch. 12).[77] Moreover, the wholehearted, single-minded devotion of Tripitaka to his scriptural quest and, ultimately, his fulfillment of it, in the end affirm the lasting, positive, religio-cultural legacy of the diffusion of Mahāyāna scriptures in China, and qualify both him and his supernatural simian companion to be rewarded with Buddhahood by the Tathāgata himself. This outcome and the Tathāgata's conferral upon them of, respectively, the titles "Buddha of Candana Merit" and "Buddha Victorious in Strike" (see ch. 100)[78] stand in stark contrast to the depressing denouement of the *Quixote* in its final chapter. There, the Manchegan hidalgo likewise assumes a new name, Alonso Quixano the Good (*Alonso Quijano el Bueno*), but only to betoken his avowed "repentance [*arrepentimiento*]" (pt. 2, ch. 74)[79] before he renounces what heretofore have served as his own equivalent of Tripitaka's sacred scriptures: the books of chivalry. As a consequence of his earlier defeat at the hands of the Knight of the White Moon (*el Cabellero de la Blanca Luna*, or, in actuality, the bachelor Sansón Carrasco; *DQ*, pt. 2, chs. 64–65), a remarkable inversion of Monkey's battle and ultimate triumph over the false macaque (*JW*, ch. 58),[80] the disillusioned, melancholic Manchegan hidalgo regains his sanity. But he does so only to fall gravely ill and bedridden, dictate his will, confess to a priest, receive the last sacraments, and then die—after "expressing with many and efficacious words his loathing of books of chivalry" (pt. 2, ch. 74).[81]

In view of the Heart Sūtra's central doctrine of emptiness (*śūnyatā*), the religious sobriquet, "Wake-to-the-Void" (*wukong*), conferred on Monkey by Patriarch Subodhi at the end of the first chapter,[82] might seem almost as connectible as the name Tripitaka to the novel's theme of scripturality. But in Wukong's case, the linkage would be specifically to the image of the wordless and hence *blank*, *empty*, or *void* scriptures, in chapter 98, with which Ānanda and Kāśyapa initially dispatched the Tripitaka and his companions homeward as a punitive prank for the pilgrims' not having offered them a gift in exchange. This prank has a profound Buddhist implication, bearing directly on the emptiness doctrine: as the Buddha explains to the indignant pilgrims when, after they realized the prank, they return to get hold of the "real" scriptures with words on them, "[T]hese blank texts are actually true, wordless scriptures, and they are just as good as those with words. However, those creatures in your Land of the East are so foolish and unenlightened that I have no choice but to impart to you now the texts with words."[83] Given this apparent use of the image of wordless scriptures as a mildly satirical reflection of the emptiness doctrine, a doctrine that thematically connects the omission of words from those scriptures with Tripitika's shedding of his physical body as he and his fellow pilgrims were earlier ferried across a treacherous river in a bottomless boat to the Buddha's realm (ch. 98), it seems only fitting that Tripitika's eighty-first and final ordeal, which brings the journey almost to its end, should be suggestive of another central Buddhist teaching, that of *impermanence*. Illustrating the truism that any and all scriptures, whether blank or inscribed, are inevitably vulnerable to physical decay, disintegration, and hence imperfection, the last ordeal occurs in chapter 99, where the giant turtle transporting the pilgrims on his back across Heaven-Reaching River dumps them and their cargo of scriptures into the waves. This misfortune requires the pilgrims, after they struggle ashore and survive an ensuing storm, to dry out the scriptures on some boulders in the sun. Despite the pilgrims' best efforts, several scrolls of the *Buddhacarita*, Aśvaghoṣa's biographical account of the Buddha, end up

> stuck to the rocks, and a part of the sūtra's ending was torn off. This is why the sūtra today is not a complete text. . . . "We've been very careless!" said Tripitaka sorrowfully. "We should have been more vigilant."

> "Hardly! Hardly!" said Pilgrim, laughing. "After all, even Heaven and Earth are not perfect. This sūtra may have been perfect, but a part of it has been torn off precisely because only in that condition will it correspond to the profound mystery of nonperfection." (ch. 99)[84]

One is reminded of that amusing satire of an inquisition and *auto de fe* (or *auto-da-fé*) early in the *Quixote*,[85] which exposes no less memorably the physical impermanence of books. There, the priest, barber, niece, and housekeeper of the mad, bibliophilic protagonist gathered over a hundred of the books from his library, which they faulted for having driven him insane, and then burned most of them, but only after inspecting and critiquing some of the volumes one by one, including one by Cervantes himself.

An Axial Moment?

What might we conclude from the correspondences we have considered between *The Journey to the West*, the *Quixote*, and *Hamlet*, specifically with regard to the phenomena of scripturality and the tale within a tale or *mise en abyme*? It is tempting to construe these three works, in view of their lack of genetic ties, as representing an axial moment in Chinese and Western literature,[86] spanning the last decade of the sixteenth century and the opening decades of the seventeenth century, when at least three classics of the two traditions almost simultaneously take it upon themselves to flaunt their own literary substance by replicating it within themselves: the play within a play (*Hamlet*), the novel within a novel (the *Quixote*), and the scriptures within a scripture (*The Journey to the West*). Historically, this phenomenon finds suggestive conceptual precedents deeply ingrained in the Buddhist and Christian traditions from which the three works emerged. Let us consider just two examples. In *The Journey to the West*, the intermittent, fragmentary allusions of Xuanzang's past existence as Gold Cicada—by which the story of his fall from the Buddha's grace gradually emerges like a palimpsest within the currently unfolding story of his journey in this new, present life of his—collectively call to mind the Jataka tales. For the literary device of enfolding one tale within another tale bears resemblance to the Jatakas inasmuch as each of the latter tales involves the recollection of one of the Buddha's past lives from the perspective of our awareness of his later, most recent life. At the same time, the imitation of

Claudius' crime in the play that Hamlet stages within Shakespeare's play, and the discussion of the *Quixote*'s first part by the characters of the *Quixote*'s second part, enact a literary technique that seems not utterly unrelated to the habit of quoting, paraphrasing, or recalling—and hence, incorporating—elements from one scripture into another that has always underlain the Christian reading of the Old Testament, beginning in the New Testament itself: "so that the scriptures of the prophets may be fulfilled" (Matt 26:56); "Adam, who is a type of the one who was to come" (Rom 5:14). Perhaps it is their playing upon the theme of scripturality that explains why, around all three of these ostensibly secular, profane texts, an aura of religiousness or sacrality has accrued over time, at least for some readers. In pondering the question, raised by Søren Kierkegaard's pseudonym Frater Taciturnus, of whether *Hamlet* is a "religious drama,"[87] Gene Fendt concludes that *Hamlet* does indeed constitute a "religious drama in Taciturnus' impossible sense, though it must be discovered, if at all, in the affects it effects, not in the representations which construct it."[88] Later, after relating *Hamlet* to the "economies" of religion set forth by Georges Bataille, Fendt goes so far as to submit: "*Hamlet* is the drama of religion; Western culture since Wittenberg is the mimesis of this play. Shakespeare did not invent this play, he felt it, as Hamlet, like someone playing at loggets with his bones."[89] Fendt does not mention the Basque philosopher Miguel de Unamuno (1864–1936), who likewise argued influentially that Cervantes did not create Don Quixote but that Cervantes was the mouthpiece through which Don Quixote sprang from the Spanish soul to become the "Bible" of humanity.[90] In fact, Kierkegaard himself, who greatly influenced Unamuno, had come to regard "Don Quixote as an analogue to Christ and to true Christians, especially when contemplating them against the backdrop of modern Christendom."[91]

As extraordinary as such claims are for *Hamlet* and the *Quixote*, they fail to exceed in enthusiasm any number of pronouncements that have been made over the centuries on the various perceived religious ramifications of *The Journey to the West*. For example, Liu I-ming asserted of this novel that its "real message completely transcends the actual words of the text"; that it is "a book of gods and immortals, quite different from those 'books by and for geniuses' "; that it "is permeated through and through with the truth of the unity of the Three Teachings" (Buddhism, Daoism, Confucianism); and that "it possesses the power to alter [the processes of] birth and death and appropriate the secrets of Creation."[92] More recently, just over a hundred years ago, Timothy Richard, a Welsh Baptist missionary to China, published his *A Mission to Heaven: A Great Chinese Epic and Allegory* (1913),[93] which, as it is analyzed by John T. P. Lai in this present volume, proffers the downright outlandish interpretation of the entire novel about the journey of Xuanzang and his disciples as a Christian (!) allegory of pilgrimage. In this regard, it is only apt for the last word to go to Yu, who contributed so much to our perception and understanding of the religious allegorical underpinnings of *The Journey to the West*—albeit *not* of the sort Richard had in mind:

> Prior to the twentieth century, every annotated edition of the full-length narrative that I know of has treated this work as a developed and sustained allegory, a text of veiled mysteries that would divide its readership into the ignorant masses on the one hand and the fellowship of the few discerning cognoscenti on the other, an esoteric manual with a secret code that transforms it into a veritable sacred text itself.[94]

3

PILGRIMAGE TO HEAVEN

Timothy Richard's Christian Interpretation of The Journey to the West

John T. P. LAI

Translation constitutes, instead of an innocent or a purely linguistic activity, a form of intercultural mediation taking place in a specific social and cultural context,[1] and it inevitably involves the negotiation of massive cultural and ideological divides, which is made manifest in the literary translations by missionaries to China. *The Journey to the West* (西遊記 *Xiyou ji*; hereafter *Journey to the West*),[2] conventionally acclaimed as one of the four great classical novels of Chinese literature,[3] was partially translated in 1913 by Timothy Richard (1845–1919),[4] for forty-five years a Welsh Baptist missionary to China, under the title *A Mission to Heaven: A Great Chinese Epic and Allegory* (hereafter *Mission to Heaven*).[5] Deeply appreciative of its literary value, Richard regards the work as "one of the world's great masterpieces of literature and must be classed with the Epics of Homer, Dante, and Milton, and Bunyan's *Pilgrim's Progress*."[6]

Journey to the West, as Anthony Yu has succinctly suggested, can be read on at least three levels: a tale of physical travel and adventure, a story of Buddhist karma and redemption, and an allegory of philosophical and alchemical self-cultivation.[7] Richard, however, interprets the whole novel as a Christian allegory of pilgrimage, depicting a group of converted sinners who travel to heaven for "the transformation of character from very unpromising materials into saints fit for Heaven."[8] The allegory is claimed to be constructed on "profound Christian philosophy,"[9] with its author being a "Christian who sought to evangelize China."[10] In this connection, Richard offers an ardently provocative Christian interpretation of *Journey to the West*, for this classical work of Chinese fiction is deeply embedded with Buddhist and Daoist symbolism and conception. Being one of the earliest English translations of *Journey to the West*,[11] Richard's *Mission to Heaven* has hitherto received little academic attention, particularly in the English-speaking world.[12] By investigating Richard's Christian interpretation of the Buddhist elements in *Journey to the West*, this article attempts to demonstrate Richard's efforts in promoting the Christian-Buddhist dialogue and comparative study of religions in the early twentieth century.

Mahayana Christianity and Buddhist Trinity

In the process of interpreting and translating *Mission to Heaven*, Timothy Richard embarks on a religious dialogue, if not syncretism, between Christianity and Buddhism, particularly advocating the notions of Mahayana Christianity and Buddhist Trinity.[13] Among nineteenth-century Protestant missionaries,[14] Richard was not only a diligent student but also one of the most radical in the appreciation of Buddhism.[15] Richard maintains that Christianity and Buddhism had "many truths in common"[16] and that "Mahayana Faith is not Buddhism, properly so-called, but an Asiatic form of the same gospel of our Lord and Saviour Jesus Christ, in Buddhistic nomenclature."[17] *The Lotus Sutra* (*Miaofa lianhua jing* 妙法蓮華經) is even taken by Richard as God's revelation for Asia, or the "Fifth Gospel."[18] Concerning the Buddhist pantheon, Richard proposes two distinct models of Trinity, namely the "Sakyamuni Trinity" of Hinayana Buddhism, in Richard's words "Primitive Buddhism," and the "Amitabha Trinity" of Mahayana Buddhism, in his words "Higher Buddhism." The "Amitabha Trinity," with Amitabha (阿彌陀佛) in the center, Ta Shih Chih (Da Shi Zhi 大勢智 Mahasthamaprapta) on his right hand, and Kwanyin (Guanyin 觀音 Avalokitasvara) on his left,[19] is contended to have a "complete identification of the attributes of the Christian Trinity."[20] Deliberate attempts are hence made to associate the "Amitabha Trinity" with the Christian Trinity in the translation of *Mission to Heaven*.

Julai as Christ, the Incarnate God

An omnipotent figure in the novel, Julai (Rulai 如來 Tathāgata) is instrumental in settling the heavenly havoc caused by Sun Wukong (孫悟空), or the Monkey, and provides the sacred scriptures for the pilgrims from the East. Literally "the absolute come" and being one of the highest titles of Buddha,[21] "Julai" is subtly distinguished from "Fo" (佛 Buddha) in *Mission to Heaven* in order to accommodate the "Amitabha Trinity" proposed by Richard. While "Fo" is said to be the "Supreme God of the Buddhists," Julai, also called the "Mighty One" (Mahasthamaprapta 大勢智), puts an end to death and to the possibility of reincarnation, and ascends to Heaven to sit on the right hand of God.[22] In *New Testament of Higher Buddhism*, Richard suggests that the term Julai should be best rendered as "Messiah in English, as it literally means the 'Model Come,' i.e., the True Model become Incarnate,"[23] or simply the "incarnate God."[24] In other words, Richard attempts to equate Julai the Buddha with the Christian notions of "incarnate God" or "Messiah," who was born on earth to provide the true model for humankind to understand and follow God and who ultimately ascended to heaven to sit on the right hand of God, as the second person of the Christian Trinity.

In line with the aforementioned interpretation, Richard addresses Julai as the "Incarnated Model" in *Mission to Heaven*. For the illustration of Julai (如來佛) in chapter 58, Richard supplies a caption embedded with Christian implication, "The Incarnate One. With the Dove settling down on Him. The Dove shows that the original artist connected the Epic with the Gospel Narrative."[25] By mentioning "Gospel Narrative," Richard makes explicit reference to the Gospel of John, which describes the descent of a dove, symbolizing the Holy Spirit, upon Jesus Christ at his baptism: "And John bare record, saying, I saw the Spirit descending from heaven like a dove, and it abode upon him" (John 1:32 KJV). In doing so, Richard establishes a direct intertextual relation between *Mission to Heaven* and the biblical account to reinforce the proposed connection between Julai and Christ.

Other than using illustrations to construct the linkage between Julai and Christ, Richard applies Christianized notions to translate the Buddhist concept of scriptures. In chapter 8, Julai announces that he had three baskets of scriptures, including a basket of vinaya (*fa* 法) that speaks of Heaven, a basket of sātras (*lun* 論) that tells of the Earth, and a basket of sutras (*jing* 經) that redeems the damned.[26] This passage was translated by Richard as "I have a Sacred Book, which is a guide to Virtue, and which discusses the three realms of saints in heaven, of men on earth, and of demons and the lost below."[27] With the deliberate replacement of the Buddhist concept of "three baskets of scriptures" by "a Sacred Book," the multiplicity of Buddhist scriptures has been reduced to a singular canonical book, reminiscent of the Bible in Christianity. This translation might even convey the message that a single sacred book would suffice for the governance of all the heavenly and earthly realms.

In addition to the provision of sacred scripture, Julai prepares for the pilgrim master several precious Buddhist objects, two of which are the "embroidered cassock" that can protect the wearer from falling back into the wheel of transmigration and the "nine-ring priestly staff" that can keep the holder from meeting harm.[28] These two objects have been rendered in *Mission to Heaven* as "a cassock of Gospel Peace, which would save the Scripture Messenger from death and re-incarnation" and "a pastoral staff, which would save him from fatal danger."[29] Supplemented by the translator, the term "Gospel Peace" makes direct biblical reference to Ephesians 6:15, "And your feet shod with the preparation of the gospel of peace" (KJV), while the "pastoral staff" alludes to the staff of the Lord, the Great Shepherd, in Psalm 23:4, "thy rod and thy staff they comfort me" (KJV). Henceforth these originally Buddhist objects have been given profound Christian association and imagination. By highlighting that the cassock of Gospel Peace may save the Scripture Messenger from death and reincarnation, Richard not only foregrounds the saving power of the Christian gospel but also affirms his argument that Julai possesses the attributes of Christ as "God incarnate, putting an end to death and transgression, and opening the way direct [*sic*] to immortality and Heaven, without a series of incarnations."[30]

Richard's Trinitarian model becomes further complicated in chapter 7, with the first encounter between the Monkey and Julai, who calls himself Shakyamuni. Julai opens the conversation with a self-introduction, "I am Śākyamuni, the Venerable One from the Western Region of Ultimate Bliss."[31] In *Mission to Heaven*, Julai says, "I am Shakyamuni, from the happiest Paradise in the West. Praise be to Amitabha." The expression "Praise be to Amitabha," in Sanskrit "Namah Amitabha" (南無阿彌陀佛), carries profound religious implication. The Sanskrit term "Namah" means "paying homage to, bow to, or make obeisance," while "Amitabha," literally "boundless light" and "boundless life," refers to the Buddha in the Land of Ultimate Bliss (Pure Land), where all beings enjoy unbounded happiness.[32] At this particular point, Richard supplies a translator's note, reminding the readers to "note the distinction between Shakyamuni and Amitabha."[33] With regards to "Shakyamuni," Richard, in the last chapter of the novel, again provides a footnote elucidating that Shakyamuni of Higher Buddhism rose from the dead after three days. The claim about Shakyamuni's resurrection from the dead further strengthens Richard's advocated connection between Shakyamuni (Julai) and Christ.[34] Concerning "Amitabha," Richard defines him as "supreme in Paradise (Western Heaven)."[35] While Amitabha does not appear as a character in *Mission to Heaven*, the translator's annotation, "note the distinction between Shakyamuni and Amitabha," highlights, the supreme presence of Amitabha and the distinction between Julai and Amitabha in the Buddhist pantheon. The suggestion is that Amitabha, the most high God worthy of Julai's praises, would also be reminiscent of the praise offered by Jesus to his heavenly Father.[36] Consequently Richard takes full advantage of the originally formulaic line "Namah Amitabha," which is turned into "Praise be to Amitabha," for the sake of affirming his model of "Amitabha Trinity" in Mahayana Buddhism.

The Mahayana Trinitarian model, however, cannot perfectly match every scenario of the novel. In the introduction of *Mission to Heaven*, Richard not only compares Julai with Christ (Messiah) but also refers Julai to Mileh Fo (Maitreya 彌勒佛).[37] Nonetheless, Mileh Fo, in the same way as Julai, appears as a distinct character in the novel. In chapter 66, the Monkey, failing to defeat the Thunder Demon, sees a bright cloud and hears a heavenly voice, "This was no other than MILEH FO (MESSIAH), THE MOST HONOURED IN THE PARADISE OF THE WEST."[38] By doing so, Mileh Fo has been explicitly equated with the Christian Messiah. It is worth pointing out that there has been a longstanding attempt to associate Maitreya with Messiah. William Soothill, for instance, defines Maitreya as "the Buddhist Messiah, or next Buddha, now in the Tuṣita heaven, who is to come 5,000 years after the nirvāṇa of Śākyamuni."[39] However, the problem in this example lies in the potential textual conflict that both Julai and Mileh Fo, two distinct characters in the novel, are the Buddhist equivalents of the Christian Messiah, even carrying the implication that the two are identical. Apparently Richard was aware of the necessity of reconciling such a textual inconsistency.

As a matter of fact, the capitalized line above was translated from the Qing dynasty edition *Journey to the West*, titled *Xiyou zhengdao shu* (西遊證道書), which only introduces Mileh Fo as the highly honored one in paradise, worthy of all hail. However, this is merely the rendition of the last two lines of the original eight-lined poem in the Ming dynasty Shide Tang (世德堂) edition, which depicts Maitreya as a joyous stoutish Buddha.[40] Richard's selection of the more concise portrayal of Maitreya from the Qing edition seems intentionally to blur the distinction between the two Messianic figures, Julai and Mileh Fo. In so doing, the figure of Maitreya has been skillfully manipulated to cater to Richard's Christian interpretation of *Mission to Heaven*, particularly the proposed Mahayana Trinitarian model.

Kwanyin as the Holy Spirit

Bodhisattva Kwanyin (Avalokitasvara) is regarded as the third member of the "Amitabha Trinity" of Mahayana Buddhism, according to Richard's *New Testament of Higher Buddhism*.[41] A vivid image of Richard's interpretation, the illustration of Kwanyin in chapter 12 of *Mission to Heaven*, is given a caption claiming that the dove and rosary served as the symbols of Holy Spirit.[42] The dove associated with Kwanyin resonates with our previous discussion of the dove settling upon Julai, alluding to the descent of the Holy Spirit upon Jesus Christ in the Gospel of John. While Julai and Mileh Fo represent the Christian Messiah in *Mission to Heaven*, Kwanyin has been claimed to be the "Buddhist equivalent to the Holy Spirit, to whom is attributed the work of conversion. She is always represented on the left of Amitabha, when one of the Trinity, but alone and behind the Trinity screen when saving someone from a sea of trouble."[43] These Holy Spirit attributes of Kwanyin were given repeated emphasis throughout *Mission to Heaven*.

Kwanyin has been depicted as the agent of repentance leading to the conversion of the individual pilgrims in chapter 8. A contemporary reader of *Mission to Heaven*, Lin Yutang (林語堂 1895–1976) saw eye to eye with Richard's Christian interpretation by commenting on the conversion experience of the Monkey, who "ate the forbidden peach in heaven as Eve ate the forbidden apple in Eden, and he was finally chained under a rock for five hundred years as Prometheus was chained. By the time the decreed period was over, Hsüantsang [Xuanzang] came and released him, and he was to undertake the journey, fighting all the devils and strange creatures on the way, as an atonement for his sins."[44] The conversion of the Monkey and other disciples is predominantly attributed to the spiritual power of Kwanyin. The imprisoned Monkey pleads for salvation by praying to Kwanyin, "I pray you to save me, and I shall henceforth lead a new life."[45] Meanwhile, the Dragon Horse, who in his previous life committed sins by setting fire to the heavenly palace and was condemned to execution, also implores Kwanyin for help in penance of his sins, "I pray you, Kwanyin, to save me."[46] In a similar manner, Kwanyin plays the role of the agent of repentance for Sha Monk by admonishing, "Why do you not repent and help to fetch the Sacred Books from the West? Then you will no more be tormented with remorse."[47] Richard deliberately opts for those expressions with Christian overtones, for instance "pray" and "repent," to emphasize the pivotal role of Kwanyin in the repentance and redemption of the pilgrims.

Apart from serving as the agent of repentance, Kwanyin is also portrayed as the giver of new life. The resurrecting power of the Holy Spirit and Kwanyin is equalized in Richard's comparison between Christianity and Buddhism: "There are dry bones in both religions. What is needed is the Creative Spirit of the Christians, called the Merciful Kwanyin by the Buddhists, to make these dry bones live again!"[48] Kwanyin's power of "making the dry bones live again" can be best illustrated by the narrative of the beheaded Dragon in chapter 10 of *Mission to Heaven*. When the Tang Emperor is haunted by the ghost of the headless Dragon, "a Taoist priestess came forward and waved a willow twig. The headless dragon, still mourning and weeping, left at once towards the northwest."[49] Richard subtly changes the plot and introduces a new ending to the scene: "Kwanyin came with her jar of water and sprig of willow and made the dragons head grow on his body again."[50] Instead of being expelled, the beheaded Dragon is given a new life, or resurrected, by Kwanyin, coinciding with the Holy Spirit's role as the "giver of life."[51] Assuming the role of the Holy Spirit, Kwanyin serves as the "chief agent in repentance and the new birth, inspiring men to follow God in works of mercy"[52] by summoning the sinners to undertake the pilgrimage, answering their prayers, and offering immediate salvation along the arduous journey to the Western Heaven.

Huen Chwang as Apostle Paul

Being the master of the pilgrimage to heaven, Huen Chwang (玄奘Xuanzang) was converted from Primitive Buddhism to Higher Buddhism in response to the calling of Kwanyin. Richard contends that Huen Chwang belonged to "Primitive Buddhism originally and despised the Higher, as Paul did the Christian, but was afterwards converted and became a leader in the Higher."[53] Henceforth, Richard attempts to compare Huen Chwang with Apostle Paul by drawing parallels between the religious experiences of these two religious leaders of Buddhism and Christianity, respectively. They not only believed in the so-called "primitive" form of the "higher" religion in their early lives but also despised the latter. While Paul had been a staunch adherent of Judaism and persecutor of Christianity, Huen Chwang in his previous life in the heavenly realm looked down on the teaching of Buddha and was incarnated on earth.[54] Both Paul and Huen Chwang experienced the heavenly revelation and converted to the religion they once despised. While Paul had the miraculous encounter with the resurrected Christ on the way to Damascus and converted to Christianity, Huen Chwang's teaching in Primitive Buddhism was renounced by Kwanyin, who instructed him to teach Higher Buddhism because "Early Buddhism cannot save the dead, but Higher Buddhism can take them to heaven, can save men from trouble, can make them long-lived without being reborn again in this world."[55] Richard pays heed to the similar post-conversion experiences of Huen Chwang and Paul, who emerged as religious leaders and preachers of the "true religion." Endowed with the heavenly mission, the apostle Paul undertook journeys of itinerant preaching in Asia Minor and the Hellenic world in face of various persecutions. In a similar manner, Huen Chwang was called by Kwanyin to travel to the Western Heaven through numerous trials and tribulations. Like Paul who left his teachings in the Epistles to the Church, formulating a major portion of the New Testament, Huen Chwang ultimately fetched the true scriptures of Higher Buddhism from the Western Heaven for the enlightenment of the people in the East. Furthermore, Richard's translation portrays an image of a Buddhist master with unswerving determination and lofty virtues by means of a substantial omission of Huen Chwang's selfishness, cowardice, and hesitation in the face of various carnal temptations.[56]

While depicting a Pauline figure in Huen Chwang, Richard, however, does not have a consistent interpretation of the allegorical role of

Huen Chwang, who is described as a "religious Master with a vow of faith in, and loyalty to, Buddha 'God,' to help and save all living beings, by doing good to them, and by self-sacrifice. . . . He has come down from Heaven . . . to save men."[57] This description obviously associates Huen Chwang with Christ's voluntary incarnation and redeeming passion. In actual fact, Richard in his autobiography suggests that Huen Chwang is an "allegorical figure of Jesus Christ."[58] Apparently Richard has overlooked the fact that Huen Chwang's incarnation was involuntary, as chapter 100 of *Mission to Heaven* reveals; Huen Chwang, once known as Kin Shen (Golden Cicada) and a leading disciple of the Buddha, was expelled from the heavenly realm due to his despising of Buddha's teaching. This makes it clear that Richard's association between Huen Chwang and Jesus Christ is not without textual discrepancy, if not contradiction. According to Richard's manipulative narrative in *Mission to Heaven*, Huen Chwang seems to have a stronger allegorical connection with the apostle Paul than Jesus Christ, on the grounds that both of them had once looked down on the true religion, experienced the downfall and conversion, and finally embarked on the pilgrimage for the salvation of humankind.

The *Pilgrim's Progress* of Nestorianism

The quest for Higher Buddhism as the "true religion" constitutes the ultimate objective of the pilgrims in *Mission to Heaven*. On the nature of Higher Buddhism, Richard not only asserts that it shares some common truths with Christianity but claims Higher Buddhism to be equivalent with early Christianity.[59] In line with this religious assumption, chapter 100 of *Mission to Heaven* defines the "great religion" (Higher Buddhism) specifically as Nestorianism through Julai's final revelation of the underlying reason for Huen Chwang's reincarnation on earth: "Holy monk, in a former life you were my disciple, second in rank, called Kin Shen. But because you did not study carefully, and looked down on our great religion (Nestorianism) you were condemned to be re-born in China."[60] Richard's deliberate addition of "Nestorianism" to annotate "great religion" jumps to the conclusion that Mahayana Buddhism is identical with Nestorianism,[61] both of which are qualified as the "great religion" or "true religion." On the basis of this provocative interpretation, Richard puts forth a bold claim that *Mission to Heaven* is the *Pilgrim's Progress* of Nestorianism,[62] and that it is a "Chinese Epic and

Allegory of Higher Buddhism by one who appears to be a liberal Nestorian Christian."[63]

Chapter 88 offers some typical examples of Richard's manipulation of *Journey to the West* to buttress his claim of Mahayana Buddhism as the equivalent of Nestorianism. Richard highlights the importance of "prayer" as a means to "get power from on high."[64] The Monkey tells the princes that "they must acquire more power and must first be taught HOW TO PRAY . . . concentrate their thoughts on some Scripture truth, and let the breath of Heaven enter their bodies, so that God's spirit might dwell in their heart."[65] In comparison to the translation of Anthony Yu, Richard's rendition explicitly replaces the originally Buddhist terms with Christianized vocabulary. First, "Burn some incense to worship Heaven and Earth" (焚香來拜了天地)[66] has simply been translated as "Pray," modifying a heavily Buddhist ceremonial scene into one with a vivid color of Christian sacrament. Second, the Buddhist term "mantras" (*zhenyuan* 真言), in Sanskrit meaning "sacred utterance" or "magical formulae,"[67] has been rendered as "scripture Truth," which turns the mystical power embedded in the Buddhist sacred utterance into the knowledge of the scripture, with the implication of the Bible. Third, the Daoist term "Divine Breath" (*xianqi* 仙氣) has been translated as "breath of Heaven," which enters the bodies of the princes and empowers them. It is worth noting that Richard is well aware of the Daoist implication of *Shen* (*xian* 仙) in the first few chapters.[68] The replacement of the Daoist term with the use of "breath of Heaven" may not only convey the concept of Holy Spirit with its double meanings "breath" or "spirit" of the Greek term πνεῦμα (*pneuma*), but also suggest the possible link of this episode with that of the creation of Adam, when God blew his "breath" into Adam and gave him life.[69] Similarly, another Daoist expression "spiritual consciousness" (*yuanshen* 元神)[70] has been rendered into the Christian concept that "God's spirit might dwell in their heart," echoing the Pauline theology expressed in the First Epistle to the Corinthians.[71] An equally drastic move is Richard's modification of the source text by supplementing a line that the princes who received the heavenly power "become the sons of God." This addition may suggest that the Monkey's teaching was rooted in "profound Christian philosophy,"[72] particularly the power of the "scripture Truth" (Bible) and "breath of Heaven" (Holy Spirit), which can make the princes obtain power from above and become born again as the sons of God. As Theo

Hermans has argued, translation may be understood as a matter of "manipulating a Source Text so as to bring the Target Text into line with a particular model and hence a particular correctness notion, and in so doing secure social acceptance, even acclaim."[73] The aforementioned examples clearly demonstrate that Richard deliberately substitutes the Buddhist/Daoist elements and brings the target text into line with the Christian framework in an effort to convince the English readers that *Mission to Heaven* is apparently a Christian allegory, or more specifically *Pilgrim's Progress* of Nestorianism, with a view to securing social acceptance in the target culture.

To further substantiate his assertion of a Nestorian *Pilgrim's Progress*, Richard spares no effort to "rediscover" any possible Nestorian elements and references in *Mission to Heaven*. The original text of chapter 88 has an eight-line poem depicting the scene of the three disciples who demonstrate their mastery of martial arts in front of the Princes of Yu Hwa (玉華縣). Richard's rendition of the first two lines of the poem, "The true Illustrious Religion is not human / The great Way, whose origin is in all space," is profoundly problematic. A footnote has been added to elucidate the term "Illustrious Religion": "The Chinese name used here is the same as that used on the Nestorian monument for Christianity."[74] As a matter of fact, "Illustrious Religion" is the literal translation of the Chinese name of Nestorianism (*jingjiao* 景教), which is mentioned in the Nestorian monument.[75] Nevertheless, the term *jingjiao* is not used in the first line of the original poem, reading *Zhen Chan jingxiang bufan tong* (真禪景象不凡同).[76] The word *jingxiang* (景象), simply meaning "view," "scene," or "sight,"[77] does not have the faintest association with *jingjiao* (Illustrious Religion). This example testifies to the strategy of liberal refashioning of the original text on the part of Richard for serving his purpose of Nestorian interpretation in *Mission to Heaven*. In fact, Richard's Nestorian interpretation and manipulation of *Journey to the West* is not confined to this particular chapter.

Predominantly, Richard strives to make a remote, if not bizarre, connection between Allopen (亞羅本), the first Nestorian missionary to Tang China, and the Daoist deity Chin Wu (真武大帝) in chapter 66. The beginning of the chapter narrates the mistranslated legend of Chin Wu (The True Conqueror), whose wife miraculously swallowed a beam of light and in AD 581 gave birth to a child who was "The Equal One with God."[78] Regarding Chin Wu, Richard even provides an annotation to assert that Allopen was the child born in the year AD 581 and that Allopen was fifty-four years old upon his arrival in China in AD 635. Richard goes further to contend that "Nestorians taught that the Spirit of their Saviour had reappeared in the person of Olopen [Allopen]."[79] Such a claim attempts to build a far-fetched connection between the miraculous birth of the Nestorian priest Allopen and that of the Christ of Christianity who was conceived by the power of the Holy Spirit and born of the Virgin Mary. Without any solid evidence, Richard makes incredible use of the myth of the birth of the son of Chin Wu to relate the novel to the history of Nestorian missions in Tang China, giving historically groundless support to his assertion that *Mission to Heaven* is a Nestorian *Pilgrim's Progress*. This once again testifies to Theo Herman's argument that translation is a goal-oriented act that implies a degree of manipulation of the source text for a particular purpose.[80]

"Multi-religious" Kingdom of God

Mission to Heaven concludes with the pilgrim's arrival and canonization in the Western Heaven in chapter 100. Probably alluding to the "new song" sung by the heavenly creatures in the book of Revelation,[81] the climatic chanting of the "New Anthem in Heaven" at the end of *Mission to Heaven* is in praise of the aim of all the founders of the great religions,[82] such as Buddha, Messiah, Mohammed (Muhammad), and Mani.[83] The purely Buddhist Western Heaven of the original text has been lavishly converted into the kingdom of God that embraces all the major world religions in a harmonious manner. Richard's portrayal of the multi-religious kingdom of God constitutes an implementation of his view on comparative religion—that is, that "the fundamental principles of Comparative Religion which recognize that true Religion comes not to destroy but to fulfil, that no religion has a monopoly of all truth, and that the best in all religions is Divine and eternal, and must be honoured."[84] Richard's view actually echoes Max Müller's (1823–1900) statement denying the monopoly of Western religions, particularly Christianity, in the possession of truth: "There is no specific difference between ourselves and the Brahmans, the Buddhists, the Zoroastrians, or the Taosze. Our powers of perceiving, of reasoning, and of believing may be more highly developed, but we cannot claim the possession of any verifying power or of any power of belief which they did not possess as well."[85] By undertaking and editing the fifty-volume *Sacred Books of the East* series, Müller for the first time "placed the historical and comparative study of religions on a solid foundation."[86] While Richard's interest in other non-Christian religions commenced as early as the 1870s,[87] Müller's view on comparative religion might have been a major source of inspiration for Richard, whose library contained a complete set of *Sacred Books of the East*.[88] In translating the *New Testament of Higher Buddhism*, Richard makes special reference to *Sacred Books of the East* for the discussion of the common ground between Buddhism and Christianity.[89] In other words, Richard's standpoint on comparative religion not only reflected but was actually influenced by the contemporary development of the comparative study of religions spearheaded by Müller in the late nineteenth century.[90]

The multireligious kingdom of God envisaged in the "New Anthem in Heaven" unveils the ultimate missionary goal of Richard, who regards the establishment of the kingdom of God on earth as the solution to multifarious human problems, including poverty, oppression, violence, ignorance, selfishness, and sin.[91] For Richard, the missionary vision of establishing the kingdom of God on earth includes not only the unity of religion but also the cooperation of Christians and non-Christians for the well-being of all humankind.[92] Nevertheless, Richard's envisioned kingdom of God encompassing multiple religions remains, in essence, Christian centered. Although he argues that the Great Religion of the kingdom of God would not be born of any particular existing religion, he also argue that the kingdom was still what "Jesus Christ commanded His disciples to preach"[93] and that it was a "kingdom of our God and of His Christ."[94] With this underlying Christian assumption in mind, it is inevitable for Richard to view Buddhism through the lens of Christianity and even equate Mahayana Buddhism with Christianity, as manifested in his proposed notions of Mahayana Christianity and Buddhist Trinity.

Conclusion

Timothy Richard's production of a Christianized rendition of *Journey to the West* coincides with his underlying interpretation that Mahayana Buddhism is an Asiatic form of the gospel of Christianity, on the basis of which he formulates his assumption that *Journey to the West* was a Nestorian *Pilgrim's Progress* with its predominant theme of a pilgrimage to heaven. One may easily criticize the "misinterpretation" of Buddhism and "inaccuracy" in the translation of *Mission to Heaven* on the grounds of the identity and proselytizing agenda of Richard as a Christian missionary from the West. Richard has undoubtedly manipulated the source text of *Journey to the West* by translating the Buddhism concepts and terminology in the Christian framework. Nevertheless, as Maria Tymoczko succinctly argued, translation is not a substitutive, metaphorical process of wholesale replacement of one language or culture by another but rather a "metonymic process of connection, a process of creating contiguities and contextures."[95] Instead of a wholesale replacement of Buddhism by Christianity, *Mission to Heaven* has been transformed into a kind of hybrid text: on the one hand, it has the flavor of the Buddhist implications of the original novel, and on the other, it is infiltrated with Christian references in the target text. It would be hardly justifiable, as Li Hui remarked, to view Richard's translation approach as a simplified and reductionist substitution of Chinese culture by Christian mentality, because Richard adopts a liberal cultural attitude by fully acknowledging the complexity of Oriental culture and the high literary value of *Journey to the West.*[96]

All in all, the translation of *Mission to Heaven* constitutes a literary experiment, if not instrument, for advocating Richard's comparative religion and realizing his vision for the establishment of the kingdom of God, not only in China but all over the world. While Lai Pan-chiu has a point when he suggests that Richard's appreciation of Mahayana Buddhism was shaped by his Christian beliefs,[97] Richard's Christian beliefs are also reshaped in the process of his intense encounter with Buddhism and other Chinese religions. We may argue that Richard attempts to transcend not only Buddhism but also Christianity in his pursuit of the establishment of a more inclusive kingdom of God, which embraces the ideals of the great religions of the world. Being one of the earliest endeavors of translating *Journey to the West* into English, *Mission to Heaven*, albeit controversial, was testament to the dawn of Christian-Buddhist dialogue and comparative study of religions in the early twentieth century.

Part II

STUDIES IN TRANSLATION
China and the Missionaries

4

REVISITING THE MISSIONARY STANCE

Conversation and Conversion in James Legge's The Religions of China *(1880)*

Trevor Hart

Translation as an Ethical Act

In his magisterial study of the phenomenon of translation, George Steiner reminds us that far from being an exceptional or specialized circumstance, to translate is in fact the basic mode of human relationship as facilitated and realized through language.[1] The logical structure of every act of linguistic communication, he argues, is precisely the same, whether we are listening to a neighbor's account of yesterday's cricket match, poring over an ancient document in the library with a barrage of lexical tools at hand, or asking for directions in a foreign airport where even the local alphabet is inconveniently unfamiliar. Acts of translation are involved in each of these circumstances—an effort (conscious or unconscious) to align our horizons of understanding with those of another to the greatest extent possible, and so to be come those "with ears to hear." We can never do so completely, of course, and in this sense, as the German philologist Wilhelm von Humboldt noticed long ago, "[a]ll understanding is at the same time a misunderstanding, all agreement in thought and feeling is at the same time a parting of the ways."[2]

Of course, the task is rather more difficult (or at least more obviously so), and the likelihood of misunderstanding correspondingly higher, when there are linguistic and cultural as well as personal differences between transmitter and receiver, and we find ourselves reminded rudely once more of the material reality of words as, at one level, mere ejaculations of sound or a forest of black marks on the page. But, despite the perpetual gap between physical signifiers and their signifieds, and the Heraclitean aspect of signification as such, as Steiner points out, "We *do* translate, and have done so since the beginning of human history. The defence of translation has the immense advantage of abundant vulgar fact."[3] Like other material realities, words and the structures we create from them can be used as barricades behind which we hide, carefully designed to exclude the other when it suits our needs to do so; but they are also chief among the ways in which we extend ourselves out into the world and make contact with others and, as such, are essential to projects designed to enhance human flourishing. If, notwithstanding the apparent difficulties, communication is possible between individuals, if translation and conversation can and does occur across the gaps posited by our own individual privacies, then we need not despair of hearing human voices speaking to us from other cultures, other times and places.

As the form to which every act of human communication is subject at some level, translation itself is ethically ambiguous in its nature and needs to be carefully monitored and undertaken. The relevant metaphors are often bold and imperialistic, providing an uncomfortable parallel, perhaps, to aspects of that very nineteenth-century missionary endeavor with which we shall duly be concerned. The translator begins with an act of faith, trusting that there is meaning to be "had," something there to be laid hold of through the hermeneutic venture. And there is an act of aggression, a trespassing into foreign territory in order to grasp something and carry it home captive. Or, employing a different metaphor, we "make sense" of the "text," placing a construction upon it that draws it securely within the horizons of our prior understanding. (Every act of translation, Steiner reminds us, is an act of interpretation, a creative "making" of meaning rather than scientific matching of linguistic equivalences.) This, though, like the literal acts of colonialism that it parallels, carries with it its attendant risks, as we bear home cargo and introduce it to our world of understanding, a process that cannot leave that world unchanged. There is, to use Steiner's preferred (and perhaps unduly negative) image, the ever-present risk of infection from imported cargo, so that we may find ourselves compelled to reckon with new and uncomfortable ways of looking at things. And then, finally, there is what Steiner calls the stage of "restitution," as the translator seeks faithfully to offer some account of the meaning that he/she brings home in terms familiar to those unable to make the intellectual (or the geographical) journey for themselves. There are elements here, then, of both action and passion, a dialectic of aggression and self-emptying, translating and in turn "being translated" into new and alien cultural environments.[4] And undergirding and driving all this is the energy of what Iris Murdoch identifies as imaginative curiosity with respect to the other and, hopefully, a respect for the other that seeks its well-being and flourishing rather than its marginalization and control.[5] For the Christian missionary, finally, even the language of "respect" for the other will be too anaemic (let alone its even more sickly cousin, "tolerance"); it is with love for the other that we must be concerned, in acts of translation as elsewhere.[6]

Legge's Open Secret

The accomplishment of James Legge in translating the Chinese classics into English can hardly be gainsaid. In the estimation of that other great sinologist of the age, Herbert Giles, "Legge's work is the greatest contribution ever made to the study of Chinese, and will be remembered and studied ages after."[7] The accomplishment was more than merely linguistic, of course, bearing on the whole perception of Chinese culture among Western readers, and thus the early shape of that other modern construction, "East-West relations." "These volumes, the outcomes of his long-continued toil," wrote Joseph Edkins of Shanghai, "contain a rich store of facts by which the foreign observer in Europe and America can judge of China so correctly, because here are the maxims which are popular, here are the ideas that rule the minds of the scholars and all the people. . . . What the Bible is to the Christian; what Shakespeare is to the student of English poetry . . . these books are to the universal Chinese mind."[8] Even allowing for the intrusion of enthusiastic overstatement ("Alas! the classics are hardly studied nowadays," another contemporary complains),[9] the importance of Legge's contribution is surely difficult to overestimate. In his eulogy at Legge's funeral on December 3, 1897, his fellow-Scot exiled together with him in Oxford, A. M. Fairbairn (then principal of Mansfield College, a haven of ecclesiastical nonconformity in the midst of a sea of Anglican establishment) referred to Legge's initiation with his predecessor Robert Morrison (1782–1834) of a new phase of intercultural work: "Namely, the promotion of the brotherhood of men by the development of mutual understanding between different groups of mankind."[10]

One might have thought this reason enough to engage in the task, and in one sense it was. Legge was certainly concerned to translate more than just the texts with which he wrestled for the best part of thirty years to bring to publication in English. He wanted to translate the ethos from which those texts issued too and to translate his Western readers in their turn into that ethos so that they might view it, as it were, from within. This feat of intercultural translation he attempted (and dedicated half of his working life to), though, not out of any merely pragmatic or academic concern (in the way that some modern scholars in earlier generations than our own were able to "make their name" academically by becoming the acknowledged expert on a particular body of literature, often regardless of its merits). Legge was wholly convinced of the intrinsic value of the texts he worked upon and the more than merely political benefits, therefore, to Western readers of becoming acquainted with them. It is worth citing him at length on this:

> It is true that their civilization is very different from ours, but they are far removed from barbarism. When we bear in mind that for four thousand years the people have been living and flourishing there, growing and increasing, that nations with some attributes perhaps of a higher character—the Assyrian, the Persian, the Grecian, the Roman, and more empires—have all risen and culminated and decayed, and yet that the Chinese empire is still there with its four hundred millions of inhabitants, why, it is clear that there must be amongst the people certain moral and social principles of the greatest virtue and power.[11]

This may read to us today in certain respects as damnation with faint praise; after all, staying power is not everything, and many things are "far from barbarism" and glad to be so, without laying any great claim to profundity or religious and moral illumination. But in Legge's own day this was exuberant in its affirmation of the worth of Chinese culture as anything more than another backward manifestation of the human spirit awaiting the gracious Enlightenment to be provided (together with suitably adjusted political and economic arrangements) by Western markets. Indeed, there may even be a deliberate and carefully aimed barb in Legge's closing accolade in the passage cited, that "in no country" (what, not even a European one?) "is the admiration of scholastic excellence so developed as in China, no kingdom in the world where learning is so highly reverenced."[12] Once placed in context and decoded, this sounds like a representative of Enlightened Western civilization going significantly "off-message." It tallies with Fairbairn's estimation that Legge "studied [Chinese culture] with an eye made luminous by love. . . . And as he loved the people, he was jealous for all that was good and true in their faith. . . . He had the insight which comes of the heart even more than of the head into their literature and religion; and he saw that the primary condition of making the West influential in the East was to make the East intelligible to the West. The missionaries who would convert a people," Fairbairn continues, "must first condescend to know the people they would convert and the religion they would displace."[13]

But there is the rub. Legge's massive labor of translation may have been undertaken with a love of the people and their culture and from the conviction that the Western world for its part had much to learn from that culture; it may have been undertaken in such a manner as to equip and enhance the work of future generations of scholars and with a weather eye to the considerable political benefits of increased mutual understanding between East and West. But finally, Legge was a Christian missionary, and his labor was far from being disinterested or dispassionate. On the contrary, it was driven by the desire that "our missionary labours among the people should be conducted with sufficient intelligence and so as to secure permanent results."[14] Legge made no bones about it. This instrumental consideration was reflected in his successful persuasion of John Dent to underwrite what was otherwise a costly publication far beyond the purse of those in the mission field, in order that they might obtain it at half the cost of production, and his continuation of the arrangement at his own cost after Dent's death. It is easy, in celebrating and exploring Legge's intellectual contribution, to picture him in his Oxford study, at ease with his books, his clutch of honorary degrees and the other paraphernalia of academe. But we do him no justice, nor any favors, if we forget that the translations on which his reputation largely rests were undertaken as a subsidiary activity alongside (and ultimately in the service of) his ministry as a pastor and a preacher purposed "to lead men to eternal life, so that the light of the Christian doctrine could shine in every corner of the earth."[15]

The question of whether this "open secret" (which everyone knows, but which it is sometimes more convenient to forget to mention) may be reckoned with honestly, and Legge's missionary stance be owned as a legitimate disposition in intercultural conversation, is one of more than merely academic concern. In other words, may we, in our engagements with otherness, legitimately be motivated by a desire to see the other "converted" (a clumsy and unfortunate metaphor, but we may as well grapple with it in its starkest version) to our way of thinking and experiencing the world or at least to some core aspects of the same? Can there be a place for "contested" truth,[16] which is either left unresolved or must be resolved by a shift in conviction on the part of one or more of the participants in a conversation? In the religious and theological context, there is rather more nervousness about the suggestion that it might be so than one typically finds among advocates of other disciplines and practices outside the sheltered "objectivity" of the natural sciences—political science say, or history, or literary criticism. No doubt in part this nervousness is occasioned by awareness of the awful history of "man's inhumanity to man" and the convenient platform religious and theological differences have often provided for getting stuck into it. Add to this the other images conjured up by that word "conversion," and one can well understand the nervousness and even begin to appreciate it. But *abusus non tollit usum*, and if religion can be toxic we at least know nowadays that officially atheist and other ideological substitutes for it typically fare no better when it comes to perpetrating random acts of violence and cruelty. If we are genuinely involved in conversation, and want to learn what it is that makes our fellow participants tick, what it is that they consider worth striving for in life, what it is that they hope for (and religion is at least as much about those things as what it is worth *dying* for), then we shall not want to encounter them shorn of many of the things that they hold to be true and important, in the bid for a liberal concensus that ends up marginalizing every particular standpoint and commitment other than that of liberalism itself. Legge's love for all things Chinese was born not of such pusillanimous strategies, but of having translated himself into Chinese culture as he found it, desirous of an unconditional encounter with it in which nothing was held back, and having offered himself back unreservedly in return.

It was this sort of openness to the Chinese classics and the many Chinese people he came to know that, in Legge's pre-Liberal context, granted him whatever love for and wisdom about their culture he possessed. But it was an openness that, as it should, provoked deep questions about facets of his own Christian faith. For, as Hendrik Kraemer notes, "To become more deeply aware of the stupendous richness and depth of religious life in *all* religions has made the question of value and truth in the non-Christian religions more, and not less, acute."[17] Legge's generation was one of the first to be compelled to reckon with this and, in the wake of Friedrich Schleiermacher (arguably the first Christian theologian to make a fully considered response), to grapple with the formulation of what these days we would call a "theology of religions." Legge did not shirk this, though his observations are scattered and occasionally indirect, arising in the midst of his positive accounts of Chinese religious traditions and his comparisons of them with Christianity.

Legge's Appreciation of Chinese Religions

It was in delivering the Spring Lectures of the Presbyterian Church of England in 1880 that Legge offered what was, if not quite an encomium, nonetheless an account of the religions of China that would perhaps surprise some among his audience in its warmth and positive discrimination.[18] It was to Confucianism in particular that the largest measure of generosity was afforded in his account, and for purposes of space, among others, I shall limit myself to that here.

By "Confucianism" Legge intended much more than the recorded teachings of the great sage himself or those of his acolytes, using the term rather as synecdoche for the wider tradition of China's ancient religion dating back five thousand years BC, which Confucius himself transmitted and modified in proportions difficult to determine. Unlike some of his peers, Legge was in no doubt that Confucius himself was in a proper sense a religious teacher rather than a mere moralist or purveyor of social etiquette;[19] but in any case, the wider tradition within which he must be situated was, Legge believed, not only religious but profoundly monotheistic, a judgment bringing it at once into the same ballpark for consideration as the religion of the ancient Hebrews, a comparison Legge himself was quick to make. Thus of the ancient noun *Tien*

(Heaven) he writes that it "has had much of the force of the name Jahve, as explained by God Himself to Moses," while the more personal *Tî* "has presented that absolute deity in the relation to men of their Lord and governor, *Tî* was to the Chinese fathers, I believe, exactly what God was to our fathers, whenever they took the great name on their lips."[20] The question of the aptness or accuracy of Legge's analogical imagination at points such as this is one to which we may return; but my interest here is more with his own reading of the circumstance, and how that duly shaped his thinking about mission and the place of Chinese religion in God's scheme of things.

Of course Legge recognized that, in a manner not quite paralleled in Hebraic religion, Confucianism was populated too with numerous spiritual beings, some associated with various facets of the created world, and to whom worship was due and was offered. Furthermore, for the ordinary man or woman, worship was chiefly linked to the veneration of one's ancestors, involvement with the worship of *Tî* or *Shang Tî* being focused on the person of the emperor alone. Such "inferior worship" (a value judgment Legge does not hesitate to make) was, he observes, all the religion that was left to the masses. But where some commentators looked and saw only an uncertain play of polytheism, Legge insists that such tendencies were held securely in check by the overarching acknowledgement of Tî alone as the one true God, and the situation of all other spirits in subordination to him and his will, being in effect the created mediators of his purposes (and thus surely bearing some resemblance at least to later Jewish and Christian angelology and to the roles played by the saints in some strands of Christian piety).[21]

Drawing on the evidence of the *Shû King* and the *Shih King*, Legge constructs a doctrine of God that certainly resonates well enough with that of biblical sources. Thus: "In both of these books many things are predicated of Heaven, *Tî*, and *Shang Tî*, that are true only of the true God. He is ruler of men and all this lower world. Men in general, the mass of the people, are His peculiar care. He appointed grain to be the chief nourishment of all. He watches especially over the conduct of kings."[22] Indeed, Legge traces something strikingly akin to the so-called "Deuteronomic principle" in these texts, whereby divine judgment (executed in history's midst) visits blessing on upright rulers and downfall on the recalcitrant and reprobate.[23] It is in the liturgy of sixteenth-century solstitial rites,[24] though, that he identifies the most striking resonances, especially with the characterizations of God found in the creation theologies of the Pentateuch, the Psalter, and the Prophets. A handful of examples will suffice to make the point.

> Of old, in the beginning, there was the great chaos, without form and dark. The five elements had not begun to revolve, nor the sun and moon to shine. In the midst thereof there presented itself neither form nor sound. Thou, O spiritual Sovereign, camest forth in Thy presidency, and didst first divide the grosser parts from the purer. Thou madest heaven; Thou madest earth; Thou madest man. All things got their being, with their reproducing power.
>
> O *Tî*, when Thou hadst opened the course for the inactive and active forces of matter to operate, Thy making work went on. Thou didst produce, O Spirit, the sun and moon, and five planets; and pure and beautiful was their light. The vault of heaven was spread out like a curtain, and the square earth supported all on it, and all creatures were happy.[25]

Interestingly, although classical strands of Jewish and Christian exegesis have tended to insist upon the sovereign creative activity of God "from above," setting God apart as Creator from any other agency, recent work by interpreters of the Hebrew Bible such as William Brown, Terrence Fretheim, and Jon Levenson, and systematic theologians such as Michael Welker, has drawn attention to the presence in biblical texts too of the notion of God (El/Yahweh) as one who, while certainly set radically apart from the world in all sorts of ways, nonetheless enlists creaturely agencies and processes into his own creative work, which proceeds *per collaborationi* rather than in splendid isolation.[26] But to resume the litany of purported resonances:

> Thy sovereign goodness is infinite. As a potter hast Thou made all living things. Great and small are curtained round (by Thee from harm). As engraven on the heart of Thy poor servant is the sense of Thy goodness, but my feeling cannot be fully displayed. With great kindness Thou dost bear with us, and, notwithstanding our demerits, dost grant us life and prosperity.
>
> All the ends of the earth look up to (*Tî*). All human beings, all things on the earth, rejoice together in the Great Name.[27]

That such sentiments would not be out of place in the Hebrew or Christian canons will be clear to anyone familiar with them. That the doctrine of God to which they point was one unknown to the larger masses of religious practitioners in China must not be overlooked, but the formal presence of such ideas and their articulation in the central rites of the cult is significant for Legge nonetheless. Where he finds them wanting, in doctrinal terms, is in their failure to face sufficiently forthrightly the problem of the human propensity for sin and evil, and the consequent lack of any sense of guilt on the part of the worshipper or concomitant apprehension of God as one who forgives and makes good the damage occasioned by sin. He cites Tang in the *Shû* as evidence of a basically optimistic Chinese anthropology, at odds with the estimations of Jewish and Christian texts: "The great God has conferred (even) on the inferior people a moral sense, compliance with which would show their nature invariably right. To make them tranquilly pursue the course which it would indicate is the work of the sovereign" (i.e., the king or emperor).[28] Legge acknowledges that other strands are more nuanced in their reading of the human circumstance, such as Shun (in the *Shû*): "The mind of man is restless, prone (to err); its affinity to what is right is small."[29] But he sees the true heir to Confucian thought in the familiar thought of Mencius that "water will . . . flow indifferently towards the east or west; but will it flow indifferently up or down? It will not; and the tendency of human nature towards good is like the tendency of water to flow down."[30] Humanity may be diverted toward evil, but its natural inclination is always otherwise. Confucius may have admitted the difficulty he experienced in following his own moral precepts; but for Legge Confucianism provides no adequate account of why this should be so, no morally robust acknowledgment of the realities of human behavior, and no theologically satisfying account of the moral and spiritual outcomes. While, therefore, he applauded the Confucian insistence upon humanity having been formed for goodness ("if it were not so, I do not see how man could be exhorted, under any system of religion, 'to eschew evil and do good' "),[31] he was obliged to conclude that "in every department of morality," theoretically and theologically at least, it was lacking by comparison with Christianity (i.e., in the latter's biblical and theological heart rather than its empirical manifestations).

Conversation, Conversion, and Universal Intent

How, then, did Legge square this descriptive and evaluative account (positive and negative) of Chinese religion with his own status as a Christian missionary? How did his interpretation of it fit within his self-understanding as one called upon to bear witness to the unique revelatory and redemptive economy of God concentrated on God's own entry into history as a creature in Jesus Christ? How did he think of the standing before God of those millions of devout souls raised within the traditions of Confucianism and seeing no particular need to change religious horses in midstream?

Perhaps the first thing to admit, in light of the first section of this essay, is that Legge's reading of Confucianism was and must necessarily have been a "construction," a "making sense" of what confronted him, and doing so by drawing it within horizons of understanding already available to him (the only way any of us is ever able to begin to make sense of anything). Just as our notions of identity are generally constructed in relation to some notion of alterity, so, correspondingly, alterity can only be grasped at all by relating it to analogies lying within the sphere of the self and its familiar territories. Thus, as Kearney puts it, "there can be no relation to the other that does not in some respect transform the other into a relative other. . . . The notion of an absolute manifestation of the other qua absolute (*kath' auto*) is impossible."[32] Again, this ethical dilemma (insofar as it is such) is true of our relationships *within* cultures and communities, as well as relationships between them. Perhaps some will suppose Legge guilty of assimilating Confucian religion too much to what he already knew and valued, and so of underestimating the genuine otherness of the texts and the people he was dealing with. Perhaps they are correct. Here, too, though, there can be no absolutes, and all of us fail all the time to discern the depths of the others who confront and encounter us. An ethics of interpretation or translation will seek to acknowledge this and so refuse to rest content with first or even second impressions, being open to the further adjustment and alignment of its perspectives to accommodate new ways of seeing things. Here, at least, Legge was anything but naive. At the very outset of the final, comparative chapter of the work to which I have been alluding, he states his proposed method and its potential downfalls, and he offers a distinctly Christian imperative for what I have called an "ethics of translation." It is worth citing him in full:

> It may be said that my reasoning will proceed from and conduct to a foregone conclusion. To some extent it must and will be so. I cannot make my mind a *tabula rasa* in regard to the faith in which I was brought up, and which, in mature years, after not a little speculation and hesitancy, I embraced for myself, with an entire conviction of its truth. At the same time, the more that a man possesses the Christian spirit, and is governed by Christian principle, the more anxious he will be to do justice to every other system of religion, and to hold his own without taint or fetter of bigotry. Looking abroad on the various forms of belief in the world, and including his own among them, he will endeavour to fulfil the counsel of Paul, to "prove all things and hold fast that which is good."[33]

This is prescient in its anticipation of an epistemological point made by numerous writers on mission and the theology of religions in the late twentieth century, and germane to the comparative study of religions more widely—namely, that where matters of a "religious" nature (among others) are concerned, "there is no objective, i.e., rationally cogent and universally valid and acceptable norm" on the basis of which to evaluate the perspectives and paradigms of others.[34] The grounds on which we judge, and the horizons from within which we judge, are those bequeathed to us (by upbringing, education, currents of wider culture) or deliberately chosen by us, and for the purposes of intellectual functioning cannot rationally themselves be exposed to scrutiny. To do that, we should have temporarily to adopt some other set, invested equally with fiduciary authority (i.e., we must trust them, for the purposes of the investigation, to be true or at least trustworthy). What we cannot do is take our stand nowhere, in religious terms or terms of any other sort.[35] This is the same point made by Lesslie Newbigin in his critical response to "comparative" approaches to religion and to currents in religious pluralism:

> It is very understandable that we should look for some point of view which would enable us to bring together . . . clashing commitments in a single framework. It is understandable, but we have to face the fact that it is impossible. The framework which I desire or discern is my ultimate commitment or else it cannot function in the way intended. As such a commitment, it must defend its claim to truth over against other claims to truth. I have no standpoint except the point where I stand. The claim that I have is simply the claim that mine is the

> standpoint from which it is possible to discern the truth that relativizes the truth. That claim is the expression of the ultimate commitment which is my true religion.[36]

Newbigin draws on the philosophy of Michael Polanyi, a philosopher of science, to stay the apparently inevitable slide into relativism here. The fact that every truth claim rests on a prior fiduciary commitment that cannot itself be demonstrated to be true does not, Polanyi insists, mean that such claims are "subjective" or that they cannot or ought not to be invested with "universal intent," a point he illustrates repeatedly and at length not from the humanities but from the ways of working of the so-called hard sciences.[37] In brief, the fact that there is no nonperspectival place from which to approach and view and engage with things does not mean that all perspectives are equally helpful (and so equally unhelpful), and the one we choose to adopt ought logically to be the one we invest with "universal intent" and for which we are prepared constructively to contend in our conversations with others. It is this, I think, and not some deregulated bar-room brawl, that Kraemer has in mind when he writes that, given this perspectival nature of our human condition, "the search for scientific and metaphysical truth will go on as a spiritual contest—full of risks and precious results, to be sure—and not as a march towards intellectual unanimity."[38] In such "contest," as part of a genuinely ethical engagement with the other, each participant will certainly hope to bear effective witness to the riches of his or her own viewpoint, but the epistemic point we have made robs anyone of the right to indulge in spiritual or intellectual arrogance. To cite Kraemer again: "As long as there is no universally acknowledged norm of religious Truth—and it is evident that there is not, indeed there cannot be one—it is, logically speaking, useless to talk about the superiority of one religion over another. It always amounts to the confident assertion of one's own religious Ego as the standard."[39]

Perhaps Legge can be forgiven for not having anticipated quite this much and so for slipping from time to time into the language of "superiority" and "inferiority" in his judgements; but certainly he did not intend by doing so to belittle or offend adherents to a religious tradition by which he had come to set great store and from which he believed Christians might learn a great deal, albeit without abandoning the fundamental shape of the faith they habitually indwelt. And, of course, the fact that two or more religious traditions must be acknowledged to offer perspectives on all manner of things that differ and clash with one another and must thus be humbly "contested" in any conversation worthy of the name does not mean that there are not significant apparent coincidences and complementarities of insight among them. Indeed, experience "does discover certain crossing-points (*Knooppunten*) or 'magnetic fields,' around which, in many converging and deeply diverging ways . . . human thinking has crystallised."[40] Legge seems to me to concur with this judgment and to be both generous and discriminating in his treatment of different religious traditions and their relationships of parity and disparity one to another. Confucianism, we have seen, he holds above all to be "not antagonistic" to the thought-world in which Christianity moves and breathes, where others (he mentions Buddhism and Brahmanism) might be judged to be.[41] Yet he refuses to do any religion the disservice of pronouncing it a *preparatio evangelica* or a version of "anonymous Christianity." To do that would indeed be to fail to treat it on its own terms and to fail to grapple adequately with its otherness. Nonetheless, Legge felt that there were a fair number of "magnetic fields" falling within the purview of Christianity and Confucianism alike and so that there was more likelihood of finding riches in the latter to be celebrated and learned from by Christian missionaries. "Let no one think any labour too great to make himself familiar with the Confucian books," he writes. "So shall missionaries in China come fully to understand the work they have to do; and the more they avoid driving their carriages rudely over the Master's grave, the more likely are they soon to see Jesus enthroned in His room in the hearts of the people."[42]

Perhaps the greatest weakness in Legge's "comparative" account of Chinese religion and Christianity is his failure to address the question of how his missionary endeavors, aimed in some sense at the conversion of those whose thought and beliefs he engaged with, were related to questions about their salvation. For it is here that something positive needs to be said, and it is here that misunderstanding can lead to an unhealthy dogmatism of one sort or another (whether "exclusivist" or "pluralist" in the terms of Alan Race's familiar taxonomy). Could Legge really have rested content with the supposition that the culture that he had come to respect and love (rather than merely tolerate), and from which he held himself to have learned so much, was condemned to an eternity of separation from God unless it swallowed his doctrine wholesale and submitted to baptism (literal or metaphorical)? These are difficult questions, and one can hardly blame Legge for not having answered them, though it is clear that he felt their force.

In moving this essay toward a close, it seems appropriate to draw on the wise, theologically sensitive, and astute reflection of another Presbyterian, the aforementioned Newbigin. Like Legge, Newbigin was for thirty years a missionary in a land alien to his own, called upon to bear Christ to those who had not yet reckoned with him but convinced by his translation of himself into the world of the "other" that he was by no means the one holding all the strong cards in his hand. Offering a brief outline of some of Newbigin's own reflections on the alleged "scandal of particularity" will help to tie up some theological loose ends and so bring closure to certain questions raised in the preceding pages. Indeed, despite the obvious anachronism involved, what Newbigin has to say seems to me to be both in shape and sin ubstance precisely the sort of stance implied by what Legge writes about Chinese religious culture and by the wider tone and manner of his engagement with it. A brief summary of it may therefore be a fitting way in which to conclude an account of his thought.

We may as well begin with the scandal and offense undoubtedly caused by Christians whose missionary activity has been premised on their prized possession of something others lack—namely, salvation, or the key to it. On this, Newbigin is forthright; no Christian he insists should assume any right to know and declare what God's final judgment on anyone will be. "This," he writes, "is not a small matter. It determines the way in which we approach the man of another faith. It is almost impossible for me to enter into simple, honest, open, and friendly communication with another person as long as I have at the back of my mind the feeling that I am one of the saved and he is one of the lost. Such a gulf is too vast to be bridged by any ordinary human communication."[43] Nor should we presume, in the manner of some religious pluralists, to assure others that, due to some religious adherence or performance within their own tradition, they *will* be saved. That too is to arrogate to ourselves a "pay grade" we simply do not possess. "The truth is," Newbigin writes, "that my meeting with a person of another religion is on a much humbler basis. I do not claim to know in advance his ultimate destiny. I meet him simply as a witness, as one who has been laid hold of by Another and placed in a position where I can only point to Jesus as the one who can make sense of the whole human situation which my partner and I share as fellow human beings. That is the basis of our meeting."[44] What this does *not* mean, though, is that the Christian has a stranglehold on truth, and that the claims of those outside the church must be false or deluded. "The Christian confession of Jesus as Lord does not involve any attempt to deny the reality of the work of God in the lives and thoughts and prayers of men and women outside the Christian church. On the contrary, it ought to involve an eager expectation of, a looking for, and a rejoicing in the evidence of that work."[45] To say this, of course, is to say that the core beliefs of Christianity itself lead us paradoxically to look beyond its borders (and not to other "religions" alone) and render ourselves vulnerable to insights and adjustments of perspective gleaned in doing so. "Christians, then, in their dealings with men and women who do not acknowledge Jesus as Lord, will meet them and share with them in a common life, not as strangers but as those who live by the same life-giving Word, and in whose life the same light shines."[46] "The church," furthermore, "as it is *in via*, does not face the world as the exclusive possessor of salvation, nor as the fulness of what others have in part, the answer to questions they ask, or the open revelation of what they are anonymously." Different religions turn on quite different axes, and each must be understood with integrity on its own terms and along the line of its own central axis. "The church faces the world, rather, as *arrabôn* of that salvation—as sign, first fruit, token, witness of that salvation which God purposes for the whole."[47] And we participate in dialogue or conversation with those of other faiths believing that they and we together share a common nature as those created by the one God and Father of all, that they and we exist by his grace and goodness alone, that they and we are responsible to him, and that he purposes the same blessing for us all. "This does not mean that the purpose of dialogue is to persuade the non-Christian partner to accept the Christianity of the Christian partner. Its purpose is not that Christianity should acquire one more recruit. On the contrary, *obedient* witness to Christ means that whenever we come with another person (Christian or not) into the presence of the cross, we are prepared to receive judgement and correction, to find that our Christianity hides within its appearance of obedience the reality of disobedience. Each meeting with a non-Christian partner in dialogue therefore puts my own Christianity at risk."[48] And, finally, when we meet with others in this way, we are eager to receive from them whatever God has given them, to hear what God has shown them. "Eagerness to listen, to learn, to receive even what is new and strange will be the mark of one who knows the word of Jesus: 'All that the Father has is mine.' In our meeting with men of other faiths we are learning to share in our common patrimony as human beings made by the one God in his own image."[49]

Newbigin, I suggest, articulates a theology of religions, and of mission, in terms of which James Legge's discriminating but positive evaluation of Confucianism can be made sense of. He furnishes positive theological reasons to suggest how (and why) Christian participants in interreligious and intercultural conversation can (and should) remain true to the articulation of their several standpoints, without ever demeaning (let alone despising) the contributions and insights of others. He provides a framework in which healthy discernment and discrimination may be exercised, and we may aspire (if not always wholly successfully) to an ethical hermeneutic in which our work of "translating" subordinates neither the Other too quickly to the Same nor the Same to the Other but construes otherness as a partner in the shared quest for the light that lightens everyone, however we may have learned to name it.

5

A STUDY OF THE "PREFACE" AND "INTRODUCTION" TO JAMES LEGGE'S *THE TEXTS OF TAOISM*

ZHAO Jing

> 圣人但为实腹而养气，不为悦目而徇物，故悉去彼外在之诸多妄，而独取此内在之一真。
>
> 吴澄[1]
>
> *The Sage nourishes the breath in order to fill his belly, but never follows the things under sensual seductions. So he removes all those external illusionaries, but remains merely this internal authentic.*
>
> —Wu Cheng
>
> 余为陈道有异同同异之辩，而言至道，终必归于大同。
>
> 王韬[2]
>
> It must be admitted that one might face a variety of differences as well as sameness in claiming for his own Tao; yet as long as the ultimate Tao is arrived at, everything converges into the great identity.
>
> —Wang Tao

As a missionary, sinologist, and translator of Chinese classics, James Legge (1815–1897) has recently received a great deal of attention by Chinese scholarship. The academic interest in Legge mainly concentrates on his proper texts of translation—that is, the texts that can be traced back to their Chinese original texts in classics. But as for the prefaces to every book, the prolegomena to every volume of *The Chinese Classics*, the introductions to *The Sacred Books of the East*, and also the commentaries—the lengths of which often exceed the proper text—one may find that these texts, equally deserving of scrutiny, have been treated with relatively less care.

The Chinese Classics,[3] recently republished in five volumes, demonstrates awareness of this problem. In every volume of this series, there is an editorial introduction (引言),[4] which offers an overall view of the features, forms, methods, and influences of the translation; academic contributions and lacunae that deal with the background of the 1860s to the 1890s (i.e., the mid-to-late Qing dynasty) are also given attention. These summary accounts of the translator's work are made possible only by a thorough reading of Legge's *Prolegomena*, emphasizing its importance. *The Sacred Books of the East*, edited by Max Müller, contains certain volumes (vols. 3, 16, 27, 28, 39, 40) translated from ancient Chinese by Legge, and each one has an academically distinguished preface and introduction. Among them, the preface and the introduction to volume 39, *The Texts of Taoism*,[5] is the most remarkable, as Taoism is the largest native religion in China apart from Confucianism, and at the time Legge was already under the influence of Müller's idea of comparative religious study. After his return to England, the shift of his personal identity, thoughts, and views on academic matters was in accordance with his changed and changing opinion on Taoism. Unfortunately, Legge's work on Taoism has not attracted enough attention in Chinese scholarship. Indeed, there are discussions concerning Legge's translation of *Daodejing*, centering on the translation strategy or Laozi's philosophical principles. But a study that grasps Legge's own academic life in a fuller sense is still absent.

The concept of "Scriptural Reasoning" (经文辩读 as Yang translates it), recently introduced to China by Professor Yang Huilin, has added a new dimension to research on Legge. This formula has its verbal subtlety: How could the sacredness implied in the word "Scripture" be compatible with the rationality of "Reasoning," especially in this era of secularity (or profanity)?

Actually, this movement of Scriptural Reasoning employs a very concrete model for practice: people (not necessarily scholars) from Judaic, Islamic, and Christian backgrounds, sitting in the same room, reading the overlapping texts in their scriptures. Within such a dialogue, open to "the other," the participants experience and share a "reasoning on a deep level," while celebrating a "trans-lateral sacred ritual."[6] In our era, the so-called "sacred ritual" is essentially a practice *of* a community that can also have influence *on* the community, enabling the temporary loosening of respective identities and allowing "the other" to be heard. In this respect, scholars try to find a potential in Scriptural Reasoning for moving beyond the borders of the Abrahamic traditions.

For obvious reasons, when talking about a "Sino-Western Scriptural Reasoning," one must exercise great caution, as exhibited by Yang in his tentative suggestion that "a certain kind of Scriptural Reasoning which is not necessarily natural" could be traced back to *The Sacred Books of the East*. A Goethean aphorism often mentioned by the editor of the series reads, "He who knows one knows nothing," which, according to Yang, well corresponds to the inner spirit of Scriptural Reasoning.[7] The same spirit is also expressed by Legge (Müller's colleague) in a quite clear tone:

> The more that a man possesses the Christian spirit, and is governed by Christian principle, the more anxious will he be to do justice to every other system of religion, and to hold his own without taint or fetter of bigotry. Looking abroad on the various forms of belief in the world, and including his own among them, he will endeavor to fulfill the counsel of Paul, to "prove all things and hold fast that which is good."[8]

Yang states, "Legge's translation and commentary works on ancient Chinese classics provided many passages between the Christian doctrinal system and ancient Chinese thinking, and left us abundant resources for the Sino-Western 'Scriptural Reasoning.' "[9] And according to Ralph Weber's analysis, the strengths of Scriptural Reasoning could be understood on three levels: (1) a deepened understanding of one's own tradition; (2) the value of persons drawn from interfaith dialogues; and (3) the intention of aiming "beyond the Abrahamic traditions" at "the fate of humanity" and reclaiming a soteriology of human beings as a whole. As Weber points out, at this level, "the theological vocabulary is the strongest."[10] Here "Scripture" and "Reasoning" both touch upon their limit, with a paramount tension between the religious and the a-religious components of Scriptural Reasoning.

The modern situation of Scriptural Reasoning has something in common with Legge's gesture over one hundred years ago. This is the reason scholars like Lauren Pfister make claims for a rereading of Legge in our "post-secular age." Legge, who had received the strictest biblical and philological training in his youth, took the interpretation and translation of the Chinese ancient classics to the West as his "duty"; this vocational incandescence found adequate embodiment only through those austere and sober textual works. Legge's religious passion seemed untimely in contrast with his contemporaries. But only in this untimeliness could one find something that transcends the temporary limitations.

The purpose of this essay is to offer a reading of Legge's preface and introduction to *The Texts of Taoism*, in *The Sacred Books of the East*, volumes 39–40. These texts, which well represent Legge's ideas and intentions, can be here taken as an entrance to his late thought and also as a paradigm of his comparative religious study.

The Literature Related to the Translation of *The Texts of Taoism* and the Inner Intention of This Selection

The Texts of Taoism were published in two volumes in 1890, when Legge was professor of Chinese language and literature at the University of Oxford. The preface first reports the structure of the book, which contains principally three important Taoist texts: *Tâo Teh King* (老子道德经, Laozi's *Daodejing*), *The Writings of Kwang-ʒze* (庄子, *The Books of Zhuangzi*), and *The T'ai Shang Tractate of Actions and Their Retributions* (太上感应篇, *Ganyingpian*). After *Ganyingpian*, eight shorter Taoist articles appear in an "Appendix."

Daodejing and *Zhuangzi* comprise the greatest part of this anthology. The texts belonging to the "Taoist religion" (道教) in a proper sense are only *Kan Ying Phien* and five articles of the eight appendices. The selection of these appendices was influenced by Balfour's *The Taoist Texts*,[11] which Legge fiercely criticized. Balfour once claimed that the research of Taoism should exclude the views of Confucianism. But the last three appendices Legge applied to his book were the commentaries and reading of Laozi and Zhuangzi written by literati from the Confucian school—seemingly a rebuttal of Balfour. Legge's general consideration of the Taoist religion (i.e., the Taoism other than Laozi and Zhuangzi) as trivial is well represented in his edition, and the proper Taoist religious (or sacred) texts are treated rather cursorily. *Ganyingpian* was included precisely "because of its popularity in China."[12] At the time, this Taoist treatise on retribution was highly emphasized by early sinologists, like Abel-Rémusat (1788–1832), Stanislas Julien (1791–1873), and Alexander Wylie (1815–1887). However, in comparison with the over five hundred pages of the French version of *Ganyingpian* by Julien,[13] Legge's translation of that work required only several dozen pages. Unlike Julien, Legge was obviously not interested in those derivative pictorial illustrations and legendary stories surrounding *Ganyingpian*, only "the Tâoism of the eleventh century in its moral and ethical aspects."[14] In his view, *Daodejing* and *Zhuangzi* are more reflective of "philosophical speculation than a religion in the ordinary sense of that term."[15] Thus the distinction between Taoism as philosophy (*Daojia*, 道家) and Taoism as religion (*Daojiao*, 道教)—a distinction made by twentieth-century Chinese scholars—was proposed early on by Legge.

In fact, Legge already had his own judgment on the nature of Chinese Taoism after the entrance of Buddhism into China. In the preface, various religious phenomena are enumerated and then criticized. Taoism is thus considered more "as a degraded adjunct of Buddhism than as a development of the speculations of Lâo-ʒze and Kwang-ʒze."[16] In this respect, "the Confucian system" won Legge's highest praise, "which, while admitting the existence and rule of the Supreme Being, bases its teachings on the study of man's nature and the enforcement of the duties binding on all men from the moral and social principles of their constitution."[17] The intention for an interreligious comparison is quite obvious here.

As the preface suggests, the primary edition of the works of Laozi and Zhuangzi that Legge used for translation is *Shiziquanshu* (十子全书), published in Suzhou, 1804. This edition was selected out of another, older edition that is more encompassing, namely *Zhuzihuihan* (诸子汇函), edited with commentary by Gui Youguang (归有光, 1506–1571), containing the works of ninety-four "philosophers" (子). Both these editions select the commentary made by "He Shang Gong" (河上公注) as the most reliable commentary on Laozi. Legge also frequently refers to *Laoziyi* (老子翼), printed in 1587 by Jiao Hong (焦竑, 1540–1620), which includes sixty-four kinds of commentary on Laozi. This selection may be influenced by Julien. The great sinologue based his French version of *Daodejing* mainly on these two editions, both influential and popular in the Late Qing period. Interestingly, Legge was influenced by a Confucian in the Yuan dynasty, namely Wu Cheng (吴澄, 1249–1333), whose commentary to Laozi—that is, *Daodezhenjingzhu* (道德真经注)—was printed in 1853, in the series of books *Yueyatangwenji* (粤雅堂文集).

When translating Zhuangzi, besides *Shiziquanshu* and Jiao Hong's *Zhuangziyi*, Legge also relied on Lu Shuzhi's (陆树芝) *Zhuangzixue* (庄子雪), Lin Yunming's (林云铭) *Zhuangziyin* (庄子因), and Hu wen Ying's (胡文英) *Zhuangzidujian* (庄子独见); these works represent the new tide of Zhuangzi interpretation in the period of Ming-Qing. Legge points out the fundamental problem in interpreting and translating Zhuangzi:

> When consulting the editions of Lin Hsî-kung and Lû Shû-kih, the reader is surprised by the frequency with which they refer to the "old explanations" as "incomplete and unsatisfactory," often as "absurd," or "ridiculous," and he finds on examination that they do not so express themselves without reason. He is soon convinced that the translation of Kwang-ȝze calls for the exercise of one's individual judgment, and the employment of every method akin to the critical processes by which the meaning in the books of other languages is determined. It was the perception of this which made me prepare in the first place a draft version to familiarise myself with the peculiar style and eccentric thought of the author.[18]

Despite these often conflicting interpretations—some quite literal, some keeping to the rules of philology, some offering interreligious inspirations, and some attaining the level of the philosophical—Legge arrives at his fundamental hermeneutical principle for Zhuangzi, that the only way to treat with this ingenious writer is to go along with him spiritually.[19] This spiritual or mindful interpretation must base itself upon not only a familiarity with Chinese literature but also an insight that could by no means be separated from his personality. However, Legge's translation of Zhuangzi is rather inferior in quality to his translation of Laozi. In several instances that refer to Zhuangzi in his introduction, one may find his translation questionable. The problem lies in Legge's lack of Chinese assistants. The preface ends with a recollection of the time in China shared with his local colleagues. He says, "I have often sorely missed the presence of a competent native scholar who would have assisted me in the quest of references, and in talking over difficult passages."[20] However, Legge promises that the quality of translation will not be influenced. Given that Zhuangzi is notoriously hard to translate, we as readers would benefit greatly had there been assistants working alongside Legge to discuss and inspire, as was the case in the production of the Confucian Classics. We might also wonder, is such cooperative translation a certain mode of Sino-Western "Scriptural Reasoning?"

The preface is attentive to the question of how to approach different commentaries on Laozi in the Chinese traditions. It is noted that Julien, looking at the large and comprehensive collection of commentaries in *Laoziyi* and analyzing the scholarly backgrounds of various commentators, concludes that the commentaries from the School of Confucians are "useless" to "obtain a just idea of his [Laozi's] doctrine."[21] Balfour, who criticized Julien in his version of *Daodejing*, actually goes even further, claiming that the study of Laozi by Confucians only has grammatical and philological values; one must rely for actual understanding upon the proper Taoist texts. But unfortunately the texts he selected from the Taoist religious tradition are considered " 'spurious' and 'ridiculous' " by both Legge and Giles.[22] Balfour's naïveté in sinology, resulting from the biased belief that Confucianism and Taoism are incompatible with each other, is not hard to dispute. For the person who has an acquaintance with Chinese traditions, like Legge, trans-traditional interpretation of ancient texts is not at all problematic. The commentary that exerted on him the greatest influence is that of Wu Cheng, a Confucian scholar. In his translation and commentary on Laozi, Wu vehemently criticizes the official editors of *Sikuquanshu* (四库全书) as "intermingling with Confucianism and Moism," "making arbitrary commentaries," and "tampering with the old text."[23] Yet Legge still gives him his highest compliment as "a bold thinker and a daring critic, handling his text with a freedom which [Legge] had not seen in any other Chinese scholar."[24] The deep influence of Wu's interpretation on Legge's version can be seen in many places in the translation; for example, the first sentence of *Daodejing* is rendered by Legge as "The Tao that can be trodden," which strictly follows Wu's notes on the same passage.[25] Wu's edition not only reordered Laozi's eighty-one chapters into sixty-eight but also made many textual changes in order to render the text compatible with his own idea. For example, in chapter 14, he changed 下知有之 to 不知有之 with no actual grounds. This change is accepted by Legge, who thought that such a shift in words might better represent the archaic living situation of the Chinese people, without of course jeopardizing the idea of the original text.[26] This is a good example of Legge's well-known practice in taking for his basic rule the Mencian hermeneutic principle "to meet the author's scope with the explainer's thoughts" (以意逆志).[27] But before this "meeting" can occur, according to Mencius, there are also required many personally cultivated and exemplary exercises like "understanding words" (知言) and "nourishing breath" (养气).[28] This "mind resource" (心源) of hermeneutics, along with "knowledge in philology," constitutes the basis upon which Wu and Legge could exert their hermeneutical freedom.

Basic Determinations on Laozi, *Daodejing*, and Its Teachings

In the introduction, consisting of five chapters and forty-four pages, one can find Legge's basic theses on Taoism: Taoism originated before Laozi; it is quite different from Confucianism, for the discussion of the Tao by Laozi and his successor Zhuangzi was essentially philosophical and a-religious and showed hardly any relationship to the one true God; Taoism afterward deteriorated under the influence of Buddhism. The reasons for these theses will be fully explored in the following discussion.

These basic judgments are constructed by answers to a series of textual, contextual, and historical questions on Laozi's personality, *Daodejing*'s authenticity, its status as a "scripture" (*jing*), its authenticity, and so on. Confronted with these knotty questions, Legge mainly relies on the historical records of Sima Qian, while his own scrutiny of old texts also offers him confidence to solve them. Although the introduction takes into account a great scope of literature, from the all-encompassing edition *Laoziyi*,[29] to a medieval Taoist collection of fairy tales *Shenxianzhuan* (神仙传),[30] even to the Qing pedagogical book *Youxuegushixunyuan* (幼学故事寻源),[31] the ultimate criterion seems to be Qian's somewhat orthodox account. The author of *Shiji* (which itself is not the original record) and Sima Qian himself take a very doubtful attitude toward who the person Laozi actually is.[32] But the prudence and erudition of the author of *Shiji* is well recognized and admired by Legge.

Since Laozi is considered a philosopher, it is therefore necessary to make a scrutiny of his philosophical work, the text of *Daodejing*. And as a result, Legge screens out the legendary or mythical elements in Qian's account.[33] The unique mythologeme that Legge suggests is related to a textual event, namely that "Lâo-ȝze wrote a book in two parts, setting forth his views on the Tâo and its attributes, in more than 5000 characters."[34] As for the provenance of the title "Laozi," Legge would rather consider it as a title of honor, meaning nothing other than "Old Philosopher" or "Old Gentleman."[35]

Western sinology questioned the authenticity of Laozi and *Daodejing*. In 1886 Herbert Allen Giles (1845–1935) wrote an essay in *China Review*, expressing strong doubt that *Daodejing* was a genuine work. At this point, Legge's view is in accordance again with the Chinese tradition. He says with confidence that "I accept the Tâo Teh King as a genuine production of the age to which it has been assigned, and the truth of its authorship by Lâo-ȝze to whom it has been ascribed."[36] The grounds of such a determination is the witness of ancient literature. Due to the many references to Laozi and to the texts of *Daodejing*, in *Hanfeizi*, *Huainanzi*, *Shiji*, and so forth, textual authenticity is easily proved. Legge furthermore mentions some important resources such as the "Account of Yueyi" in *Shiji* (史记·乐毅列传), *The Catalogue of Han Royal Library* (汉书·艺文志), and *The Catalogue of Sui Library* (隋书·经籍志), and provides an outline of how *Daodejing* was circulated through time. He also acutely points out that the various texts suggest the likelihood that there were several manuscripts of *Daodejing* from the beginning.[37]

The debate between Giles and Legge concerning the authenticity of *Daodejing* was a great event in nineteenth-century sinology. Norman Girardot, one of Legge's biographers, recounts Legge's belief in "the coherence of ancient classics and the integrity of sage authors" as "reverent methods," which is in contrast to Giles' "deconstructive irreverence."[38] The hermeneutical divergence reflects the turning point of the developments in academic study. Legge's quite traditional reverence now encountered the "more irreverent, critical, historical, and destructive"[39] methods of an emerging professional sinological orientalism. We are not here to judge these two methodologies. What is important for us to recognize here is that Legge's judgment on the authenticity of a text comes from his personal expertise in ancient texts, which was based upon his biblical training and reinforced by over thirty years of diligent study. The profundity of such so-called "reverent" methodology should never be underestimated.

After the justification of the authenticity of the text, Legge carries out the philosophical interpretation of the concept of "Tao," which is central in characterizing Taoist belief. Legge first presents a brief historical review on the understanding of Tao by Western sinology. As is easily seen, this work has a comparative nature from the outset.

In a Latin manuscript presented to the Royal Society by Matthew Raper, which might be the earliest translation of *Daodejing* in a Western language, "Tâo is taken in the sense of *Ratio*, or the Supreme Reason or the Divine being, the Creator and Governor."[40] This piece was probably from the Jesuit figurists. "The chief object of the translator or translators" of it, as determined by Legge, "was to show that the 'Mysteries of the Most Holy Trinity and of the Incarnate God were anciently known to the Chinese nation,'" while "the version as a whole is of little value."[41] Although the figurists might share the same theological goal as Legge, their all too optimistic postulation was easily disputed and inevitably criticized, under the sober eyes of academic rigidity. Abel-Rémusat went even further along the lines of figurism, claiming that the Tao has the meaning of "sovereign Being," "reason," and "word,"[42] the only adequate rendering of which would be the Greek *logos*. He picked out the three characters used to describe the Tao in chapter 14 of *Daodejing*—*Yi*, *Xi*, *Wei*—and claimed that with these three sounds together, the name of the Hebrew god "Yahweh" is heard. He even depicted the road map of Laozi's expedition to the West. In his opinion, Plato, the Stoics, even the evangelist John, those believers in reason (*sectateurs de la raison*), can all find their remotest origin in Laozi.[43] This is fantasy, and was criticized by his disciple Julien, but it may find its counterpart in the Chinese Taoist tale that Laozi went westward and civilized the Indians to create Buddhism (老子化胡). Legge takes it as "a mere fancy or dream."[44]

Another popular hermeneutical trend took "Tao" as equal with the concept of "Nature" in Western thought.[45] Balfour abruptly rendered all "Tao" in his version as "Nature," with the same meaning as the Spinozan concept *natura naturans* in the *Ethics*, while Laozi's "all things" (*wanwu*, 万物) meant the same as Spinozan *natura naturata*. Such comparison could be pertinent in some sense. However, if without attentive textual and contextual treatment, any explication based upon superficial similarity will eventually seem less legitimate. No wonder Legge mentions it as "barbarous phraseology."[46]

Yet the relationship between "Nature" and "Tao" is still of interest. Modern Chinese uses a term of pre-Qin Taoist origin, *ziran* (自然), to render the English term "nature." *Ziran* appears five times in *Daodejing*. Legge's translation does not conceptualize this word with one fixed English word but translates it every time differently within its various contexts. Laozi's famous formula *Dao faziran* (道法自然) is translated as "The law of the Tâo is its being what it is,"[47] in which a certain theological subtlety can be detected. This may remind us of the Mencian saying taken by Legge as his *modus operandi*: "Literal expression should not harm the senses" (不以文害意).

Archdeacon Charles Hardwick, who held the office of Christian Advocate in the University of Cambridge, also understood "the centre of the system founded by Lâo-ȝze . . . resembl[es] the 'Nature' of modern speculators," and he maintained that "the indefinite expression Tâo was adopted to denominate an abstract cause, of the initial principle of life and order, to which worshippers were able to assign the attributes of immateriality, eternity, immensity, invisibility."[48] However, Legge found the term "worshipper" problematic. Legge himself provides an answer to the question of pre-Qin Taoism's religious character:

> Neither Lâo nor Kwang says anything about the worship of the Tâo, about priests or monks, about temples or rituals. How could they do so, seeing that Tâo was not to them the name of a personal Being, nor "Heaven" a metaphorical term equivalent to the Confucian Tî, "Ruler," or Shang Tî, "Supreme Ruler." With this agnosticism as to God, and their belief that by a certain management and discipline of the breath life might be prolonged indefinitely, I do not see how anything of an organised religion was possible for the old Tâoists.[49]

After clarification of the nonreligious nature of Laozi and Zhuangzi's philosophy, Legge does not criticize Hardwick's reference to nature but rather takes that a step further. Legge cites the opinion of Canon Farrar, envisioning nature as "a distinct, living, independent entity," and acutely adds:

> But it seems to me that this metaphorical or mythological use of the word nature for the Cause and Ruler of it, implies the previous notion of Him, that is, of God, in the mind. Does not this clearly appear in the words of Seneca?—"*Vis illum (i.e., jovem Deum) naturam vocare, non peccabis:—hic est ex quo nata sunt omnia, cujus spiritu vivimus.*"[50]

Seneca[51] noticed that the face of Jupiter (Jove/*Deus*) may be recognized hidden in the midst of nature. At the time of Legge's early period in China, Jupiter was still thought of as a pagan god quite different from the Chinese ancient Shangdi.[52] But in the 1880s and 1890s, Legge was likely aware of his colleagues' findings in religious studies: Max Müller said, etymologically, that Ju-piter is properly the name of "heaven-father."[53] "Nature" is never able to be an equivalent to "Tao," yet naturalness is the Tao's most apparent and important character. For Legge, the natural Tao, in its metaphorical or mythological sense, does imply a supreme being above nature. For Müller, the idea of nature, which in turn links to German philosophers such as Feuerbach and Schelling, refers only to the origin of all primordial religions. An encounter of the two concepts may allow a certain kind of Scriptural Reasoning between philosophy and theology. But Legge has no intention to let that exchange happen, simply quoting the ancients and eschewing the hazard of overinterpretation. That might be the proper manner of a scholar in philology and also in accordance with Laozi's doctrine *Xi yanziran* (希言自然, Rarely speaking is the most natural) and Confucius' *San jian qi kou* (三缄其口, Sealing one's mouth with triple seals so as to keep him in silence).

After these laborious discussions, Legge's main interest is becoming manifest here. With the help of a paragraph he borrowed from Kwangzi, an ontological statement of Tao is put forward:

> The Tâo therefore is a phenomenon; not a positive being, but a mode of being. Lâo's idea of it may become plainer as we proceed to other points of his system. In the meantime, the best way of dealing with it in translating is to transfer it to the version, instead of trying to introduce an English equivalent for it.[54]

"A mode of being"—note that Legge's phraseology or terminology is much more civil and careful than Balfour's—differs clearly from the substance (positive being). The Tao is thus separated from God, the Supreme Being. Clearly the relationship between God and Tao commands Legge's attention in the "philosophical" portion of the introduction, and Legge seems to give a clear-cut answer: "The old Tâoists had no idea of a personal God, when they wrote of Thien of Heaven."[55] Although Tao functions as the point of origin of all things, and Tao itself is also called "Transformer" (造化), this process can only be called "evolution."[56]

"Monotheistic" Views on Taoist Religion

Similar to his treatment of Laozi, Legge's view on the Taoist religion grew also out of a monotheistic stance. Taoist tradition in China is notoriously problematic, as Ma Duanlin (马端临) says: "The Taoist arts are miscellaneous and complex."[57] He also separates later Taoists from Laozi: "How could we find such things in Laozi's 5,000 characters? Probably the more years distanced them from Laozi, the more inauthentic were they."[58] In modern academic study, Taoism is commonly divided into "the Taoist School" (道家) and "the Taoist Religion" (道教)—as Xu Dishan (许地山) called it, "the Tao with respect to thought" and "the Tao with respect to religion."[59] Such a division was already made by Legge, who also postulated a more ancient Tao that preceded Laozi and Confucius. In the course of lectures in London in the 1880s, later published as *The Religions of China: Confucianism and Taoism Compared with Christianity*, Legge makes the distinction:

> Tâoism is the name both of a religion and a philosophy. The author of the Philosophy is the chief god, or one at least of the chief gods, of the religion; but there is no evidence that the religion grew out of his book. It was impossible, indeed, as you will see, for it to do so in many of its aspects. Any relation between the two things is merely external, for in spirit and tendency they are antagonistic.[60]

"Tâoism" refers comprehensively to the Taoist school and Taoist religion. In the preface and introduction of 1890 such terminology continues. That which could bring together "the antagonistic" pair "in spirit and tendency" must be an archaic common origin of the two. So Laozi was no longer considered the founder of Taoism.[61] About its origins, the texts of *Daodejing* give very few clues, except that "there are some references to earlier sages whose words the author was copying out, and to 'sentence-makers' whose maxims he was introducing to illustrate his own sentiments."[62] The "sentence-maker" (建言) appears in chapter 41 of *Daodejing*; Legge proposes that he is cited directly by Laozi. Furthermore, Taoist texts give descriptions of the archaic, innocent world. Legge's translation of Zhuangzi's *zhidezhishi* (至德之世) or *zhizhizhishi* (至治之世) as "happy time" even gives it equivalence to a "paradisiacal state," with apparent theological implication. Being quite aware of the allegorical technique of Taoist writers, he still seeks to find a tradition behind Laozi:

> I find . . . a ground for believing myself that to Tâoism, as well as to Confucianism, we ought to attribute a much earlier origin than the famous men whose names they bear. Perhaps they did not differ so much at first as they came afterwards to do in the hands of Confucius and Lâo-ʒze, both great thinkers, the one more of a moralist, and the other more of a metaphysician.[63]

A Taoism before Laozi and a Confucianism before Confucius thus converge. Such an assumption of a single origin for every school was never strange for the Chinese academic tradition. Zhuangzi said the different Tao and their techniques under heaven "shared a common origin, 'the One.'"[64] What is the One? Legge had his own point of view, named by scholars as "Confucian Monotheism" (儒教一神论).[65] In a book published in 1852, he writes,

> My thesis is—that the Chinese possesses a knowledge of the true God, and that the highest Being whom they worship is indeed the same whom we worship. But they do not only worship Him; they worship a multitude of beings besides, and with their knowledge of God have associated a mass of superstitions and follies.[66]

In the 1850s Legge thought that Confucians were the defenders of the ancient monotheist "state religion,"[67] while Taoists were the destroyers. The first emperor of Qin summoned a Taoist to seek for longevity, as did the Wu Emperor of the Han dynasty. And according to the record of *Kongzijiayu* (孔子家语), the name *wudi* (五帝, the five *Di*) that undermines the uniqueness of God was heard from Laozi but never mentioned by Kongzi.[68] Legge concluded, "*Wudi* is the invention of Taoism."[69] It is then not difficult to imagine Taoism's negative and superstitious role in Legge's mind. But in 1880, back in England, he expressed the view that Christianity, Confucianism, and Taoism belonged together under the label of monotheism: "At any rate, Christianity, Confucianism, and Tâoism, all allow the element of the supernatural, all assert the fact of revelation, all acknowledge the existence of God."[70] By this time, Legge had already corrected his notion that there was no revelation in ancient China, in his preface to volume 3 of *The Sacred Books of the East*.[71] Here

"Tâoism" mainly referred to Laozi and his *Daodejing*, essentially different from the books full of weird tales and superstitions like *Liezi* and *Zhuangzi*.[72] Laozi's *Tian* (天, heaven) was thought to be immaterial, referring to God.[73]

In the introduction of 1890, his view changed again. Taoist writers did not consider *Tian* to refer to any personal godlike being: "Never once is Thien used in the sense of God, the Supreme Being. In its peculiarly Tâoistic employment, it is more an adjective than a noun."[74] As Zhuangzi said, "Acting without action, this is what is called Heaven" (无为为之之谓天). Thus this adjective's predicates must be described as "vacancy, stillness, placidity, tastelessness, quietude, silence, and non-action" (虚静, 恬淡, 寂寞, 无为).[75] Zhuangzi's "age of Perfect Virtue" is then conceived as an atheistic age, in which humans live with creatures equally, where "there is not the slightest allusion to any sentiment of piety as animating them individually, or to any ceremony of religion as observed by them in common."[76]

With Tao and Tian ruled out as monotheistic ideas, Legge's moral view on later Taoism could be easily inferred. In the beginning of the preface, he criticizes the various Taoist "superstitious" techniques, while the introduction ends with a criticism of the Zhang family whose head held the title of "Master of Heaven" (张天师).[77] He holds that these monstrous phenomena should not be linked with the "Old Philosopher":

> A visitor to one of the larger of these temples may not only see the pictures of the purgatorial courts and other forms of the modern superstitions, but he will find also astrologers, diviners, geomancers, physiognomists, et id genus omne, plying their trades or waiting to be asked to do so, and he will wonder how it has been possible to affiliate such things with the teachings of Lâo-ʒze.[78]

The translation of *Ganyingpian* (as well as the small Taoist texts in the appendices) was said to represent the "moral and ethical aspects" of Taoism. In fact, those moral and ethical aspects as Legge understood them are better represented in his reproach of the tutelary temples (城隍庙), which were seen as temples of the city god and the state gods. During Legge's time in Hong Kong, his second wife, Hannah, complained about such temples as places of "filthy heathens."[79] Those complaints should be taken into account for Legge's experience of Taoism and might well explain his negative attitude toward the Taoist religion, an attitude that could lead him to cite the Qing dynasty's Penal Code to reproach "the Master of Heaven."

Comparative Studies

Max Müller's comparative method in religious studies influenced Legge at an essential level. In this young discipline, Christianity attained a special status. According to Müller, who defined comparative religious studies as comparative theology,[80] every religion speaks with a pharisaical tongue but not a popular tongue, and only Christianity is an exception. Thus the Christian religion is the most humanistic and universal among all others, whose attitude toward Judaism must be the first lesson of comparative religious study.[81]

Legge insisted upon this priority of Christianity in his comparative studies, while nevertheless the three Chinese religions (*san jiao*, "three teaching systems") can give another lesson less pharisaical. The commentary of *Daodejing* is itself a history of the interactions between the three religions, wherein an early development of what we call Scriptural Reasoning can be detected. Legge clearly noticed this. Although he was deeply involved with the Chinese literary tradition as a scholar, his concern as a missionary still dominated. As his daughter writes, "Dr Legge believed and was sure that the literature, to know which he lived laborious days and nights, revealed on its pages that the grey fathers of this race 'knew God.' "[82] The constant search for "God" makes his interreligious studies literally a comparative theo-logy, practiced in his subtle treatment of the notion of "Nature" with its implication for "God." This concern can be traced back to his missionary period in China. In his early work, Legge analyzed the Chinese god Di or Shangdi (together with the main gods of other peoples such as Jupiter, Vishnu, Shiva, and so on) with respect to the Christian God.[83]

Another aspect of this comparative study is the ethical and practical level of religion. The criterion of this evaluation is still Christian and monotheistic. Legge criticizes Taoist popular religion as idolatrous, and Taoist philosophy as atheistic, while Confucianism receives approval since the ancient Confucians had a knowledge of God. Accordingly, the Confucian concept of duty is praised:

> There had been indeed, all along the line of history, a groping for the rules of life, as indicated by the constitution of man's nature.

> The results were embodied in the ancient literature which was the lifelong study of Confucius. He had gathered up that literature; he recognised the nature of man as the gift of Heaven or God. The monitions of God as given in the convictions of man's mind supplied him with a Tâo or Path of duty very different from the Tâo or Mysterious Way of Lâo.[84]

The contrast of Laozi's mysterious Tao with the Confucian path of duty (which is Legge's translation of Tao in Confucian texts) best explains the old principle that "those whose Taos are different cannot lay plans for one another" (道不同不相与谋).[85] Another major deficiency of Taoism for Legge is its despising of knowledge:

> We can laugh at this. Tâoism was wrong in its opposition to the increase of knowledge. Man exists under a law of progress. In pursuing it there are demanded discretion and justice. Moral ends must rule over material ends, and advance in virtue be ranked higher than advance in science. So have good and evil, truth and error, to fight out the battle on the field of the world, and in all the range of time; but there is no standing still for the individual or for society. Even Confucius taught his countrymen to set too high a value on the examples of antiquity. The school of Lâo-ʒze fixing themselves in an unknown region beyond antiquity,—a prehistoric time between "the Grand Beginning of all things" out of nothing, and the unknown commencement of societies of men,—has made no advance but rather retrograded, and is represented by the still more degenerate Tâoism of the present day.[86]

Here a tone of progressivism is clearly heard—even an orientalist voice, one might say. As Girardot said, this "reflect[s] his own deep predilections for a Divine order or fixed imperial design and traditional moral civility."[87] Order must overwhelm (oriental) chaos. Chaos is a very compelling word that represents the essentials of Taoist teaching, both theoretically and practically. Zhuangzi's metaphor on chaos surprised Legge a great deal:

> So it was that Chaos passed away before Light. So did the nameless simplicity of the Tâo disappear before Knowledge. But it was better that the Chaos should give place to the Kosmos. "Heedless" and "Hasty" did a good deed.[88]

The pun on "chaos" shows his mastery of the text. But Zhuangzi's most subtle metaphor, touching upon every Chinese person's mind, Legge ultimately finds uninteresting. The lack of sympathy here reminds us that every hermeneutic has its limitation. Legge identifies the difference between philosophical Taoism and the Taoist practices for longevity or immortality, but misses the inner identity of the two, which, to some extent, forms the identity of the Chinese. As Lu Xun says, "[T]he root of the Chinese tradition totally lies in Taoism" (道教).[89]

With regard to its ethical aspects, Legge considers the central teaching of Laozi as "absurd."[90] By criticizing the absurdity of the Taoist belief in a prehistoric perfect society and the possible practical results of such a belief, Legge betrays his most profound hope for the future world:

> "All very well in theory," some one will exclaim, "but, the world has not seen it yet reduced to practice." So it is. The fact is deplorable. No one saw the misery arising from it, and exposed its unreasonableness more unsparingly, than Kwang-ȝze. But it was all in vain in his time, as it has been in all the centuries that have since rolled their course. Philosophy, philanthropy, and religion have still to toil on, "faint, yet pursuing," believing that the time will yet come when humility and love shall secure the reign of peace and good will among the nations of men.[91]

In this comment there shines a "postmillennial eschatology," about which Lauren Pfister's work is quite inspiring.[92] The principle of this theological position (formed in Legge's youth in Scotland) is the transferal of hope for the second coming of Christ into personal duty and practices, embodying the "Victory of Christianity" in a sociohistorical (also political) process. Thus a happy and peaceful world would arrive before the second coming and the universal judgment. The importance of this Scottish Christian tradition should not be underestimated. However, when the postmillennial theology encountered the Taoist tradition, did Legge himself ignore the political and messianic aspects of Taoism, given the fact that almost every peasant uprising in Chinese history had a Taoist background? Even the word *Taiping* (太平, lit. "great peace"), used by the insurgents in 1851 to predicate their Heavenly Kingdom, is an old concept shared by Confucians and Taoists in their particular understanding of the coming human society. One may dare to call it a

Chinese millennialism, and in this idea lies an appeal for further pursuit of Scriptural Reasoning.

Ma Duanlin's claim that the Taoist tradition is in a process of ever becoming inauthentic (失真) is quite representative of the Chinese literati who "believ[ed] in and lov[ed] the ancients."[93] The object of this essay is thus to show Legge's interpretation and introduction to Taoism and to make manifest how he sought for the authentic element, for the truth of the texts. As *Li Ji* formulates it, the basic goal for all Chinese student who have entered *xue* (学, the school, the academy) for a whole year is to see "whether they could read the texts intelligently, and what was the meaning of each."[94] What this essay has argued and discussed is nothing other than such an elementary work.

6

THE HERMENEUTICS OF TRANSLATING CHRISTIAN THEOLOGY FOR THE EVANGELIZATION OF CHINESE SCHOOL CHILDREN IN LATE IMPERIAL CHINA

B. H. McLean

Contemporary scholarship has devoted much attention to the study of how the Bible was translated into the Chinese language. This scholarly attention seems to have been motivated by the assumption that the work of biblical translation consumed most of the energies of missionaries in China. Yet, as Chloë Starr has observed, correspondingly little scholarly attention has been paid to missionary tracts.[1] Moreover, what scholarly attention one can speak of has largely been focused on the period after the Treaty of Nanking in 1842, when missionaries were granted unimpeded access to China, and particularly focused on the period after the 1880s, when missionaries established large numbers of schools and colleges.[2]

But when one considers the importance that the London Missionary Society (LMS) missionaries themselves accorded to their own tracts for the purposes of evangelism, this lack of scholarly attention is very striking. A case in point is the tracts of the LMS that were written before 1842. When the Qing dynasty denied missionaries the legal right to operate in China, the LMS determined that evangelism in China could best be carried out remotely, by printing tracts and then arranging for their distribution in China.[3] Robert Morrison of the LMS believed that such Christian tracts could trigger in their Chinese readers an awareness of their own sinfulness, which, in turn, could lead them to seek out a

Christian teacher or pastor, who would provide further instruction.[4] On the basis of such convictions, Morrison established the Ultra-Ganges Mission Press in Malacca (Singapore), whose mission was to print tracts for circulation in China. According to Patrick Hanan, "the tracts written by missionaries were more acceptable to [Chinese] readers than their translations of the Bible, because the style of the tracts was in a more genuine Chinese [style]."[5] Walter Medhurst, also of the LMS, actually admits that the tracts of the LMS were "well calculated to instill into the tender mind of Chinese children correct ideas of the true God and the Saviour of Men."[6]

This essay will discuss two of these pre-1842 tracts of the London Missionary Society: Walter Medhurst's *Sanzijing* (三字經, *Three character classic*) and Sophia Martin's *Xunnü sanzijing* (訓女三字經, *Three character classic for the instruction of young ladies*).[7] Though the texts of these two trimetrical tracts are frequently cited in the scholarly literature, their actual contents have been virtually ignored. To the best of my knowledge, neither has been published or translated in full. In the case of Martin's tract, this lack of attention, as Ryan Dunch observes, fits into the larger pattern of the scholarly neglect of the work of *women* missionaries in particular.[8]

The Confucian *Sanzijing*

Both Medhurst's *Sanzijing* and Martin's *Xunnü sanzijing* were named after, and modeled on, the venerable Confucian classic, the *Sanzijing* (三字經, *Three character classic*). As such, let us begin with a brief overview of the purpose and contents of this Confucian text. The *Sanzijing* is attributed to the Confucian scholar Wang Yinglin (王應麟) of the Song dynasty (1223–1296). This text is arranged in three-character couplets. A comma following the first couplet introduces a pause, which, when repeated line after line, creates a steady rhythm. Many of its stanzas also rhyme. School children over the centuries—indeed to the present day—have recited this text in unison, often swaying their bodies back and forth in time with its poetic rhythm. Given the terse literary style of the trimetrical form, it is appropriate to translate this text by an unadorned, concise English style.

Through the study of the *Sanzijing* (abbreviated below as 三), children were first introduced to many of the basic characters of the Chinese language and to the basic terms and concepts of the Confucian tradition. As Robert Morrison himself recognized, "by committing to memory and copying these tracts" Chinese children were first "initiated in reading and writing."[9] The *Sanzijing*, the *Baijiaxing* (百家姓, *Hundred family surnames*), and the *Qianziwen* (千字文, *Thousand character classic*) are collectively known as the *Sanbaiqian* (三百千), a term composed of the first Chinese character of the titles of these three works. From the Song dynasty onward, the study and rote memorization of the *Sanbaiqian* formed the basis of the early elementary education of children and functioned as the de facto point of reference for assessing the literacy of children. As the *Sanzijing* itself explains, "primary school is finished" (小學終, 三[57]) with the learning of the *Sanbaiqian*. At this point, children began the study of the *Sishu* (四書, Four Books—namely *Analects*, *Book of songs*, *Book of rites*, and *Spring and autumn annals*, 三[57]), and then the *Liujing* (六經, Six Classics, 三[66]). Thus, the mastery of Confucian texts lay at the heart of the education of all children.

The structure of the *Sanzijing* can be divided into five parts. It begins with an affirmation of the goodness of humankind and stresses the value of education (三[1-53]). Part 1 commends the observance of filial piety and respecting the primary social relationships of Confucian society. It then introduces students to many basic cultural concepts such as the "three forces" (天地人, 三[25]), the "three lights" (日月星, 三[26]), the three primary relationships (三[27-31]), the four seasons (三[29]), the four directions (三[30]), and the five elements (三[33-34]). Next are presented the "five constant" virtues (*wǔcháng*, 五常, 三[35]) of Confucianism: benevolence (*ren*, 仁), right conduct (*yi*, 義), ritual propriety (*li*, 禮), wisdom (*zhi*, 智), and honesty (*xin*, 信). After this comes a list of the six grains (三[19]), the six types of domestic animals (三[20]), and the seven Confucian emotions (情喜怒懼愛惡欲, 三[41-42]). The first section ends with a list of the nine generations that make up a family "clan" (族, 三[45-48]).[10]

Christians Emulating the Style of the *Sanzijing*

Missionaries of the LMS held the conviction that both Chinese translations of the Bible and Christian tracts should be composed in the literary style of the Confucian classics, which is to say, "classical" Chinese. Missionaries coined a special term for this style: *wenli* (文理) or *wenyan* (文言). Given the importance of the Confucian classics in Chinese society at large, it is not surprising that they decided to translate their texts into what amounted to *noncolloquial* Chinese. Robert Morrison and William Milne have the distinction of being the first to translate the entire Bible into *wenli* Chinese.[11] However, in an effort to remain as close as possible to the syntax and language of the original Hebrew and Greek biblical texts, their translation departed markedly from elegant literary Chinese. One could say that their literalist style had a strong "western accent." For Morrison, being "convinced that the Bible's words were inspired by God," also believed, as Patrick Hanan has observed, "that the mere reading of the [biblical] text might be enough to convert people"; as a result, most translators of the LSM refused, as a matter of principle, "to depart very far from the words and syntax of the original Hebrew or Greek."[12]

Walter Medhurst's assessment of Morrison's translation was more critical. According to Medhurst, Morrison's translation was "barbarous," "unidiomatic, difficult, foreign, obscure, stiff, unbending, unfinished (and) verbose."[13] For his part, Medhurst advocated for the adoption of a dynamic translation style, one that imitated the "idiom and phraseology" of what he termed the "genius of the [literary] Chinese language."[14] But in the minds of many of his colleagues, his dynamic translation style yielded "little more than a human paraphrase of the Word of God."[15] Medhurst preferred to describe his translations as "free renderings" rather than "paraphrases." His preference for a truly literary Chinese style is most evident in his 1836 translation of the Bible, which he assigned the remarkable title *Xin yizhao shengshu* (新遺詔聖書, *The sacred book of the newly bequeathed oracles*).[16] Though Morrison and Medhurst disagreed on matters of translational practice, both recognized that the greater the degree of the adoption of classical Chinese style, the greater the necessity of abandoning the original literary style of the biblical text.[17] Needless to say, the trimetrical tracts of Walter Medhurst and Sophia Martin are good examples of this principle. Both are written in the literary style of the *Sanzijing*. In contrast to Morrison's Bible, which Morrison termed a *shu* (書, book), Medhurst termed his tract a *jing* (經), a most apposite term, because it designated in Chinese both a "classic" text and a "sacred" text. Indeed, by imitating both the style and title of the illustrious Confucian primer, both Medhurst and Martin implicitly claimed similar honor for their own compositions.

Medhurst's decision to model his own tract on the trimetrical style of the *Sanzijing* school primer was strategic in other ways as well. The Confucian *Sanzijing* continued in use in the nineteenth century, not only in Chinese schools, but also in many *mission* schools, because it contained no religious doctrine, and its moral teaching was generally held to be congenial with the moral teaching of nineteenth-century Protestantism.[18] Since the *Sanzijing* lay at the very core of the formal education of young boys, it made good sense to many missionaries to take advantage of this fact for the purpose of Christian evangelism. Efforts to improve literacy of children in school could be linked to Christian evangelism by the introduction of a Christian version of the *Sanzijing*. Thus Medhurst's adoption of the trimetrical form of the *Sanzijing* in his own tract to communicate the Christian gospel was very strategic. Both his tract and the tract of Martin were used over many decades in the LMS schools that were established for Chinese students in Malaysia, Singapore, and China.

Medhurst's *Sanzijing*

Walter Medhurst (麥都思, 1796–1857) was originally recruited by the LMS as a printer and typesetter. He arrived in Malacca (Malaysia) in 1816, newly married to Elizabeth Martin, whom he had met in Madras while en route. His *Sanzijing* (abbreviated below as "M") was first published by the London Missionary Society Press (*Mohai shuguan*, 墨海書館) in Hong Kong in 1823. Following the signing of the Treaty of Nanking (1842) at the conclusion of the First Anglo-Chinese War (1839–1842), Medhurst settled in Shanghai where he lived for the next fourteen years. His *Sanzijing* became a Christian classic in its own right and was revised, expanded, and republished in Shanghai (1851, 1857) and Peking (1863).[19] Ten editions were published in total.[20] The version transcribed in appendix 1 (below) was obtained from National Library of Australia.[21] It is dated to "the sixth year of the reign of [the Qing emperor] Xianfeng [咸豐]," which is to say in the year 1857, which, coincidently, was the year of Medhurst's own death.[22]

Translating the Name for God

At the outset of composing his *Sanzijing*, Medhurst had to come to a decision on a controversial matter: the appropriate Chinese term to designate the proper name of Elohim in the Old Testament, and to translate the term *theos* (God) in the New Testament. Morrison had already set a significant precedent with his use of the generic term *Shen* (神, god, spirit) in his translation of the Bible. In Medhurst's time, this so-called

"*Shen* usage" in Morrison's Bible had become the *locus classicus* for all subsequent translators of the LMS. Nonetheless, the independently minded Medhurst went his own way on this matter. He was the first to employ the term *Shangdi* (上帝), meaning "most-high God" or "highest deity," to designate the Christian God. In his *Sanzijing*, Medhurst employs the term *Shangdi* nine times.[23]

To appreciate the significance of Medhurst's choice, one has only to observe that the name *Shangdi* was also the specific name for the "Jade Emperor" (*Yuhuang*, 玉皇) in both Chinese folk religion and Taoism; the Jade Emperor was also known as *Yuhuang shangdi* (玉皇上帝). Thus, Medhurst's use of the term *Shangdi* would have been immediately recognizable to his Chinese readers as the proper name for the supreme God of heaven. His preference for *Shangdi* was also informed by his own theology of revelation, which, according to his contemporary James Legge, was a theology of "progressive revelation in the Biblical text" that "affirms the possibility that God could leave a witness elsewhere in the world, even if," as Legge concedes, "this witness was quickly distorted by other corrupting influences."[24] In Medhurst's case, the use of the term *Shangdi* implied that the infinite God addresses all people through their own, diverse religious traditions: the use of the term *Shangdi* in early Chinese texts was evidence that the Chinese people had already acknowledged, at least in some fashion and to some degree, the one true (Christian) God. But Medhurst's use of *Shangdi*, with its implicit theology of progressive revelation, also posed some risks. As the British orientalist Solomon Caesar Malan observed, the "*Shangdi* usage" possessed an equivocal nature: its use could have the unintended effect of instilling in Chinese people a greater devotion to their own Jade Emperor.[25]

Medhurst's preference for *Shangdi* was a minority position at the time, for Morrison's *Shen* was widely accepted as authoritative in the LMS. Even Sophia Martin followed Morrison in the use of *Shen* almost exclusively (twenty-seven times) in her tract.[26] Martin's preference for *Shen* is to be expected in a tract written as early as 1832, given the influence of Morrison's translation of the Bible (1823). Like Medhurst's "*Shangdi* usage," the "*Shen* usage" was also informed by a theology of revelation, but one that was particularist in nature. Its use implied a disjunction between God's self-revelation in the Bible and Chinese religiosity, implicitly consigning the latter to the category of paganism and idolatry.

The *Shen/Shangdi* controversy came to be known as "the term question." To settle this controversy, the LMS convened a special meeting of its translators in Shanghai in 1843.[27] There could be no doubt as to the outcome of this meeting. Morrison's Bible, though deeply flawed in Medhurst's eyes, had taken on the proportions of a monumental text in the estimation of the LMS, while there were longstanding conflicts between the LSM and Medhurst concerning his own general principles of translation.[28] Thus, Medhurst's side was outvoted.[29] Though the outcome was disappointing to Medhurst, both sides in this debate were responding to the same challenge, which was the necessity of mediating meaning within a plurality of languages, cultures, religions, and so forth.[30] This necessity transformed the space of biblical translation into a *conflicted zone*. Morrison's attempt to be faithful to the biblical witness and Medhurst's attempt to be faithful to the Chinese tradition both demonstrate how the translator must always "serve two masters," where the translator encounters resistances on both sides.[31] For his part, Medhurst seems to have recognized that, since there are no exact equivalences between any two languages, the language of theological discourse could never be precisely duplicated in the Chinese language.[32]

Comparing Medhurst's *Sanzijing* to the *Sanzijing*

The formal similarity between Medhurst's tract and the *Sanzijing* extends beyond their shared title and shared trimetical form. The starting point of *Sanzijing* is the birth of the individual, which is to say, the point when a child's education begins:[33]

> 人之初, 性本善; 性相近, 習相遠。苟不教, 性乃遷; 教之道, 貴以專。
>
> People at the beginning, are naturally good.
> Their natures are similar; their habits become different.
> If, negligently, not taught, their nature deteriorates.
> The right way to teach, is with absolute concentration.

It is likely not a coincidence that the third character of the first line of the *Sanzijing* and of Medhurst's tract are the same: *chū* (初, beginning). But in the *Sanzijing*, this "beginning" refers to the beginning of a child's life, whereas in Medhurst's tract it refers to a metaphysical beginning, at a time antecedent to human civilization: "In the *beginning*, there was highest God" (自太初, 有上帝, M[1]). Of course, this stylistic echo also alludes to the first verse of the prologue of the Gospel of John (太 初 有 道, 1:1) and to Genesis 1:1, and it may even hint at the first line of the *Thousand character classic*, which similarly describes a time before human civilization: "The sky was black and earth yellow; space and time vast, limitless" (天地玄黃; 宇宙洪荒).

Next, Medhurst establishes *Shangdi* as the Creator of all people and things (M^{2}). In this section, he makes effective use of the double negative *wubu* (無不, not lacking) to define God in negative terms:[34] God is "*not lacking* [無不] knowledge, not lacking [無不] existence, not lacking [無不] ability" (M$^{3-4}$). The tract returns to negative theology in M$^{7-9}$, where it states that God is divine "without [無] physical traces, without [無] movement, without [無] voice and physical appearance"; indeed "he is a beginning without [無] beginning, and he is without [無] ending."

The *Sanzijing* also makes frequent use of the character *yue* (曰, we speak of) as a rhetorical devise, employing it ten times in total.[35] Medhurst takes up this usage twice in his clarification of the distinction between body and soul: "*We speak of* [曰] a body, *we speak of* [曰] a soul" (曰身體, 曰魂靈, M^{37}). This statement forms the basis of his dualistic theological anthropology, which is distinctly at odds with Pauline theology.[36]

> These are two entities; these should be kept distinct.
> The body has substance. The soul is without form.
> The body must die. The soul survives.
> If you do not nourish the body, life does not last long.
> If you do not nurture the soul, you bring disaster on yourself.
>
> (M$^{38-42}$)

From time to time, Medhurst even cites phrases from the *Sanzijing*. For example, the *Sanzijing* enumerates the three social bonds of Confucianism: namely, the "duty between sovereign and subject" (君臣義), the "love between father and child" (父子親), and the "harmony between husband and wife" (夫婦順) (三$^{27-28}$). Medhurst quotes the latter two of these bonds in M^{28}. These bonds obviously fit within a Christian moral framework. But given St. Paul's own position on civil obedience in Romans 13:1-7, Medhurst might also have also cited the *first* social bond, the bond of "duty between a sovereign and a subject." However, in the context of imperial China, civil obedience to the Qing sovereign (who was opposed to Christian proselytizing) would have necessitated disobedience to God's will, at least in Medhurst's mind.

As noted above, the *Sanzijing* lists the six types of domestic animals: "horse, ox, sheep, chicken, dog, pig" (三[39]). Medhurst cites these animals in exactly the same order (M[43]). His purpose was not pedagogical but theological: in this section he explains how animals differ from human beings—human beings have a soul, which makes them answerable to God for their actions in life. In contrast, domestic animals

> do not proceed into the next world (heaven).
> When they hunger they eat;
> when they eat their fill, they go away.
> They lack cleverness, they do not think.
> The birds and animals have a less intelligent character.
> They do not do good or evil.
> Therefore there is no judgment for them.
>
> (M[44-48])

The *Sanzijing* refers to history books and ancient Chinese chronicles and exhorts the young to "recite them with your mouths, and examine them with your hearts" (口而誦, 心而維, 三[140]). Medhurst quotes this line exactly (M[157]). But in the wider context of Medhurst's version, those that one "recites" are not historical chronicles but one's prayers (M[156]) and sins (M[153]). The stanza that follows reads: "If you do not do this, *it is not proper*" (若相反, 非所宜, M[158]). This statement picks up yet another line from the *Sanzijing*: "If a child does not study, *it is not proper*" (子不學, 非所宜, 三[11]).

References to Confucianism and Christian Scripture

In contrast to Sophia Martin, Medhurst does not list the four directions or the five constant (*wuchang*, 五常) virtues. Of the seven emotions (joy, anger, grief, fear, love, hatred, desire, 三[41-42]), Medhurst mentions only "desire" (欲), which he qualifies negatively as "selfish desire" (私欲, M[95]). It is also noteworthy that he does not mention "love" (*ai*, 愛), which appears thirteen times in Martin's text. Perhaps Medhurst does not consider Christian "love" (αγαπη) to be an "emotion" (*qing*, 情) but rather consideres it a virtue comparable to the Confucian term *ren* (仁, kindness, benevolence), which he *does* employ twice (M[5, 75]). *Ren* is the foremost of the Confucian virtues and is contrasted with "selfishness" in the Confucian tradition.

Medhurst's account of human history begins with the creation of human beings. The statement "the Lord made human beings; they resemble his own image" (主造人, 象己像, M[15]) is a direct reference to Genesis 1:27. He portrays Adam (亞當) in a very Confucian manner as the "first ancestor" (始祖, M[17]). When tested, Adam was confused by the lies of the devil (魔鬼, cf. John 8:44) and ate the forbidden fruit. Having offended *Shangdi*, he hid himself in the "Happy Garden" or Paradise (樂園, M[17-22]). Medhurst then skips over the remainder of the Old Testament to take up a discussion of the sinfulness of human nature and the coming judgment of God (M[23-50]).

Medhurst next turns his attention to the life of Jesus (M[51-61]). This section seems to be modeled on the Christ hymn of Philippians 2:1-16, for neither text makes explicit mention of Jesus' crucifixion, focusing instead on Jesus' willingness to give up his honor and authority: "He was in possession of great authority. He governed everything. He departed from the heavenly palace to descend to the material world. He left behind riches and honour to experience suffering" (M[56-58]). In allusion to the Lucan nativity story, we are told that Jesus was born in humble circumstances: "When Jesus was born from above, they put him in a manger" (M[59]). Like most Chinese peasants, Jesus lived a life of hard work: "From birth to death, he laboured hard" (M[60]). The tract later explains that Jesus "underwent hardships to redeem transgressions" (歷艱難, 贖愆尤, M[69]). Next the tract describes the appropriate human response (M[62-88]), which Medhurst then sums up in terms of three specific instructions:

> If you believe in Jesus, three things are important:
> If you lack one of these, you cannot perfect the truth.
> Believe in his presence; Follow his commandments;
> Depend on his virtue.
>
> (M[89-92])

Medhurst then lists the three things necessary that have been established by God to "obtain eternal happiness" (M[112]): namely, a teacher (師傅), scripture (經籍), and ritual propriety (禮儀) (M[113-14]), the latter being subdivided into baptism (施洗)[37] and "conferring the [holy] meal"

(授餐, M[120]). Medhurst then describes God's coming judgment in terms that clearly allude to Revelation 20:12-14:

The Lord judges from on high.
The masses and the heavenly God face one another from a distance.
He unrolls his scroll [展其卷] to verify their number [核其數].
It is appropriate to examine carefully good deeds and faults.
Good and evil angels in front.
Righteous and unrighteous, all standing to be distinguished.
He interrogates his people to determine rewards and punishments.
The good must be commended; the evil must be cut off.
Some rise to the heavenly palace [明宮],
others fall into the gloomy mansion [暗府].

(M[131-39])

In the above passage, the reference to God "unrolling his scroll" (M[133]) alludes to Revelation 20:12.[38] The reference to a "number" that is "verified" (M[133]) may point to Revelation 7:4.[39] The mention of a "heavenly palace" (明宮) and "gloomy mansion" (暗府) must refer respectively to "heaven" (*tian*, 天) and "hell" (*diyu*, 地獄), which are specifically named a few stanzas below: "One person ascends to heaven, anther descends to hell" (M[145]). As I shall discuss below, belief in hell was a conspicuous component of both folk Buddhism and Chinese folk religion, as well as nineteenth-century Christianity. From a Confucian perspective, the greatest tragedy of hell is not the physical torment (which was temporary) but rather the breaking up of one's ancestral clan (族) and family relations. Medhurst seems to have been aware of this, as shown by his appeal to Confucian sensibilities in the following section:

Good and evil people are different and must be separated.
Elder brother and younger brother, elder sister and younger sister.
Even though they are part of one clan,
it is difficult to return to one another.
One ascends to heaven, one descends to hell.
One suffers, one attains blessing.
One is joyful, one is fearful.
One is resentful, one praises.

(M[142-48])

Thus the primary bonds of family life between father and son, wife and husband, elder brother and younger brother, elder sister and younger sister may be broken at the time of death, with some family members ascending to heaven and others descending to hell.

Sophia Martin's *Xunnü sanzijing*

In contrast to Medhurst, little is known about his sister-in-law, Sophia Martin (馬典娘娘). According to Alexander Wylie, she lived in Batavia (Jakarta) before moving to Singapore "in quest of health."[40] Wylie also states that she worked in "Chinese schools." But according to David K. Y. Chng, Martin actually *founded* a Chinese girls' school in Kampong Glam, a fact that provides a context for the composition of her own school primer.[41] Martin published her trimetrical primer, *Xunnü sanzijing* (訓女三字經, *Three character classic for the instruction of young ladies*) (abbreviated below as "S") in Singapore in 1932. I have transcribed and translated this tract based on a copy obtained from the Harvard-Yenching Library (see appendix 2).

The reference to "young ladies" (小女) in the title of her tract indicates more than the gender of the tract's intended readers. For this tract makes special mention of young ladies at numerous points (S[1, 7, 45, 83, 95, 183, 189, 195]).[42] Martin probably modelled the title of her tract, *Xunnü sanzijing* (訓女三字經, *Three character classic for the instruction of young ladies*), on classical instructional manuals directed toward the behavior of girls, such as the *Nüxun* (*The instruction of girls*) from the Han period (206 BC–AD 220), the *Nüxun* from the Tang period (618–907), two *Nüxun* from the two Ming periods (1368–1644),[43] and two more dating from the Qing period (1644–1911).[44] The Qing trimetrical-rhymed primer titled *Nü sanzijing* (*Three character classic for girls*), written in 1905 by Zhu Hao (朱浩) and Wen Xingyuan (文星源), provides an even closer parallel to Martin's title.[45] Like Martin's tract, this manual was written in imitation of the original *Sanzijing*.

As would be expected, the traditional texts enumerated above promote the conventional Confucian attitudes and rules that should govern the behavior of women. For example, Empress Renxiao's *Nüxun* includes chapters on respecting the husband (*jingfu*, 敬夫), a woman's bedroom and private sitting room (*guixun*, 閨訓), giving birth to children (*renzi*, 妊子), benevolence toward the children (*ciyou*, 慈幼), educating children (*jiaozi*, 教子), seriousness and quietness (*shenjing*, 慎靜), and sparingness and simplicity (*jiesu*, 節俗). Similarly, *Nü sanzijing* includes chapters on the inferiority of women to men, how a girl is to behave before marriage (e.g., binding of feet, obedience to the parents), and obedience toward one's husband and parents-in-law after marriage.

When considered against the backdrop of these manuals, Sophia Martin's tract is radical indeed: it sets out a program for girls to read and study intensively, which was very much at odds with the customary rules for women at the time. When compared with these traditional manuals for young ladies, the beginning of Martin's text is almost revolutionary: "All young ladies should go to school. Reading every day is useful. If a girl does not study, it is improper" (凡小女, 入學堂; 每日讀, 就有用, 女不學, 非所宜, $S^{1\text{-}3}$). Next, and perhaps even more surprising, Martin directly quotes perhaps the best-known stanzas of the venerable *Sanzijing*, which were traditionally intended for young *boys*. The original *Sanzijing* ($三^{12\text{-}14}$) reads:

> 幼不學, 老何為。玉不琢, 不成器。人不學, 不知義。
>
> If one does study while young, how will one act when old?
> Jade that has not been polished cannot be used.
> One who has not studied cannot know righteousness.

Curiously, Martin makes one small change to this passage ($S^{4\text{-}6}$): the final character has been altered from *yi* (義) to *li* (理, right principles).[46] Robert Morrison's own translation of the *Sanzijing* may shed light on this alteration, for he translates *yi* (義) as "justice."[47] In light of this, Martin may also have interpreted *yi* (義) as "justice" (cf. $M^{5,\,136}$) and deemed "justice" to be too spiritual a virtue to be attained by mere study, apart from the *modus vivendi* of one's whole life. Perhaps Martin's rootedness in the Protestant tradition remained under the surface of her own compositional work, even mediating her comprehension of the meaning of Confucian values.[48]

Martin returns to the subject of education for young ladies in $S^{46\text{-}50}$. This section begins with this command: "You, young ladies, should read every day, study every day. Write letters clearly. Listen to good advice." If this command to write Chinese characters clearly seems unremarkable to the modern reader, one must bear in mind that even Empress Dowager Cixi lacked this skill.[49] In a culture in which literacy was linked with power, the ability to write was essential for the upward mobility of young women. Martin evidently recognized this. Though that which follows seems more conventionally Confucian, it would nonetheless have been good advice for all young ladies seeking social advancement.

> Do not talk. Do not argue.
> Put things in your mind until you do not forget.
> If you proceed in the following way, it will be very useful.
>
> (S[48-50])

Martin's Use of the *Sanzijing* and Confucian Categories

In contrast to Medhurst's tract, Martin's text includes many of the basic Chinese characters found in the *Sanzijing*. For example, in S[30] she names the "four directions" (從南北, 到西東, cf. 三[31]), cleverly interweaving them with an allusion to Hebrews 4:13:[50]

> There is nowhere to dwell that God does see,
> "from south to north, west to east" [quoting 三[31-32]].
> In the sea, beyond it,
> in the depths, in the heights [cf. Ps 139:7-8].
> There is no one whom he does not see.
> There is nothing he does not consider.
>
> (S[29-34])

In S[59-62], Martin returns to Hebrews 4 a second time:

> God's teaching can be compared with a knife.
> A knife having two edges cuts into two parts [cf. Heb 4:12-13].
> It cuts the human heart in two, it divides one's bones.
> He who has evil thoughts, it makes them known.
>
> (S[59-62])[51]

Further on, she lists the five constant virtues (*wǔcháng*, 五常) of Confucianism: "We speak of benevolence, righteousness, ritual propriety, wisdom, integrity" (曰仁義, 禮智信, S[57]; cf. 三[35]). Martin does not list all "seven emotions" (三[41-42]): her tract takes special interest in the emotions *ai* (愛, love) and *e* (惡, hate), which she names thirteen and seventeen times respectively.[52]

The command to "honor your father and mother" (孝父母) in S[13] seems to allude to both 三[181] and Exodus 20:12 simultaneously. Here we find a good example of how compatible some aspects of Confucianism were to Christian morality. Martin even uses the verb *xiao* (孝, show filial piety), as does Morrison in his translation of Exodus 20:12 (孝父母). This verb is also employed elsewhere in the *Sanzijing* as praiseworthy behavior in children (三[18, 21, 65, 108]). But the parallel to S[13] in 三[181] actually uses a different verb, *xian* (顯), which means "to glorify" or "to honor." Perhaps Martin sensed that *xian* (顯) was too close to the practice of ancestor worship. Of course, Martin could have employed the verb *jing* (敬), as does the Union Version (敬爾父爾母, Exod 20:12), but her choice of the verb *xiao* (孝) is more fitting to her overall strategy of demonstrating the commensurability of some Confucian values with Christian morality.[53]

One of the strongest themes in Martin's tract is that of the rich and the poor. She uses the character *fu* (富, wealthy) nine times and the compound form *fucai* (富財, S[89]) once.[54] The contrasting character 貧 (poor) is used ten times, and the compound term *pinqiong* (貧窮) is used three times (S[87, 93, 105]).[55] Martin's emphasis on the troubles of the poor is ethical in import: the rich, who are honored in society, may have far less honor in God's eyes than those who are poor. For the poor, who live an honorable life, will be raised up to a life of blessedness in heaven, while the rich, who appear to be honorable in this life, may actually be sent to hell. This principle provides the context for her retelling of the story of Lazarus (Lasasa, 拉撒路) and the rich man (Luke 16:19-32):

> But at that time, he [Lazarus] lies in front of the rich man's door.
> The rich man's dog [狗] comes and licks [舐] him. [cf. Luke 16:21][56]
> Not many days later, the poor man dies.
> People abandon his body.
> But his spirit enters into heaven.
> He neither suffers nor worries.
>
> (S[155-60])

In this story, Martin focuses particularly on the fate of the rich man, who was indifferent to the plight of the poor man who lay at his door. In death, his high status and wealth on earth do not benefit to him because he did not fear God (不畏神) and did not do good works:

The rich man also passes away.
People inter his body.
But spirit suffers greatly,
because on earth his transgressions were great.
During his life, he did not fear God.
The good of the matter is that he was suddenly unimportant.
He obtained suffering, not because he was rich,
but he worried because he had not been good.

(S[161-68])

Martin leaves us in no doubt as to the name of the place to which the rich man was sent: "hell" (*diyu*, 地獄). Indeed, she employs the term "hell" five times in her tract (S[10, 23, 78, 172, 194]), in marked contrast to Medhurst's single mention (M[145]). While the concept of hell as a place of postmortem punishment was widespread in nineteenth-century Christianity, it is virtually absent in the New Testament and Septuagint. In fact, with one exception, the New Testament makes no reference to a place of postmortem punishment. The Greek term *adhis* is most closely associated with the English term "hell":[57] it designates a subterranean realm, where all the dead linger in shadows. Hence *adhis* is often translated as "hades" or as the "netherworld." Thus, *The Union Bible* translates the term *adhis* in Luke 16:23 by the term *yinjian* (陰間, the netherworld). The term *adhis* was also employed by Septuagintal translators as the translation equivalent for the Hebrew term *she'ol*. For example, in the story of the martyrdom of Eleazar, the persecuted Eleazar actually commands his torturers to send him to "Hades" (2 Macc 6:1-23).

The Authorized (or King James) Version (1611) has the distinction of being the first English translation to translate the Greek lexeme *adhis* as "hell." Martin certainly had this usage in mind when she composed her tract. Robert Morrison also employed the term *diyu* (地獄, hell) to translate the Greek term *adhis* in Luke 16:23, no doubt under the influence of the Authorized Version. It is no accident that Martin chose the story of Lazarus and the rich man to illustrate "hell": this is the only example in the New Testament where the Greek term *adhis* designates a place of punishment and torment—we are told that the rich man lives "in anguish" in "flames" (Luke 16:25). So that no one can miss the point of the story, Martin reiterates the moral: "If you do evil deeds, your body and soul will enter hell" (身靈魂, 入地獄, S[77-78]). Later, in S[188], she warns that for those who are evil, "in the next world everything will be burning" (皆一燃).

We should not suppose that Martin's Christian proclamation of hell would have seemed strange or exotic to her Chinese readers. If possible, Chinese folk Buddhism was more interested in hell than the LMS missionaries who sought to convert them. One of the most widely circulated folk Buddhist tracts of the time was titled *The Jade Record* (*Yuli chao zhuan jing shi*, 玉歷鈔傳警世), which was printed in various editions throughout the course of the nineteenth century.[58] According to the prologue of *The Jade Record*, this tract was jointly submitted to the Jade Emperor (*Yuhuang shangdi*, 玉皇上帝) by Yan Luo and the Bodhisattva of Compassion, Guanyin Pusa (觀音菩薩). This is a moralistic tract that narrates the march of souls through the ten courts of hell, drawing a clear connection between wicked deeds committed on earth and their postmortem punishment in hell. Dead souls (*hunling*, 魂靈) must first pass through the court known as the "Mirror of Reflection," where they see reflections of their former sins, including the sin of having weak faith in Buddha. In the sixth court, sinners are tortured in a variety of ways.[59] The ruler of hell is identified as King Yanluo (閻羅王), whom Christian missionaries would later conflate with the devil.

As *The Jade Record* demonstrates, many of the key concepts of LMS missionary tracts were familiar to their Chinese readers, including the concept of a most-high God (上帝), of souls (魂靈) that survive death, and of heaven (天) and hell (地獄). These concepts, far from being novel, actually constituted a point of convergence between the Christian missionaries and the Chinese people. As odd as it may at first seem to us, the Christian doctrine of hell actually provided the Chinese with a means to affirm their own religious identity and religious tradition, and, at the same time, open themselves to some of the unfamiliar aspects of Protestant religious teaching.[60]

A case in point is the life of Liang Afa (梁阿發) (1789–1855), a devout Buddhist who was, by trade, a carver of wooden printing blocks. He was hired by William Milne for the printing of Christian tracts. He subsequently converted to Christianity and was baptized in 1816.[61] Following Milne's death, Liang was recruited by the LMS and ordained by Robert Morrison. On weekends, he and Reverend Edwin Stevens would travel the countryside of Canton distributing their tracts. Liang is best known to us as the author of *Quan shi liang yan* (勸世良言, *Good words to exhort the age*), published in 1832.[62] (This is the same year that Sophia Martin published her own trimetrical classic.) Liang's lengthy text actually consists of nine separate tracts.[63] Included among the themes of tract 7 punishment in hell for the wicked. As the tract demonstrates, Liang was well acquainted with Buddhist stories of hell by virtue of his former life as a Buddhist. It seems probable that he titled his own tract in direct challenge to *The Jade Record*. For, whereas the purpose of *The Jade Record*, according to its full title, was to "*warn* the age" (*jingshi*, 警世), the purpose of Liang's tract was to provide "good words [i.e., good news, or the gospel] to *exhort* the age" (*quanshi*, 勸世). With this promise to "exhort" rather than "warn" his readers, Liang positioned his own tract in direct relation to *The Jade Record*.

The Hermeneutics of Translation

This study of the religious tracts of Medhurst and Martin illustrates the diverse ways in which the space of translation can become a "conflicted zone" where one must "serve two masters."[64] In the case of Medhurst and Martin, these "two masters" were the Protestant and Chinese traditions. As their dualist anthropology, use of *Shangdi* and *Shen*, and reflections on hell all demonstrate, contradictions and negations are inherent properties of translational process.

Marianne Moyaert has described the conflicted zone of translation as "fragile" space and laments the inevitable loss of meaning that it entails.[65] But from a Gadamerian perspective, we can view this space more positively. The religious tracts of Medhurst and Martin were each products of their own historically effected consciousnesses.[66] Their own translational practices actually *constituted* not only their own participation in tradition but also its continuity in their own time. From this perspective, their trimetrical tracts *embodied* the very "happening" of the Protestant tradition as it engaged the traditions of Confucianism, gender-specific childhood education, and folk religion in nineteenth-century China.

From this vantage point, there are no grounds for lamenting any *loss* of original meaning in the trimetrical primers of Medhurst and Martin. Their primers should more properly be understood as the very vehicles by which the Protestant theological tradition was embodied in nineteenth-century China. In order to translate this tradition into the genre of Chinese trimetrical primers, Medhurst and Martin had to re-conceive their relations of belonging to the Christian tradition, which had formed them, in light of their new relations of belonging to their "Chinese present." In so doing, they found themselves in the position of beginning again, as all translators inevitably must do. But by beginning again, they managed to arrive at a fresh experience of their own religious tradition in their unfinished Chinese present.

Appendix 1[1]

WALTER MEDHURST, 三字經 (1823, 1857)

咸豐六年

上海墨海書館印

1 自太初, 有上帝; 2 造民物, 創天地。 3 無不知, 無不在; 4 無不能, 眞主宰。

5 至仁義, 至清潔; 6 至矜憫, 至誠實。 7 乃神靈, 無形跡; 8 無方向, 無聲色。

9 始無始, 終無終; 10 宜寅畏, 宜敬恭。 11 感其恩, 凜其威; 12 億萬眾, 頌上帝。

13 斯世人, 或作偶; 14 欲配主, 眞差謬。 15 主造人, 象己像; 16 性維善, 心維良。

17 考始祖, 為亞當; 18 享福祉, 樂園藏。 19 在園中, 有果實; 20 主所賜, 俱可食。

21 惟一樹, 禁甚厲; 22 食之者, 犯上帝。 23 有魔鬼, 以妄言; 24 迷眩人, 獲罪天。

25 自此時, 人心變; 26 惟作惡, 不務善。 27 祖獲戾, 生裔冑; 28 迄叔世, 仍卑陋。

29 人自幼, 及老邁; 30 德已喪, 行更敗。 31 凡宇內, 無不然; 32 干律法, 蹈罪愆。

33 私欲熾, 眞理昧; 34 貪婪興, 公平廢。 35 忘天道, 棄永福; 36 戀貨財, 耽宴樂。

37 曰身體, 曰魂靈; 38 此二者, 當詳明。 39 體有質, 魂無形; 40 身必死, 靈常存。

41 身不養, 生不久; 42 靈不葆, 自取禍。 43 馬牛羊, 雞犬豕; 44 無前因, 無來世。

45 饑則食, 飽則颺; 46 無機謀, 無思想。 47 彼禽獸, 少慧性; 48 無善惡, 無報應。

49 爾庶民, 行為偏; 50 墮艱苦, 自難免。 51 惟上帝, 憐爾曹; 52 遣耶穌, 救億兆。

53 夫耶穌, 至尊貴; 54 軼天使, 超儕輩。 55 參天帝, 督宇宙; 56 攬大權, 統萬有。

57 離明宮, 降塵寰; 58 去富貴, 嘗憂患。 59 耶穌誕, 置馬槽; 60 生至死, 惟劬勞。

61 有耶穌, 將救世; 62 用何法, 濟乃事。 63 一傳道, 一著功; 64 一受難, 為至用。

65 用其道, 正人心; 66 從訓者, 百福臨。 67 建厥功, 立師表; 68 我希榮, 當則傚。

69 歷艱難, 贖愆尤; 70 我信之, 可得救。 71 凡爾眾, 無富貧; 72 必悔罪, 信福音。

73 改前非, 向眞道; 74 如是者, 為從教。 75 上帝子, 普深仁; 76 我篤信, 蒙其恩。

77 主誕降, 為兆民; 78 補過失, 施矜憫。 79 我懷疑, 主弗救; 80 功自誇, 過難宥。

81 如旭日, 光徧燭; 82 覆盆下, 有不及。 83 如藥石, 療諸疾; 84 不入口, 自無益。

85 人悔改, 畧有四; 86 棄前非, 無二志。 87 一憂思, 一怨艾; 88 一任過, 一順理。

89 信耶穌, 有三要; 90 苟缺一, 不成道。 91 信其有, 遵其命; 92 賴其德, 乃為盛。

93 凡悔改, 從眞理; 94 必赦宥, 蒙綏祉。 95 此世人, 狥私欲; 96 善不為, 惡是作。

97 維天父, 惠無窮; 98 降聖神, 牖其衷。 99 欲遷改, 整厥躬; 100 必祈禱, 無倦容。

101 求上帝, 望恩鴻; 102 賴耶穌, 以誠通。 103 藐我體, 無功績; 104 自為義, 有何益。

105 惟耶穌, 勳至赫; 106 默籲時, 賴其德。 107 如誠求, 必有得; 108 適爾願, 因不輟。

109 由斯世, 躋樂國; 110 有善途, 宜竭力。 111 法有三, 上帝設; 112 宜遵行, 得永樂。

113 一師傅, 一經籍; 114 一禮儀, 以循習。 115 有聖經, 可明道; 116 所宜信, 所當造。

117 有師傅, 善指示; 118 勤講貫, 儆斯世。 119 有禮儀, 著二端; 120 一施洗, 一授餐。

121 人于世, 壽無長; 122 老與少, 必死亡。 123 既沒後, 身歸土; 124 此靈魂, 仍如故。

125 有今世, 有來生; 126 身與靈, 必相分。 127 迄叔季, 死復活; 128 身與靈, 再相合。

129 當此時, 耶穌至; 130 得大榮, 享福祉。 131 主聽訟, 居高位; 132 眾天神, 遙相對。

133 展其卷, 核其數; 134 宜詳審, 功與過。 135 善及惡, 侍於前; 136 義不義, 皆立辨。

137 鞫斯民, 定賞罰; 138 善必奬, 惡當絕。 139 升明宮, 墮暗府; 140 從此離, 難相顧。

141 父子親, 夫婦近; 142 善惡殊, 必相分。 143 兄與弟, 姊與妹; 144 雖一族, 難同歸。

145 升天堂, 下地獄; 146 一受苦, 一得福。 147 一怡悅, 一驚恐; 148 一怨懟, 一讚頌。

149 爾小生, 宜寅恭; 150 賴上帝, 德至隆。 151 宜祈禱, 朝而夕; 152 恒若此, 毋休息。

153 先頌美, 以任過; 154 求矜恤, 後蒙嘏。 155 心必正, 意必誠; 156 祈若此, 事以成。

157 口而誦, 心而惟; 158 若相反, 非所宜。 159 恒厥心, 畏上帝; 160 及老死, 不可廢。

Appendix 2[1]

SOPHIA MARTIN, 訓女三字經 (1832)

1 凡小女, 入學堂; 2 每日讀, 就有用。 3 女不學, 非所宜; 4 幼不學, 老何為。

5 玉不琢, 不成器; 6 人不學, 不知理。 7 多小女, 只玩耍; 8 真精伶, 言惡話。

9 你無怕, 若做惡; 10 死那時, 入地獄。 11 在此世, 敬畏神; 12 常懇来, 其大恩。

13 孝父母, 惜兄弟; 14 若不如, 無盡禮。 15 信耶穌, 學好道; 16 在後世, 無煩苦。

17 因始祖, 得罪天; 18 其後代, 不好愆。 19 從始初, 到今時; 20 人不隨, 好道理。

21 若不愛, 做好事; 22 必得法, 無奈何。 23 身靈魂, 入地獄; 24 無平安, 無納樂。

25 神足大, 造世人; 26 大於小, 报其恩。 27 神在天, 明看下; 28 你不取, 與人罵。

29 無何處, 其不看; 30 從南北, 到西東。 31 在海內, 在於外; 32 在底下, 在於高。

33 無何人, 其不看; 34 無何物, 其不筭。 35 人若思, 愛去窨; 36 神之手, 亦能持。

37 去道遠, 上到天; 38 人不脫, 到人見。 39 在於光, 在於暗; 40 皆相同, 皆一樣。

41 神之目, 透人心; 42 其省察, 到深深。 43 人何思, 人何去; 44 能神看, 皆而知。

45 爾小女, 該小心; 46 常日讀, 常日念。 47 字寫明, 聽徽音; 48 不可言, 不可爭。

49 放在心, 到不忘; 50 若如此, 有多用。 51 神之道, 比燈先; 52 照人路, 指以天。

53 兩比之, 以木鐸; 54 警戒人, 減自惡。 55 無一好, 其不教; 56 人該隨, 幼到老。

57 曰仁義, 禮智信; 58 其亦教, 到無盡。 59 神之教, 比於刀; 60 有刃口, 到兩個。

61 刺人心, 刺其骨; 62 人想惡, 其能著。 63 神之書, 人心讀; 64 因其指, 樂其路。

65 而已學, 始到終; 66 若不隨, 無何用。 67 人該來, 聖神風; 68 來而印, 在心中。

69 若聖風, 感人心; 70 無何好, 其不成。 71 敬神天, 信耶穌; 72 免聖風, 人不做。

73 人若愛, 升上天; 74 皆惡事, 其該恨。 75 人拿刀, 刺自己; 76 何人信, 其不死。

77 亦如此, 人作惡; 78 身靈魂, 入地獄。 79 如一刀, 斷人身; 80 罪如此, 敗靈魂。

81 人食毒, 壞其身; 82 而做惡, 壞其靈。 83 凡小女, 該好行; 84 若不如, 不好名。

85 富於貴, 人所貪; 86 貧與賤, 人所惡。 87 智者信, 人貧窮; 88 若好名, 更有用。

89 昔一人, 甚富財; 90 但其惡, 人不愛。 91 賤足多, 心驕傲; 92 人藐視, 人恨惡。

93 再一人, 定貧窮; 94 無幾久, 其為王。 95 或小女, 足要知; 96 人何如, 更愛之。

97 說雖貧, 人甚好; 98 惡之事, 其不做。 99 心信實, 行慷慨; 100 常愛行, 所公義。

101 王那時, 心謙遜; 102 民甚愛, 足要順。 103 彼一人, 雖甚富; 104 因其惡, 生無久。

105 此一人, 雖貧窮; 106 因畏神, 亦敬重。 107 生足久, 得鴻恩; 108 死那時, 升上帝。

109 爾勿想, 人若富; 110 但不好, 無煩惱。 111 人若貧, 但愛好; 112 今後世, 無萬苦。

113 神主造, 眾世人; 114 萬國方, 萬世民。 115 其亦養, 萬人者; 116 自國君, 到乞丐。

117 萬人者, 其亦管; 118 其神使, 幾千萬。 119 人布秧, 以為禾; 120 神不祝, 生無則。

121 神使日, 連日照; 122 其使爾, 屢次落。 123 眞實的, 神不存; 124 皆世人, 立到亡。

125 少女貧, 望神主; 126 其不忘, 其不棄。 127 蓋神天, 足可憐; 128 要眾人, 得其恩。

129 神若允, 以世人; 130 其自然, 踐前言。 131 從古時, 到而今; 132 總不識, 食其言。

133 神之愛, 比母親; 134 心足慈, 愛其子。 135 母忘子, 或無有; 136 但神天, 不如此。

137 神之愛, 到無盡; 138 無何終, 其可憐。 139 再一次, 我能言; 140 古之事, 于二人。

141 一人富, 賤十萬; 142 每日穿, 甫整衫。 143 大間屋, 長隨多; 144 無一物, 其不有。

145 他別人, 患與貧; 146 無朋友, 無何親。 147 其身體, 滿於瘡; 148 衫補釘, 足大慘。

149 忽一日, 人可憐; 150 因不行, 而擡之。 151 放在前, 富人面; 152 或其心, 有可憐。

153 其求食, 只飯粒; 154 求更加, 其不欲。 155 但在時, 在門前; 156 人之狗, 來舐之。

157 無幾日, 貧人死; 158 其身體, 人棄之。 159 但其靈, 入天堂; 160 又無苦, 又無煩。

161 彼富人, 亦過世; 162 其身體, 人之葬。 163 但其靈, 足煩苦; 164 因在世, 大其過。

165 生那時, 不畏神; 166 好之事, 其忽輕。 167 其得苦, 非因富; 168 但得煩, 因不好。

169 人若富, 亦敬神; 170 其自然, 死上天。 171 又人食, 亦愛惡; 172 自然死, 入地獄。

173 但此人, 雖大苦; 174 其不愛, 做惡事。 175 小女看, 人煩苦; 176 該可憐, 不可笑。

177見朋友, 做惡事; 178 該教之, 來做好。 179 女如此, 神足愛; 180 但不可, 必得害。

181 凡小女, 勿說謊; 182 勿偷取, 再勿搶。 183 若小女, 做此事; 184 足弊的, 可恨之。

185 生那時, 可羞辱; 186 死那時, 煩到熟。 187 在此時, 而討嫌; 188 在後世, 皆一燃。

189 小女惡, 死那時;	190 靈魂來, 把之去。	191 因生時, 在此世;	192 聽其言, 隨其意。
193 魔鬼悅, 若其子;	194 入地獄, 分其禍。	195 勿小女, 聽其言;	196 其若引, 你做惡。
197 常求天, 求耶穌;	198 但不要, 無偷走。	199 免耶穌, 無別名;	200 能救孜, 人靈魂。
201 我勸爾, 懇求神;	202 今後世, 福無盡。		

7

THE "ISHMAEL" OF SINOLOGY

H. A. Giles' History of Chinese Literature *(1901) and Late Victorian Perceptions of Chinese Literature and Culture*

Elisabeth Jay

> *We most of us transact our moral and spiritual affairs in our own country.*
>
> —Henry James[1]

This paper is premised on the argument that the way in which British sinologists conceived of China and the Chinese had more to do with the social structures and ideological debates of nineteenth-century Britain than with any great degree of interest in, or familiarity with, the contemporary culture variations and ethnic diversity to be found throughout China's vast territories.

Recent anthropological thinking about identity construction and perception has seen a change in which static, monolithic notions of national societies have given way to models more sensitive to generational change and composed as much in terms of class, educational background, religious formation, or gender as in terms of territorial concepts. Recognizing the differently typical, or sometimes highly individual, career and vocational choices that led nineteenth-century British men and women to engage with Chinese culture makes it more possible to acknowledge the tensions that operated between the individual viewpoint and that of the "national" outlook they often asserted. Their claims to very different understandings of "the Chinese" were often formed upon a battleground that, in retrospect, appears to have had a great deal to do with Victorian social structures and the intellectual and ideological debates being waged in the closing decades of nineteenth-century Britain. If, as the *Oxford Dictionary of National Biography* entry claims, Herbert Allen Giles' "clearest contribution to Chinese studies was his ability through his writings to 'humanize' China for a Western audience," then his own formation had a considerable bearing on the picture he gave. This paper will explore the interaction of varied, formative "home" backgrounds with an equally complex but differently structured Chinese civilization to arrive at an understanding of why Herbert Giles was introduced to his second wife's family as "the 'Ishmael' of sinology."[2]

"The Chinese"

Although those who had spent any length of time in nineteenth-century China were usually careful to insist on its geographical variety, this did not seem for the most part to lead to deeper reflection on the diversity of its contemporary ethnic composition. When Herbert Giles contributed *The Civilization of China* (1911) to the popular self-education series The Home University of Modern Knowledge, he aimed, in 268 pages, to "suggest a rough outline of Chinese civilization from the earliest times down to the present period of rapid and startling transition." His opening paragraph ended, "What is meant by China?" "Taken in its widest sense," this would include, he admitted, "Mongolia, Manchuria, Eastern Turkestan, Tibet, and the Eighteen Provinces," but he nevertheless elected to confine his survey to that portion of the whole "which is known to the Chinese as the 'Eighteen Provinces,' and to us as China Proper." Despite Giles' attempt to legitimate his chosen area by capitalizing the concept of "China Proper," this was not a formulation recognized by the China of his day, and it inevitably reduced the Chinese Empire's cultural diversity. Describing his chosen subject as demarcated by "Peking, the capital, in the north; Canton, the great commercial centre in the south; Shanghai on the east; and the Tibetan frontier on the west," Giles proceeded to ridicule "the absurdity of asking a returning traveller . . . 'How do you like China?'" He replied, "Fancy asking a Chinaman, who had spent a year or two in England, how he liked Europe!"

Giles' answer to his own rhetorical question speaks volumes: a more appropriate response to the question he posed might have been to ask how the "Chinaman" liked the British Empire, in all its rich ethnic variety. Although Giles proceeded to write at length about the varied topography and produce of the Eighteen Provinces, his concession to considering the difference between their inhabitants was first to apply the kind of pseudo-ethnography favored by such nineteenth-century European luminaries as Ernest Renan and Matthew Arnold: "The inhabitants of the coast provinces are distinguished from dwellers in the north and in the far interior by a marked alertness of mind and general temperament." His second concession to national diversity was to mention how the Franco-British forces in 1860 had been able to deploy the mutual loathing of the various provinces to further advantage.[3] A career in the diplomatic service was likely to encourage the professionally convenient notion of conceiving of China as a homogenous political entity, whose internal geographical and ethnic divisions were of interest only when they could be exploited.

Coupled with the liberal humanist approach characteristic of late-nineteenth-century literary studies, this mindset had the effect of collapsing the many centuries of China's culture, treated in Giles' *A History of Chinese Literature* (1901), into a curiously monochrome affair. Despite organizing his survey of Chinese classics by dynasty, in trying to convey the "essence" of Chineseness, Giles adopted the notion of the transcendent timelessness of good literature (which was still favored some thirty years later by E. M. Forster, who decided to treat several centuries of English novelists "as seated together in a room, a circular room, a sort of British Museum reading-room—all writing their novels simultaneously"[4]). It would be a foolhardy literary scholar today who—basing his or her remarks on the poem *Beowulf*, a roughly contemporary work[5]—collapsed all the ethnic identities that have contributed through the centuries to multicultural Britain and declared the poem's sentiments typically British. Yet this collapsing into one dehistoricized entity is precisely what happens when Giles is discussing a roughly contemporary text by Tu Fu (AD 712–770) in his *History of Chinese Literature*. Apropos of one of Tu Fu's "short-stop" poems, so named because it appeared to cease at its penultimate moment, Giles declared this favorite Chinese form to be "based upon a disease common to all Chinese, poets or otherwise,—nostalgia."[6] Furthermore, both the vocabulary of pathological condition and the implicit moral imperative to the active life that we see here are also redolent of a Victorian distrust of such backward-looking emotions as "nostalgia." Giles often seemed to find Chinese poetry redolent of the "dis-ease" that had led Matthew Arnold to write to his fellow poet Arthur Hugh Clough (in November 1853) about his poem "The Scholar Gipsy":

> I am glad you like the Gipsy Scholar—but what does it *do* for you? Homer *animates*, Shakespeare *animates* . . . the Gipsy Scholar at best awakens a pleasing melancholy. But this is not what we want.[7]

There was one further significant factor influencing Giles' representation of the Chinese and their literature. Despite the fact that he had spent twenty-six years in the British consular service in China, which distinguished him from the so-called "armchair sinologists" who had introduced oriental studies to French academia earlier in the nineteenth century, the scholarly expertise that finally won him the professorship at Cambridge was largely based on textual scholarship undertaken in the seclusion of his own study. This produced a strong tendency to derive, or "confect," "Chineseness" from its literary culture and thus to see China as composed of two disparate peoples: the highly educated civil servant cadre, or "literati," who had traditionally been schooled, examined, and promoted in terms of their knowledge of traditional texts, and "the people" who, in Giles' binary mode of thinking, became characterized as ignorant, uneducated,[8] and superstitious. Any further subcategorization of the Chinese in his writing was precisely what we might expect from a man who had, through his consular employment, encountered Chinese civil servants, the occasional merchant, and "servants," a category that he appeared to regard as a class apart and whose members were mutually interchangeable. Writing of the Chinese fondness for opium, for instance, he advised the instant sacking of any servants found taking it because they would almost certainly steal to fund an addiction perfectly permissible in a better-paid clerk.[9] Elsewhere he described Chinese servants as loyal, dependable, but less easily brow-beaten than their Indian counterparts, and he alerted naïve readers to these same servants' habit of taking a commission on all the purchases they negotiated for their masters.[10] His second wife's short stories similarly represent Chinese servants as self-serving and driven by a host of familial rites and loyalties that remain inscrutable to their European employers.[11]

The pragmatic approach that drove Giles' study of the Chinese, their literature, and their language characterized the career paths of many of Britain's earliest academic sinologists who had first acquired their knowledge through serving in the field as either missionary or diplomat. Yet, despite his grudging admiration for the Scottish missionary James Legge, who became Oxford's first professor of Chinese (1876), Giles and his fiction-writing second wife frequently portrayed the missionaries in China as peculiarly ignorant, destructive meddlers. The next section of this essay explores the nature of Giles' route to becoming the second diplomat occupant of the Cambridge Chair of Chinese and suggests something of the diversity in the intellectual background and training of Britain's nineteenth-century missionaries to China.

Diplomatic and Missionary Routes to China

Until 1856, the primary qualification for the British diplomatic corps had been financial: candidates had to have a private income of over four hundred pounds. They also had to put in two months at the Foreign Office and secure the Foreign Secretary's nomination, partly, one would guess, to ensure their "clubbability": diplomacy was a genteel occupation, not a profession. In 1856 an entrance examination was introduced, and the requirement shifted to the caliber of a candidate's handwriting and his grasp of foreign languages. Given his bellicose temperament, it was just as well that Giles had been born on the right side of this chronological divide. Having passed the Foreign Office exam in 1867, he went out to Peking that May, with the humble grade of "student interpreter"—that is, to learn the language, a task he began with an abbreviated form of Robert Morrison's *Dictionary of the Chinese Language*,[12] "in which the aspirates were not marked; much as if an English-Chinese dictionary, for the use of the Chinese, were published without the letter *h*, showing no difference between the conjunction *and* and the *[h]and* of the body."[13] Next, he embarked on Thomas Wade's primer,[14] and he swiftly made three entirely characteristic decisions: first, that the primer was "ill-arranged and pedantic"; second, that learning "Radicals" (a method of categorizing Chinese characters and locating them within a dictionary) was a waste of time; and third, to strike "out on a line for himself."[15]

Giles had something of the instincts of the autodidact and an entirely pragmatic approach to language acquisition. In his peculiar memoirs, titled "Autobibliographical etc.," published only in 1997,[16] Giles noted almost with pride the successive years when he abandoned first Greek (1869) and then Latin (1871). This was not simply the relief of a laggard schoolboy, happy to put his years of classical schooling behind him, for, having completed four years at public school[17] (the equivalent of private American schooling), he found himself at age eighteen living in Paris, where he contributed a word-for-word translation of Aeschylus' dramatic trilogy to his father's fifty-volume series, *The Keys to the Classics*, completing a further two volumes—Longinus' *On the Sublime* (1870) and Cicero's *De Natura Deorum* (1872)—during his early years in China. It would appear that Giles' father, of whom more later, thought his youngest son had the makings of a classical scholar and able assistant who could benefit from attending Charterhouse, where he himself had been a pupil for the bare six months necessary to achieve an Oxford scholarship. In the Charterhouse records, Herbert Giles is recorded as the fourth son of the family (perhaps others had died in childbirth), but the only other surviving son, who ended up in the Bengal police service, had clearly not been considered suitable material for this educational opportunity. Despite the investment, both financial and educational, Giles apparently had no qualms in jettisoning his classical baggage when learning Chinese proved the focus of his career.

Unlike others who had followed this route into the consular service, Giles did not waste time going through Wade's primer again and again to anchor its ill-judged lessons, but he decided to attempt learning to read Chinese as if he were a native, first learning a Chinese classic by heart, and then attempting to decipher every kind of writing from "official letters, dispatches," and "proclamations" to "handbills," before immersing himself in bilingual versions of Confucius, Chinese novels, drama, poetry, and contemporary journalism. It is worth noting that though Giles makes very occasional mention of native Chinese tutors, his learning is almost entirely based on literary rather than conversational sources. Indeed he attributed his subsequent numerous translations, upon which he based his *History of Chinese Literature*, to his early years of omnivorous reading.[18] He says little or nothing of his own conversational powers, though he does remark that his first wife, Catherine Fenn, whom he married during his 1869 furlough, "after a residence of two years became quite a good speaker of Northern Mandarin."[19] For a trainee diplomat, accuracy in literal, word-by-word translation was the most important language acquisition, and for this Giles' classical studies had amply prepared him.[20]

For missionaries, on the other hand, the most urgent linguistic requirement was to be able to make oneself intelligible to potential converts. However, the amount of preparatory training missionaries received before embarking on their duties varied considerably, as did their previous educational attainments. Legge, for instance, began his Chinese studies in London with Samuel Kidd, a recently returned missionary, learning the dreaded "Radicals" before sailing for the Anglo-Chinese college on the Malay peninsula where he had two or three years of further study before reaching Hong Kong. Here again his role, as principal of both a seminary and a school, was more that of missionary scholar than travelling evangelist. Though he was an expert translator of classical Chinese texts, his conversational mode was Cantonese, the *lingua franca* of the British colony, and he apparently never attained easy mastery of Mandarin.[21]

By contrast the interdenominational China Inland Mission (1865) sent its recruits, chosen for their spiritual ardor rather than any previous educational or ecclesiastical qualifications, straight out to the mission's language schools in China. The mission's priority of seeking to evangelize the whole of China, by making inroads on hitherto unreached inland provinces and working and living alongside the Chinese, placed a high premium on the ability to communicate. There was a reluctance to send out Chinese Christian translators with these evangelists, "for the reason so well understood in China, that the witness of Christians (especially in small and young churches) who have been taken into employ is so much less powerful than that of those who are entirely independent,"[22] but many of the young English recruits were distinctly mortified by their own slow progress. William Cassels (1858–1925), one of the university-educated "Cambridge Seven" who went out under the mission's auspices in 1885, reported that, in his first venture out beyond Shanghai, the difficulty of conversing with the Chinese he met in the villages through which he passed meant that much of his first year was spent in bringing already established missionaries to a new sense of their being "born again."[23]

Ten years later, my grandfather W. H. Aldis, a land surveyor turned Christian youth worker,[24] neither ordained nor linguistically proficient when he left England, was sent to a Shanghai language school by the China Inland Mission for his first three months before being sent to join Cassels in remote Langzhong (then Paoning), Sichuan. Here Aldis found the language barrier at first so insuperable that he spent a time of "enforced dumbness" and resorted to "evangelism by prayer," focusing on "one particular man" and "praying that he might be led to attend the preaching and thus converted."[25]

The presumptuousness of such evangelizing endeavors now seems staggering to us, especially in the light of the fact that my grandfather, who had received no higher education, had been sent to a city renowned as a center of learning: it was here that the last imperial dynasty held its administrative examinations. Six years later he had launched an evening Bible class "for literary men" but still seemed astonished that, when a prize was offered for "the best essay on 'the difference between the Gospel and the teaching of Confucius,'" nearly sixty entries came pouring in.[26] William Cassels, by then bishop of Western China, had offered the prize, and it would be agreeable to today's mores to infer that this was because he was more attuned to the milieu in which he and his younger aide, Aldis, found themselves. However, Cassels' initial naïveté in such matters is worth recalling—his biographer related the following story of an encounter he had had shortly before embarking for China:

> Mr Cassels said he was talking the other day to a man in a railway train who had travelled in China. He was one of those people who considered that every religion was of about the same value, and when he heard he [the speaker)] was going to China to preach the Gospel there he thought it was a most presumptuous thing to do. He proceeded to say how wise and clever the Chinese were, and he told him that his arguments would be defeated. He [Cassels] felt at the time that, from his point of view, the man was distinctly right; but there was one consideration that he did not bring to bear when he was speaking, and it was that which made all the difference. They were going to China because they knew that the gospel was the power of God unto salvation.[27]

Even Legge—whose respect for Chinese culture resulted in his magnum opus, the seven-volume *Chinese Classics* (1861–1872), and the later contribution of volumes on Confucianism (vols. 3, 16, 27, and 28) and Taoism (vols. 39 and 40) to Max Müller's *Sacred Books of the East* (50 vols.; 1879–1910)—had, during the missionary phase of his career, been tempted to represent Christianity as unquestionably the supreme "light to lighten the Gentiles." Irritated by an American-pirated edition of his work on Confucius, in which the author had not only removed Legge's parallel Chinese text but dared to question his views, Legge reluctantly produced his own popular version, *The Life and Teachings of Confucius* (1867), in which, claiming that Confucianism lay at the heart of the Chinese educational system, he also declared that the only hope for this nation, humiliated by a series of "unequal treaties," was to abandon its "ancient sages" and turn to Jesus. Perhaps his then vantage point from the recently acquired British Crown Colony of Hong Kong, and his sense that Confucius' remarks about foreigners as mere suppliants stood in the way of evangelism, act as some excuse for his statement: "Of the earth, earthy, China was sure to go to pieces when it came into collision with a Christianity-civilized power."[28]

The widely distributed and long-lived missionary journal the *Chinese Recorder*, though it took to publishing long scholarly articles on such matters as "Chinese Conceptions of Paradise," continued to welcome such ideas of immortality as it could discern in the teaching of Buddhists and Taoists only insofar as "all these ideas are pulling up the great mass of the people out of the sordid and animal life which threatens all who lose the faith in future existence. Christianity comes with its glorious message to fill these age-long aspirations of the Chinese people."[29] If men of the erudition of Legge, or Lewis Hidous (author of this article and subsequently professor of Chinese culture in an American seminary) could make such remarks, how did less well-educated missionaries fare in China?

My grandfather's biographer, himself a university graduate, was clearly embarrassed by Aldis' humble educational background: "Possibly he exaggerated the handicap of not having been to public school or university, but the confident bearing which marks those descended from a patrician family was not his."[30] Indeed Aldis (known in China as Pastor Yao) was suspicious of the enthusiasm shown by "the scholars and the gentry" of neighboring Chinese cities for the missionaries to provide a "Western Education for their sons, fearing that they had less interest in Christianity, and that the mission would soon be 'inundated with scholars of the better class.' "[31]

Nevertheless, in 1902 Aldis became the first principal of a school "run on Western lines for Chinese boys" who it was hoped would mature into Christian evangelists. Aldis seems to have had no qualifications of any sort to become a boys' school headmaster before he set about teaching English, arithmetic, and the Bible to his pupils. Nor is there any evidence that his sister Kate Aldis, who became the headmistress of the accompanying girls' school, had any formal training.[32] Though by 1902 he spent five years in China, "his knowledge of Chinese was painfully limited,"[33] and one of his first pupils recalled that because of "the teacher's initially inadequate (though later fluent) Chinese he did not quite grasp what Aldis wanted to tell the boys about Christ."[34]

Aldis' fear that "Western education" would attract literate Chinese without any real interest in Christianity, rather than extending the mission's influence to the uneducated Chinese peasantry, was to prove right and wrong in almost equal parts. The pupil mentioned above, Yan Yangchu (known later as "Jimmy" Yen, or Y. C. James Yen), was recruited from exactly the class Aldis had predicted. His father was a scholar, poet, and writer and had accepted a job teaching Chinese to missionaries in the China Inland Mission station at Bazhong, a small town in northern Sichuan province. He was so convinced of the worth of the "Western education" the missionaries offered that he was prepared to send a barely ten-year-old boy, who up until then had been taught (in the traditional Chinese way) to learn by heart the Four Books of Confucius and portions of the Five Classics, over a thousand kilometers away to the CIM school at Langzhong.[35] Yet Yen's subsequent work for mass literacy—honored worldwide,[36] and first practiced among the thousands of illiterate Chinese manual workers employed by the British government in France during the First World War, and then in China and the Philippines—must have served to mitigate my grandfather's doubts, as would the coupling in Yen's posthumous tribute: "It was Mr. Aldis who introduced me to Christ and to modern education."[37]

My grandfather's career is illustrative of two further features distinguishing the different ways in which the British missionary and diplomatic cohorts experienced China. Since the treaties ending the Second Opium War in 1860, the entire country rather than merely the five coastal cities had been opened up to missionary activity. The very name of the China *Inland* Mission is an expression of the desire to touch just those remotest areas that diplomats, who largely continued to operate from the coastal cities, were unlikely to encounter.

The other factor worth noting is the premium placed on education both in China, where it had long been prized, and in Great Britain, where, in combination with talent and industriousness, it achieved a greater class mobility during the nineteenth century than at any time before or since. It was still possible, that is, for a family where two generations of males had lapsed from university attendance to rejoin the educated genteel classes: all three of Aldis' sons attended public schools and were university educated. Anglican orders had long been a means of securing a stable middle-class identity within a generation or so.

However, expatriate communities are notorious for their tendency to a social conservatism more marked than that to be found in their members' countries of origin: When newcomers arrive so frequently, how else can standards be policed? Where missionaries might be forgiven rough edges on account of their spiritual zeal, the same tolerance was unlikely to have applied in the diplomatic service. Furthermore, the fact that the diplomatic service had ceased to be a matter of class privilege only in 1856 will have made the more senior officials hypercritical in their social evaluation of the candidates like Herbert Giles who constituted the first generation of those who had entered by the examination route.

"That 'Ishmael' of Sinology," Herbert Giles

In his "Autobibliography," Giles recalled that Legge had introduced him in 1882 to his prospective second wife's family as "the 'Ishmael' of sinology," a remark that he decided contained "a fair admixture of truth."[38] The fact that Giles had not been to university is important in understanding his personality and the way in which he interpreted China for his British readers. By the time that Giles succeeded to the Cambridge Chair of Chinese in 1897, he was fifty-two and indeed only able to take up the post because he was supported by a full Foreign Office pension.[39] Although most of the Anglophone chairs in sinology, a discipline only recently admitted to English academia, went to those with experience in the field, few of them will have had as little previous experience of collegiate academic life as Giles, nor would the post alter this, since during his tenure it consisted largely of curatorial librarian's duties and carried no college membership.

The time spent laboring over *Keys to the Classics* seems to have convinced him of the virtue of making learning widely accessible, while also leaving him with an almost unassuageable yearning for scholarly recognition, mixed in almost equal measure with an attitude amounting to paranoia at any hint of academic criticism. The honorary degrees and awards that Giles finally accumulated never seemed to have entirely erased in his own mind the social stigma of not having attended university. Legge's gibe about Giles as an "Ishmael," or outcast, is pertinent, especially when we consider Legge's own position (addressed in David Jasper's essay in this volume) as a Scottish Nonconformist in Anglican Oxford.[40] It is notable, for instance, that Giles, in his introduction to his *History of Chinese Literature* (1901), flourishes the fact that he had been invited to contribute this to the series *Short Histories of the Literatures of the World*, which Edmund Gosse edited for Heinemann. Although Giles' upbringing, in an Anglican parsonage, was far less eccentric than that of Gosse, raised in the seclusion of the Plymouth Brethren, Giles seems to have admired this man who, with an even less orthodox education and distinctly less scholarly rigor, had gained both access to Establishment circles of social and political power and a literary reputation, largely on the back of extensive journalism. Giles too had tried his hand at newspaper journalism while in the Far East but, typically, strayed far beyond Gosse's literary territory into the kind of political controversy unlikely to advance his career.

Giles' second wife, Elise, unkindly caricatured the early career of coastal missionaries, while they were learning the language, as "nothing to do—but enjoy yourself, see the place, call on our ladies,—or, study any subject you happen to have a hobby for. We have never had a botanist, or a geologist, in our Mission here. There are splendid fields for those subjects, if you have any taste for them."[41] Giles was no hobbyist, but the fact that his own education had been largely limited to the classics was both help and hindrance. His classical training persuaded him that the way in which the Chinese valued and relied upon their literary inheritance as their prime educational medium was not that dissimilar from Europe's long-lived reliance on the classics. The Chinese examination system that seemed to many Westerners absurdly antiquated was not, he pointed out, that different from recruiting members of the Indian Civil Service by testing their knowledge of the classical texts of Greece and Rome.[42]

Yet the limitations in Giles' own reading detract from his ability to communicate with an Anglophone readership. His classical education almost certainly did not include the *De Consolatione Philosophae* of Boethius, which Legge read at his Scottish university,[43] and whose meditations, consequent on falling from his emperor's favor, would have made such a useful comparison with the ample Chinese literature generated by similar reversals in fortune. The comparisons and contrasts Giles was able to draw are limited to the core diet of the average nineteenth-century middle-class reader (Shakespeare, Bunyan, Wordsworth, Dickens, Tennyson, J. S. Mill, and Herbert Spencer) combined with a smattering of more popular material such as Lewis Carroll's *Alice through the Looking Glass* or the plays of W. S. Gilbert. His poetic tastes were also those of a conservative Victorian rather than those of a Modernist, favoring regular meter and rhyme over free verse,[44] and frequently finding occasion to deplore the Chinese valuing of form over content.[45] In aesthetic terms, far longer than fourteen years separate Giles' renderings from Ezra Pound's translations in *Cathay* (1915).[46]

On the one hand, as a recent critic has observed, Giles is to be admired for trying to discover and represent the central canon of Chinese literature rather than diverting his energies into becoming a specialist in a small and possibly eccentric area.[47] On the other hand, his strictly chronological account from the earliest to the latest phases becomes bewildering, partly because his translations, almost always rendered in a way that would have appealed to readers of contemporary Georgian poetry, have a tendency to merge into an indistinguishable continuum. His judgments, formed largely by deriving the biographies of ancient authors directly from their texts, have a distinct aura of the W. C. Sellar and R. J. Yeatman parody of English histories, *1066 and All That: A Memorable History of England, comprising all the parts you can remember, including 103 Good Things, 5 Bad Kings and 2 Genuine Dates* (1930).

It is clearly unfair to compare Giles' volume with a modern work such as Sabrina Knight's *A Very Short Introduction to Chinese Literature* (2012) in that her account is throughout informed by a radical sense of the difficulty of deciphering the meaning/s of texts from previous civilizations. When Giles encountered indecipherability, he swiftly dismissed the source text and embraced the opportunity for sideswipes at the perversity of other scholars in pretending to understand it:

> As may be readily inferred from the above extract, no one really knows what is meant by the apparent gibberish of the Book of Changes. This is freely admitted by all learned Chinese, who nevertheless hold tenaciously to the belief that important lessons could be derived from its pages if we only had the wit to understand them. Foreigners have held

> various theories on the subject. Dr. Legge declared that he had found the key, with the result already shown. The late Terrien de la Couperie took a bolder flight, unaccompanied by any native commentator, and discovered in this cherished volume a vocabulary of the language of the Bák tribes. A third writer regards it as a calendar of the lunar year, and so forth.[48]

However, if we take *The Cambridge History of English Literature*, begun in 1907, as a more reasonable comparator for the standards of literary criticism in vogue at the start of the twentieth century, a degree of professional specialization is already noticeable: subdivided by volume into different periods, this literary history contained chapters commissioned from experts on the various different subjects and genres.

The Background to Herbert Giles' Attitude to Religion

On the face of it then, Herbert Giles, son of an Anglican clergyman but lacking higher education, would have seemed as appropriate a candidate for missionary service as for the diplomatic corps, but in his writings he rarely failed to take a potshot at Christian missionaries' influence in China. Indeed, newly promoted to the rank of second assistant at the consulate of Tientsin (Tianjin), his reviews in the Anglophone press of China brought him a summons from the acting consul "to hear a letter to him from Sir T[homas] Wade, in which he was told to instruct me to 'leave the missionaries alone' for the future. I told [him] that I considered myself bound, as a Consular officer, to leave all official and political topics alone, but that I claimed the right to discuss such matters as religious literature, etc., without let or hindrance: and this I continued to do."[49]

Not only was Giles the son of a clergyman, but his second marriage (1883) was to the daughter of a biblical scholar. However, these two mid-nineteenth-century clerical fathers were not the kind whose children were ever likely to become evangelical missionaries. Giles' father, John Allen Giles (1808–1884), classical scholar manqué and reluctant clergyman, had a turbulent career. Suffice it to say that his inability to manage money or men, and the family's frequent relocations, combined with his advanced theological views, and a spell in prison for falsifying a parish marriage register, meant that only Herbert's four years, at Charterhouse (1859–1863), from ages fourteen to eighteen provided any relief from this troubled upbringing.[50] No record that I have seen accounts for those four years in between Herbert Giles leaving Charterhouse and joining the Foreign Office, when the school he went to and his father's early career and election to a fellowship of Corpus Christi College, Oxford, would have made university a natural progression.

Nevertheless, by the time that Herbert Giles married for the second time in 1883, he had achieved a reputation as a published sinologist. His new wife was the highly educated Elise Williamina Edersheim (1861–1921), who had "studied Hebrew with her father," Alfred Edersheim (1825–1889), an Austrian-born, Jewish biblical scholar and convert to Christianity.[51] Like her husband, Elise had been pressed into service in the family firm, spending the years between sixteen and twenty-three assisting her father's scholarship, meanwhile publishing a shorter book in her own right, *The Laws and Polity of the Jews* (1883), to be followed by *The Rites and Worship of the Jews* (1890). When her father's magnum opus was republished in a one-volume format the year after his death, his acknowledgments of his daughter's help had been removed, owing, Herbert Giles believed, "to the agnostic views which she adopted and in which she continued to the end."[52] Given that her father twice held Oxford's Grinfield Lectureship on the Septuagint (1886–1888; 1888–1889), her outspoken views must have constituted an embarrassment. Her short stories, *Chinese Coast Tales* (1897–1899), published under the pen name "Lise Boehm," depict Anglophone expatriate communities in China with something of E. F. Benson's mordant wit, combined with E. M. Forster's belligerent anti-clericalism. The most persistent of her satirical shafts were directed at Protestant missionary enclaves. One story includes the encounter of a newly arrived Baptist missionary with one of his predecessors who has "gone native" by abandoning the mission for the post of tutor to a Chinese official's son. When the younger man starts to abuse "the Classics, and comparing—most threadbare of controversies—the Golden Rules of Confucius and Christ, the wiser man's patience gave way." The following tirade ensues:

> "The Classics immoral, Confucius inferior to Christ? Only the profoundest ignorance, could excuse such statements. Only profoundest ignorance, too, could ever excuse any man coming out to teach the Chinese. What could a missionary teach them? Morality? Compare the morality of the Classics with the obscenity of some of the Old Testament stories. Was the Bible a fit book to put into the hands of such

> a moral nation as the Chinese? Hell, and punishment after death? The Chinese had all that in their own low-class literature, and their punishments were not to be shirked by a death-bed repentance."[53]

The stories' commentary on missionary ineptitude, based on a failure to understand Chinese culture, suggests that this couple's views were remarkably similar. For so thin-skinned a man to have accepted his wife's eagle-eyed scrutiny suggests the strength of their bond: after her death, Giles claimed that "in all those thirty-eight years [of marriage] not a syllable came from my pen which was not examined by her and approved for publication."[54]

Herbert Giles' Treatment of Chinese "Religions"

Giles' own life's work might be said to be enmeshed in a late-nineteenth-century British war, still hotly contested by today's historians, between the forces of secularism and religion in its various guises. Like many another militant agnostic of his day, Giles found it easier to cast aside the old orthodoxies than to imagine or create the wholly secular virtuous life. Happy to disparage the superstitious rituals observed in Chinese peasant worship, he become a committed Freemason in London in 1870 and rose to become master and warden of various colonial lodges during his service in China.[55]

Trevor Hart rightly argues that "there is no nonperspectival" standing ground from which to engage with "the other,"[56] and in truth, when writing of Chinese literature and culture Giles was entering an ideological battleground not of his own making. Almost from their inception, Western histories of China had imposed their own oppositional religious templates. As T. H. Barrett reminds us, the fact that it was a Jesuit, Matteo Ricci (1552–1610), who first reported on "Various Sects of False Religion among the Chinese" was almost bound, in post-Reformation Europe, to bring about a counterposed Protestant sinology.[57] The short story by Giles' wife, quoted above, represented the young Baptist missionary as "totally ignorant of the possibility of there being two sides, much less two answers, to any question," and as spending the long outward voyage to China reading "volumes upon volumes of missionary reports, missionary letters, and missionary views on heathenism in China!" In the course of his reading,

> [h]e found out that there were Roman Catholic missionaries in China, and that they were engaged in trying to undo everything the Protestant missionaries wanted to do. But he was not told—the Baptist Mission did not consider it necessary for him to know—that they had been there for centuries, long before Protestant missionaries, treaties, and gun-boats, when Christianity meant torture and death.[58]

Giles himself nailed his anti-Protestant colors to the mast, by similarly espousing the Jesuits' cause. Had their learning, understanding, and respect for Chinese culture prevailed, Giles claimed, Roman Catholicism might well have prevailed in China, but first the Dominicans' refusal to tolerate Chinese rites and then Protestant divisions over the status of ancestor worship had sealed Christianity's fate. Instead, Confucianism had triumphed, making its way into the heart of the more tolerant Buddhism and Taoism. Ideally, Giles considered, if these latter "degraded superstitions" could be displaced by a form of Christianity that recognized Confucianism in its "true" sense as a "pure cult of virtue, with commemorative ceremonies in honour of its founder and of family ancestors who have gone before, one great barrier between ourselves and the Chinese would be broken down forever." Yet, earlier in this same chapter, Giles had acknowledged that the chief stumbling block, as he saw it, in the way of a fusion between Confucianism and Christianity, lay in Confucianism's belief in man's essential goodness, and "his lapse into evil . . . wholly due to his environment."[59]

As a rationalist agnostic, Giles seems simply not to have been able to take seriously the importance of doctrine to credal religion. A gratuitous aside in his *History of Chinese Literature* makes the point even more clearly. The golden rule of Confucianism is, Giles asserts, "What you would not others should do unto you, do not unto them!" He continues, "It has been urged by many who should know better that the negative form of this maxim is unfit to rank with the positive form as given to us by Christ."[60] By wholly ignoring the understanding of self-sacrificial and atoning love exemplified in the life and death of Christ, Giles reduces Christianity to an ethical system that can, by this maneuver, be fruitfully compared with Confucianism, which he similarly empties, in the "pure" form envisaged by its founder, of ritual and worship:

> It is recorded of him [Confucius] that "he made his oblations as though the dead were present," which need not be pressed to mean more than

> that his observance of the ceremony was earnest rather than perfunctory. The general public, however, are inclined to interpret the words literally, and it is now customary to add a short prayer asking for the blessing of the departed upon all family undertakings. From the general spirit, however, of the teachings of Confucius, it seems clear that he would not have sanctioned superstitious rites.[61]

In 1901 Giles had seen no problem in positioning Confucianism as the opening chapter to a book titled *Great Religions of the World*; but by 1911, in a chapter titled "Religion and Superstition" in *The Civilization of China*, he claimed that the Chinese were "emphatically not a religious people," then he salvaged Confucianism by claiming that it was not a religion but a moral code and so not to be confused with Buddhism and Taoism, which he represents as vessels for a multitude of unorthodox and occult practices (divination, fortune telling, geomancy, planchette, and hypnotism) bearing distinct similarity to the privatized belief systems and practices abounding in late Victorian Britain.[62]

Ultimately, Giles applied a simple "by their fruits ye shall know them" ethical sieve to the beliefs he encountered. Medical missionaries, he argued, were quite wrong to campaign against the Chinese use of opium, since, in moderation, it did not wreak the damage of cocaine or morphia. More importantly, they would be better occupied addressing British alcohol abuse: "Where opium kills its hundreds, gin counts its victims by thousands."[63] Confucianism's advocacy of filial piety[64] seemed to produce a nation where cruelty to children or infanticide was less known than in Christian England, so since Confucianism was ineradicable, missionaries would do well to adopt its best elements. Giles' account of Confucianism was, at base, a flag-waving exercise, championing his own "pick and mix" attitude as against Legge's missionary-inspired scholarship, which he characterized in Legge's own words: "Let no one think any labour too great to make himself familiar with the Confucian books. So shall missionaries in China come fully to understand the work they have to do; and the more they avoid driving their carriages rudely over the master's grave, the more likely they are to see Jesus enthroned in his room in the hearts of the people."[65]

Giles' inability to respond to religious spirituality worked together with his classical training in literal translation, and what David Jasper has termed his "cold eye of critical discernment," to blind him to the notion of the ancient texts as embodiments of experience that demanded more than a straightforward logical or aesthetic response. His objection to Müller's blanket use of the word "sacred" in his collected *Sacred Books of the East* became almost a leitmotif of Gilesian criticism:

> Legge's *Tao Tê Ching* ought never to have been included in the Sacred Books at all. It should have been excluded on precisely similar grounds to those which exclude, for instance, Esdras from the Old Testament: (1) that it was certainly not written by Lao Tzŭ, and (2) that it has no pretensions to be revered as the production of an inspired person. I wrote to Max Müller on the subject, but received no reply. I managed, however, by a newspaper protest, to cause Dr Legge to reconsider and dismiss his intention of adding the work of Lieh Tzŭ, an imaginary personage, to the same series.[66]

> Dr Legge had also been working upon a translation of this ancient philosopher [Chuang Tzŭ], and his version was subsequently published in the *Sacred Books of the East*; quite improperly, for *Chuang Tzŭ* is no more a Sacred Book in the eyes of the Chinese than is the *Novum Organum*, or *A Tale of a Tub* with us.[67]

As the first example above illustrates, for Giles the Chinese Classics stand on a level with the Bible, or indeed the Western classics of Greece and Rome, to be appraised simply as textual constructs. In as far as it is possible to divide the "lower" from the "higher" forms of German criticism, Giles stands more in the "lower" criticism camp. Other than looking to Bible revision and translation for comparable rules of editorial engagement,[68] Giles displays virtually none of David Friedrich Strauss' interest in comparative mythology. To the rationalist Giles, all such stories are "superstition" and "fairytales" and so scarcely worthy of remark. The way in which later Chinese commentators took seriously the legends and parables of earlier classics is to Giles virtually inexplicable. In claiming that although "with us, commentaries upon the classics are not usually regarded as literature, they are so regarded by the Chinese, who place such works in the very highest rank, and reward successful commentators with the coveted niche in the Confucian temple,"[69] Giles might be said to have effectively dismissed the entire tradition of Jewish midrash. Similarly he often misses an opportunity to remark on a comparison that might give the Western reader pause to consider the reason for the inclusion of legend and folktale in either Eastern or

Western texts. A brief episode in Huai-nan Tzŭ, "On the Nature of Tao," for instance, where a man from one army manages to make his way into the opposing general's private quarters and to return to his own camp with a small intimate memento as proof, would strike any literary critic familiar with Propp's morphology as analogous to the story of David sparing Saul in 1 Samuel 24.

Perhaps Giles' concluding remarks about Huai-nan Tzŭ's work, given below, best encapsulate the driving forces behind Giles' work in popularizing Chinese literature. In them we can recognize the trace of Matthew Arnold's desire to offer literature to Britain's newly literate classes, as a means of shoring up the moral values threatened by the waning authority of religion. Giles' desire to divine a "pure" ethical ancestry to Taoist teaching both resonates with the Victorian obsession with "origins" and speaks to his own preferred form of "origin," while his coupling of "immortality" and alchemical myth anchors him firmly in the theological debate that for so many Victorians had seemed at the heart of the Christian belief:

> Like the work of Lieh Tzŭ, it is interesting enough in itself; and what is more important, it marks the transition of the pure and simple Way of Lao Tzŭ, etherealised by Chuang Tzŭ, to the grosser beliefs of later ages in magicians and the elixir of life. Lao Tzŭ urged his fellow-mortals to guard their vitality by entering into harmony with their environment. Chuang Tzŭ added a motive, "to pass into the realm of the Infinite and make one's final rest therein." From which it is but a step to immortality and the elixir of life.[70]

For all his aggressive proclamations of his freedom from the trappings of his Victorian Protestant heritage, Giles found himself ineluctably bound to work against and therefore within its parameters.

8

TWO NINETEENTH-CENTURY ENGLISH TRANSLATIONS OF *THE TRAVELS OF FA-HSIEN (399–414 AD)*

An Episode in the Translation of China in England

David Jasper

When James Legge became the first professor of Chinese language and literature in Oxford in 1876, he could, with some justification, lay claim to being the preeminent scholar in his field in Europe. In 1875 he had been the first recipient of the Julien Prize in Paris, presented shortly after the death of Stanislas Julien, the formidable doyen of Chinese studies in Paris. In the same year, the *Pall Mall Gazette* commented that universities in Paris, Vienna, Berlin, and St. Petersburg all had chairs in Chinese, although there were none at all in England, and it concluded that "we are glad to remove this national reproach by the institution of a Professorship of Chinese in the University of Oxford. It is proposed that the first nomination to the Chair should be conferred on Dr. Legge."[1] Yet, in spite of his formidable learning, his laborious scholarly revision in Oxford of his translations of the Chinese Classics, and his contributions to Professor Max Müller's massive *Sacred Books of the East*, Legge—a former missionary and Scots nonconformist—and Chinese studies were never quite accepted into the rigid and still very Anglican world of Oxford University. A portrait of Legge still hangs in Corpus Christi College, but it is consigned to a wall on a staircase and largely unnoticed. As Norman J. Girardot has well noted in his book *The Victorian Translation of China*:

> Legge, as a Scots Nonconformist professor of an exotically irrelevant language, was always to some degree on the margins of university life, but there is reason to believe that in his waning years, in contrast with his earlier outspoken challenges to the accepted order, he gradually came to accept his respected, but peripheral status within the cold bosom of Oxford.[2]

The text that is the focus of this essay is itself, furthermore, somewhat peripheral to the enormous corpus of work that is the legacy of Legge, who never claimed to be primarily a scholar of Buddhism and was a latecomer to the study of the religions of China in the West. Indeed, the travel narrative of Fa-hsien[3] is a work that is relatively little remarked on at all. But precisely for these reasons (and that it was translated both by Legge and by the younger sinologist Herbert Giles, who was to become the professor of Chinese at the University of Cambridge in 1898, the year after Legge's death), it provides some interesting insights into the changing reception of China in the West at the end of nineteenth and the beginning of the twentieth centuries.

The work that Legge ponderously titled *A Record of Buddhistic Kingdoms: Being an Account by the Chinese Monk Fa-Hien of His Travels in India and Ceylon (AD 389–414) in Search of the Buddhist Books of Discipline* is mentioned only once (and that very briefly) in the standard two-volume *Cambridge History of Chinese Literature*, which describes Fa-hsien's (Faxian) work merely as "the first extensive travelogue written by a Chinese about his experiences in foreign lands."[4] Herbert Giles' own pioneering work, *A History of Chinese Literature*, published in 1901 as volume 10 of *Short Histories of the Literature of the World* under the general editorship of Edmund Gosse,[5] merely quotes two pages of his own translation, saying little more than the descriptive and typically Gilesean sentence: "The narrative of his [Fa-hsien] adventurous journey, as told by himself, is still in existence, written in a crabbed and difficult style."[6] Lauren Pfister's weighty two-volume analysis of the work of Legge (*Striving for 'The Whole Duty of Man': James Legge and the Scottish Protestant Encounter with China* [2004]), focusing mainly on his years in Hong Kong, consigns *A Record of Buddhistic Kingdoms* to one remote footnote.

Professor Pfister's reason for this neglect is, perhaps, to a degree indicated by the sentence in his text to which the footnote refers. Pfister, referring to Legge's later years as a missionary in Hong Kong, writes, "If

Legge still retained serious doubts about the general effect of both Buddhism and Daoism among the common people, he always had a much more positive impression about Ruist [Confucian] influences."[7] Quite simply, although, as we shall see, Legge had made several attempts to read Fa-hsien's book before 1870 while he was still in Hong Kong, fuller access to it and to other Buddhist literature did not become available to him until he was in Oxford, while he admittedly did not hold Buddhism in much esteem in China. Indeed, Legge's important book *The Religions of China: Confucianism and Tâoism Described and Compared with Christianity* (1880) does not even list Buddhism as a religion indigenous to China. Giles, in his survey work on Chinese literature, is concerned with Buddhism only "under its literary aspect."[8]

As we turn now to the translations of *A Record of Buddhistic Kingdoms*, its significance for Legge, however, though in an understated way, becomes apparent. For all his quiet conservatism as a missionary and a devout Scots nonconformist, nurtured in a serious Christian faith, Legge was utterly convinced that only the careful, sympathetic, and dutiful study of the literature, religions, and culture of other civilizations was a proper preparation for the work of Christian mission. Thus under the tutelage of the exuberant Max Müller in Oxford and the more conservative and older Legge, there was a growing sense in the study of "comparative religion" that the notion of a "sacred" text could not be restricted merely to the unique and exclusive witness of the Bible—in Girardot's words, the Christian missionary task itself "hinged on an encounter with the sacred and profane pluralities of world literature rather than on an unbending conviction about the static finality of the one and only Christian Bible."[9] This was a startling suggestion that earned Legge a perhaps understandable degree of suspicion among more conservative missionaries in China—the former missionary turned academic seemingly turning against the unique revelation of God in Holy Scripture.[10] When he reads the narrative of Fa-hsien, even though he might dismiss much of the narrative as "unreliable and grotesque," still Legge is prepared to acknowledge that "we have from him the truth as to what he saw and heard."[11] The implication in this quiet remark is that, in the end, Fa-hsien was a man of genuine faith.

Yet Legge was not, and did not claim to be, primarily a scholar of Chinese Buddhism after the manner of Ernst Eitel (to whose *Handbook for the Student of Chinese Buddhism* [1870] he refers in his preface to

Fa-hsien) or Joseph Edkins, with whom he toured North China in 1873 when they famously recited a Christian doxology, barefoot in the Temple of Heaven in Beijing. During his time as a missionary in China, Legge was wont to complain of the "vulgar and ignorant" priests to be met with in some Buddhist and Daoist temples, and by the time of his final return to Europe he had, in Pfister's words, "dabbled only occasionally in the still relatively uncertain realms of Chinese Buddhism."[12] In company with most other sinological scholars of the time, when Legge did give attention to the Mahayana tradition, it was almost entirely in terms of its Indian or Aryan sources—a reflection, perhaps, of a deep-rooted Western pressure to establish the roots of all religion in the Indo-European (and therefore ultimately biblical) tradition.[13] The complications of the doctrinal and ethical sutra literature, together with what Legge admits to be "the difficulty occasioned by the Sanskrit words and names," go some way to explain the emphasis in nineteenth-century sinological study that was laid upon pilgrim and travel literature, of which the book of Fa-hsien, as Legge's first major translation of a Buddhist text, is a prime example.

It was only some time after his appointment to the Oxford professorship that Legge began to develop a serious interest in both Daoism and Buddhism. His publication of the *Record of Buddhistic Kingdoms* and the occasion it provided for an argument with the younger Giles provides, therefore, an insight into not only Legge's remarkable, and largely forgotten, place in the developing comparative study of religions but the manner in which his old-fashioned, often uncritical, and yet surprisingly "radical" readings and translations of the sacred texts of non-Western traditions came to be superseded by the more modern critical assumptions and methods of Giles, whose "secular" background in China was not within the missionary community and who was well versed in the processes of higher criticism—a field of biblical studies almost entirely unknown to Legge. Perhaps it might be more strictly accurate to say that this field was not so much unknown but eschewed by him as disruptive to the faith that he held dear. Giles, a polemicist by nature and an accomplished sinologist (if without the profound philological learning of Legge), had already engaged in sometimes vitriolic exchanges of a highly technical nature with another member of the diplomatic service in China, Edward H. Parker, in the pages of the *China Review*. Parker had defended Legge as old-fashioned and "too unimaginative" yet solid and steady in his scholarship.[14] The stage was set for an argument between Legge and Giles over their respective translations of the travels of Fa-hsien, and academically, at least in his time, Giles was the victor. In the longer term, perhaps, Legge oddly proved to be more radical precisely because he was more conservative in matters of religious belief.

When Legge finally published his translation of Fa-hsien in Oxford in 1886, he was clearly depending on earlier scholarship, and he freely admits it. When, toward the end of his long life, he returned to Great Britain as a missionary turned academic in the University of Oxford, Legge records that, while he was resident in Hong Kong, he had several times attempted to read the text that he calls the *Narrative of Fa-hien*. In 1878 he had begun to lecture in Oxford on Fa-hsien, admitting that he was also drawing on the expertise of one of his Davis Chinese scholars,[15] "who was at the same time Boden Sanskrit scholar."[16] Legge was also, by his own admission, deeply influenced by the work of T. W. Rhys Davids, who was an Orientalist working at University College, London, and one of the leading scholars of Buddhism in late Victorian England. Rhys Davids read and corrected the whole of Legge's "Translation and Notes," and, generally, Legge was happy to take his advice.

A Record of Buddhistic Kingdoms is a record of the travels of a fifth-century Chinese Buddhist monk, usually now known to us as Fa-hsien, who travelled to India across the Gobi Desert, visiting such places as Benares and Patna (Patliputra), returning after many years to China, and bringing back with him a collection of books of the Buddhist Canon and images of Buddhist deities. The two copies of the text first used by Legge in Hong Kong presented a challenge to him, despite his formidable linguistic skills, not least in their phonetic representations of Sanskrit words. Furthermore, these two copies in Hong Kong were, Legge records, printed on poor quality paper and with worn blocks rendering the text almost illegible. It was only much later when he was in Oxford, returning to a study of this narrative, that Legge came into possession of a much better copy, sent by his friend Bunyiu Nanjio, not from China but from Japan. It was this acquisition that enabled him to publish, with the resources of Oxford and fellow Orientalists, an English translation in 1886, replete with copious notes and a Chinese text taken from his Japanese copy.

However, Legge's *A Record of Buddhistic Kingdoms* was not the only (and by no means the first) European translation available of this fascinating journey between China and India, and he freely admits to his frequent recourse to these earlier translations, including that of Herbert Giles himself. Fa-hsien had first been translated from Chinese into French and published in Paris in 1836 by M. Abel-Rémusat, the formidable predecessor of Julien at the French Institute in Paris and the founder, as early as 1822, of the *Journal asiatique* (which largely focused on Sanskrit and the Indo-European tradition). Rémusat's work was titled *Revu, complete, et augmente d'eclaircissements nouveaux par MM. Klaproth et Landress.* It was a massive volume of some 424 pages. Heinrich Klaproth, using Rémusat's translation, had taken the original continuous text and divided it, somewhat arbitrarily, into forty chapters, rather like a book of the Bible, a convention later followed, "excepting three or four instances," by Legge. Giles, never one to give much credit to fellow sinologists, wrote of Rémusat's version: "Its style is terse and difficult, but not without a charm of its own."[17] In 1869 Rev. Samuel Beal, who had been a British naval chaplain in the Far East, published an English version that was essentially a translation and revision of Rémusat's French text and that was added, in a revised form, as a prefix to Beal's *Buddhist Records of the Western World* (Trübner's Oriental Series, 1884). Recently, in his book *Singular Listlessness* (1989), T. H. Barrett has remarked that Legge was the first British scholar to win an international reputation in Chinese studies with the "possible exception of Samuel Beal."[18] Nevertheless, in typically curt and cutting manner, Giles writes dismissively of Beal that "he reproduced all Rémusat's mistakes while adding many more of his own."[19] In 1877 Giles himself, as then a member of the British consular service in China, published the first of his two versions of the work, as he puts it (with the merest touch of modesty), "correcting many of Beal's glaring mistakes, but leaving behind some of my own."

Finally, in 1886 Legge published his translation in Oxford, for which, he writes with typical scholarly nicety, "I hold myself more especially responsible. Portions of it were written out three times, and the whole of it twice."[20] Giles' comment on Legge's work, however, is scathing, more or less accusing him of plagiarism: "[H]e borrowed largely, without acknowledgement, from my corrections of Beal, and managed to contribute not a few mistakes of his own."[21] In 1923 Giles, by then transferred from his diplomatic post to his academic position in Cambridge and long after Legge's death in 1897, published a "closely revised" edition of his 1877 text, shifting from the strict academic style of Legge to something more designed for the general reader; for—he writes,

> while giving, so far as possible, a strictly literal and accurate rendering, I have attempted at the same time to make the narrative appeal to the general reader by the omission of foot-notes which most people dislike, and of references to authorities which are usually altogether ignored. Thus, it is hoped that there will be no check to the enjoyment of the reader as he travels along with Fa-hsien on his stupendous journey.[22]

Lastly, and for the sake of completeness, it should be noted that Legge also refers to the work of T. Watters, the British consul at I-Chang and an amateur sinologist, who in the *China Review* in 1879 and 1880 wrote a series of articles on "Fa-hsien and His English Translators," which, Legge notes, "are of the highest value, displaying accuracy of Chinese scholarship and extensive knowledge of Buddhism." Watters' articles, among other things, make a comparison between the translations of Beal and Giles and the "many points of contention between them." Legge rather drily concludes in his preface that he prefers to avoid controversy (not easy, as he was later to find when dealing with the "pugnacious" Herbert Giles), and states "I have endeavoured to eschew those matters, and have seldom made remarks of a critical nature in defence of renderings of my own."[23]

Clearly there are the makings here of a minor academic argument between Giles and Legge, a domestic squabble between Cambridge and Oxford, though its implications are of much larger significance, for more interesting than any such exchange is the illumination that their differences throw upon their critical methods and their understanding and interpretation of a difficult and ancient Chinese text. Legge is quite explicit as to his purpose, expressing some modesty as to his notes, which he readily admits are largely a selection and condensation of the earlier work of others:

> My first object in them was to explain what in the text required explanation to an English reader. All Chinese texts, and Buddhist texts especially, are new to foreign students. One has to do for them what many hundreds of the ablest scholars in Europe have done for the Greek and Latin Classics during several hundred years, and what the

> thousands of critics and commentators have been doing of [*sic*] our Sacred Scriptures for nearly eighteen centuries. There are few predecessors in the field of Chinese literature into whose labours translators of the present century can enter.[24]

Legge is self-consciously following two traditions of Western scholarship—that of the critical reading of the classical traditions of Greece and Rome, and that of biblical interpretation. In the case of the latter, it is not, however, an exercise in the processes of higher criticism but a more traditional form of appropriation of the sacred text stretching back to the earliest Christian commentators. Both of these traditions of reading become evident in his notes with their numerous allusions to and comparisons made with both classical writers and the Bible. Even in the preface, Legge (originally an accomplished classical scholar educated at the University of Aberdeen) quotes Horace (*Nullius addictus jurare in verba magistri*), assuming here that his reader will be on perfectly familiar ground with classical Latin. Legge assures his learned reader that he has consulted the best scholarship not only in Chinese but in Western works and with the further assurance that the irrefutable presence of the Bodleian Library is close at hand to answer all academic emergencies. "My principal help has been the full and masterly handbook of Eitel[25] . . . often referred to as E. H. Spence Hardy's 'Eastern Monachism' (E. M.) and 'Manual of Buddhism' (M. B.) have been constantly in hand, as well as Rhys Davids' Buddhism, published by the Society for Promoting Christian Knowledge, his Hibbert Lectures, and his Buddhist Suttas in the Sacred Books of the East, and other writings." We can rest content, in other words, that what we read has the full authority of the scholarship of the West about China and Buddhism behind it.

Legge's footnotes to his text—apart from their object of explaining unknown names, places, and terms—have one recurring characteristic: comparisons with biblical texts. For example, in the description of an offering made in Buddha's alms-bowl in Peshawar, we read: "When poor people throw into it a few flowers, it becomes immediately full, while some very rich people, wishing to make offerings of many flowers, might not stop until they have thrown in hundreds, thousands and myriads of bushels, and yet would not be able to fill it."[26]

In his footnote, Legge compares this to Luke 21:1-4, the story of the widow's mite, not entirely an apposite or accurate comparison with the miraculous nature of the Chinese narrative, it has to be admitted. Later in the text is the extraordinary narrative of the thousand little boys found floating in a box on the river Ganges, who grow up to be tall warriors. As they unwittingly attack the kingdom of their real father, their mother proves her identity to them by sending five hundred jets of milk from each of her breasts that miraculously land in the mouths of the thousand young men, thus proving that she is indeed their mother. Legge's rather dry footnote to what he calls this "absurd" story reads: "The first part of Fa-hien's narrative will have sent the thoughts of some of my readers to the exposure of the infant Moses, as related in Exodus."[27] Perhaps his sometimes dour and distinctly puritanical Scottish nonconformist background prevented him from further comment on other aspects of a story that has interesting parallels with other, quite distinct, fabulous stories from ancient cultures.

Legge is clearly always aware of who he is translating and writing for and of the biblical and scholarly demands and context of his readership. Giles' review of Legge's book in the *Journal of the North China Branch of the Royal Asiatic Society* (1886) is mainly a carping of Legge's (actually entirely acknowledged) copying from Giles' own earlier work. Giles comments that "it would have been a cheap and graceful compliment from an old Sinologue to the early effort of a young student to admit that he had borrowed my renderings and served it up in different words."[28] More interesting among the largely respectful reviews of Legge's book are the anonymous comments in the *Saturday Review*, February 19, 1887, which accuse Legge of an overly Christian bias and an insistence upon the "evident" superiority of Christianity and a lack of "sympathy with alien faiths."[29] Actually, in this work Legge is far more sympathetic toward Buddhism and comparative in spirit than he had been in earlier major translations of texts for the Chinese Classics and the *Sacred Books of the East*. More perceptive is the review of Thomas Pearce in the *China Review*, which suggests that Legge tends to draw Buddhism too closely into conformity with the Confucianism with which he was far more familiar and for which he had an ever-growing sympathy and admiration. In fact, what is remarkable about this late work is just how far Legge moves toward a position of comparativism, leading Girardot to suggest that "during the twilight of his scholarly career, he was more assiduously trying to fashion a hybrid method uniquely appropriate to the Chinese tradition."[30]

The tone of Giles as a translator is somewhat different. Far more "secular" in his concerns than Legge could ever be, he wants his more relaxed reader to enjoy the extraordinary narrative of Fa-hsien. He omits the rather biblical chapter divisions of Legge, inherited from Klaproth and the earlier French version, and writes so that "the *unbiased* reader may perhaps obtain a furtive glimpse of the grandeur of the Buddhist religion in the early years of the 5th century AD."[31] Giles' approach to religion generally was invariably objective and external. While by no means abandoning his scholarly high tone, not to say his sense of his own academic and critical superiority, Giles clearly has in mind the "general reader," even to the point of providing a technical glossary of "terms used by Fa-hsien," including the "Ten Commandments" (of Buddhism) and the "Three Refuges"—that is, the "Three Persons of the Buddhist Trinity" and the "Buddhist Creed."[32] At only one point in his work does Giles come close to admitting his limitations as a scholar, and he does this, with scholarly flourish, by hiding behind nothing less than some words of the *Descriptive Catalogue of the Imperial Library* (1795) in which, he admits, "in the present edition, the original text is given word for word, in order to carry out the [Confucian] precept about 'putting aside points of which we are in doubt.' "[33]

In his introduction, Legge is almost entirely descriptive of Fa-hsien's narrative, apart from a rather verbose obsession with the relative number of Buddhists there are in the world "ranking below Christianity, Confucianism, Brahmanism, and Mohammedanism, and followed, some distance off, by Taoism,"[34] a not untypical concern with the missionary spirit whose ultimate object was to bring *all* to Christ. Such league tables could therefore be matters of some anxiety in the race that is set before us. But Legge's principal concern is, as always in his translation work, to present the mind of Fa-hsien to the reader—as he put it, following a principle of Mencius, in his own "Translator's Preface" to the *Book of Changes* (*I Ching*): "In the study of a Chinese classical book there is not so much an interpretation of the characters employed by the writer as a participation of his thoughts;—there is a seeing of mind to mind."[35] Yet, and this is the creative paradox, in seeing into the mind of the Buddhist Fa-hsien, the Christian mind of the missionary never quite left Professor Legge—his vision a Christian one with universal sympathies.

Giles' introduction to *The Travels of Fa-hsien (399–414 AD)* is very different, being far more academically theological and a kind of preliminary exercise in the study not of comparative religions but of the nature of religion itself. His methods are derived from a tradition of biblical criticism that Legge steadfastly resisted—that of German higher criticism, with its historical niceties, its ultimate skepticism, and its finally cold eye of critical discernment. Giles asks questions of religious belief and observance, both Christian and Buddhist, without commitment and without religious hierarchy. He begins by asking, dispassionately, what kind of "Faith" drove Fa-hsien and his Chinese fellow monks on such an extraordinary journey into India, the ancient lands of the Buddha, "in the glow of which the journeys of St. Paul melt into insignificance."[36] Then much of his discussion focuses on "the frequent reference to the Precious Trinity, of which it may be said in passing that 'Precious' best translates the Chinese term, and leaves 'Blessed' and 'Holy' to the Trinities of the Roman Catholic and Protestant churches, respectively."[37] Giles is by no means incompetent as a scholar of the history of Christian theology. In comparing these various "Trinitarian" faiths, he is perfectly well aware that in the history of Christianity the doctrine of the Trinity was comparatively late, "enunciated in detail as a mystery in the so-called Athanasian Creed, of (?) 4th century, AD." It does not appear in the New Testament, except by the hand of some "pious but dishonest monk" in a late and spurious addition to 1 John 5:8, exposed centuries later by the classical scholar Richard Porson and omitted, as one would expect, from the most up-to-date and scholarly Bible of the time, the Revised Version of 1881. Giles' point in telling us all of this is that the received understanding that the Buddhist Trinity emerged lately as a result of the influence of later forms of Gnosticism should, in fact, be reversed and the greater antiquity of the Buddhist form of the doctrine be acknowledged. In his exposition of the Trinity of Buddhism, Giles engages in a scholarly reference within the history of Chinese Buddhism that Legge, in his detailed referencing of Western scholars, never does. Giles refers to the work of a Chinese scholar—the writing of "Chu Hsi, the great Chinese philosopher and historian of the 12th century"—in his exposition of the form of the Buddhist Trinity that "comprised (1) the spiritual body of Buddha, (2) his joyful body, as rewarded for his virtues, and (3) his fleshly body, in which he appeared on earth."[38]

Furthermore, Giles refers to the Ten Commandments of Buddhism, as a result of which, he admits, "the beneficent influence of this religion as a moral factor is undoubted."[39] Beginning with the prohibition "Thou shalt not destroy life," Giles, without reference to Christianity or its possible superiority, readily admits to the benign and peaceful influence of Buddhism in China and its "greatest men, rationalists at heart." He concludes his introduction with two lines from a Chinese poet of the eighth century, Ts'ên Ts'an, on a visit to a Buddhist shrine:

> O thou pure Faith, had I but known thy scope,
> The Golden God had long since been my hope![40]

In Giles, China is allowed to speak for itself. But there is a cold note to his scholarly claims that was to characterize the twentieth-century rather than the nineteenth-century academy and consign the more Christian and even perhaps more Romantic Legge to an older age. But, as we shall see, the older wisdom preserved a radical insight that Giles, in his brashness, somehow lost sight of.

Both Legge and Giles note the prevalence of the miraculous in Fa-hsien's narrative. Legge dismisses it with some contempt and with echoes of an older prejudice toward the "vulgar and ignorant" Buddhist priests to whom he had referred in his Hong Kong days. Legge writes, "Much of what Fa-hien tells his readers of Buddhist miracles and legends is indeed unreliable and grotesque."[41] Giles is more ready to admit the almost inevitable presence of the miraculous in most religious traditions (including Christianity): "The Record is packed with interesting incidents. Miracles, without which no supernatural religion seems to have a chance of attracting worshippers, are to be found in abundance."[42] Some of these miraculous tales have, indeed, a distinctively biblical, if not universal, resonance—at times not noted even by Legge. For example, Fa-hsien's final voyage on his return journey to China almost step by step (until the final denouement, at least) follows the story of Jonah. A storm arises and the sailors seek to lighten their ship by throwing overboard everything not essential. Even Fa-hsien throws overboard his "pitcher and washing-basin, with some other articles," though his precious books and images he preserves. The ship survives, but then in a further stage of the voyage to China from the island of Java, Fa-hsien again finds himself on a ship so buffeted by wind and wave that it threatens to sink. Some of his fellow travellers conclude that he, as a foreigner, is the source of their danger: "It is having this Sramana on board which has occasioned our misfortune and brought us to this great and bitter suffering. Let us land the bhikshu and place him on some island-shore. We must not for the sake of one man allow ourselves to be exposed to such imminent peril." However, a "patron" intercedes for Fa-hsien, and he is preserved through a harrowing voyage.[43] Jonah was not so fortunate.

But also, it should be noted, Fa-hsien's travels to the India of Buddha read very much like the records of certain early Christian travellers to the Holy Land, such as the Spanish nun Egeria and even up to the more popular narratives of medieval pilgrims of the late fourteenth century to Jerusalem and Sinai. Indeed, as their miracles are intended to show the nature of Buddha, so these narratives seem not far from the texture of the writings of the early Desert Fathers and Mothers, or the later miraculous legends of Voragine's *Golden Legend* from the twelfth century. As the universality of the literary form is recognized, so issues in comparative religion subsequently must necessarily be presented.

This brief comparison of two late-nineteenth-century translations of *The Travels of Fa-hsien*, or *A Record of Buddhistic Kingdoms*, suggests a number of things of interest to the early years of sinology, or the study of Chinese language and culture, in England at the end of the nineteenth century. James Legge and H. A. Giles were, respectively, professors of Chinese at the universities of Oxford and Cambridge. Legge, indeed, as we have seen, was the first man to be appointed to such a chair at the ancient English universities. Neither of them began their careers as professional academics: Legge was a missionary in China, and Giles was a diplomat. We witness between them in their work on this text a small scholarly squabble, all too familiar in the academic world, as Giles testily dismisses the careless mistakes—and worse, the unacknowledged copyings—of his rival. Both men are applying certain rules of Western scholarship to the translation and interpretation of a somewhat obscure ancient text but doing so in very different ways. In 1888, two years after the publication of his translation of Fa-hsien, Legge, despite his professed unwillingness to enter into academic disputes, was finally moved to respond in print to Giles' carping criticisms of his scholarship on the matter of Daoism on which Legge had written with a considerable degree of sympathy in his book *The Religions of China*, which refers pointedly also to our "so-called Christian nations," some eight years previously.[44] Some years after that, Legge published an important article in the *British Quarterly Review* (1883) titled "The Tao Teh King," and he consistently lectured in Oxford in the 1880s on Daoism, Laozi, and Zhuangzi. Increasingly his views on ancient Daoism (and Laozi in particular) are sympathetic and favorable, recognizing with a remarkable degree of reverence the spiritual profundity of the ancient texts while remaining true to his conservative sense of Christian universality. God speaks in many and mysterious ways—such was the lesson of Legge's decades of immersion in the ancient literature of China. Giles is altogether different—more secular, sceptical of *all* religious traditions (including Christianity), historical in temperament, and ultimately less capable of perceiving the wisdom of holding, within an overall vision, two finally irreconcilable positions in faith. In 1885 Giles published an article in the *China Review* in which he takes Legge to task in the matter of Daoism. He dismisses the view of Legge and others of his generation[45] that there was an ancient time of pure Daoism (a form of primitivism from which Christianity is not immune). Giles even rejects the historicity of Laozi himself on the grounds of lack of any hard evidence. In other words, like much of the Bible and especially the Old Testament, this ancient Chinese literature should be regarded as of a largely legendary nature, the *Dao De Jing* being a patchwork of bits and pieces put together by later redactors. The comparison with higher critical approaches to the Bible is clear, reducing the sublime unity of the sacred texts to a heap of phrases and scraps containing little more than what Giles describes as "feeble" and "inane" ideas.[46]

Both Legge and Giles are dealing with the problems of approaching an ancient (and, at the time, largely unknown) religious tradition with the beginnings of what was developing, not least under the leadership of Legge and Müller in Oxford, into the field of the comparative study of religions: Legge, it has to be said, with a considerable element of the missionary and the missionary vision for Christianity still present in him; Giles with more dispassionate, perhaps more coldly analytic scholarly attention. Their two translations open up the question of issues in translation itself. Legge's style is somewhat ponderous, seeking exactitude and anxious to be as precise through phrase and footnote as possible. Giles seeks to let the energy of the narrative be apparent to his reader, without the weight of a scholarly *apparatus criticus* or the distinctly arbitrary, not to say biblical, division of the text into chapters. What these editions make available to an English reading public is an example of literature that expands our sense of world literature, a narrative that takes its place beside Western texts with which it resonates in extraordinary and imaginative ways. For just as so much of the early Christian literature opens us to a world that is not doctrinal, dogmatic, or abstract but alive with human energy and divine mystery, so Legge is clear about his purposes in translating these pages: "to teach myself first, and then others, something of the history and doctrines of Buddhism. I have thought that they might be learned better in connexion with a lively narrative like that of Fa-hien, than by reading didactic descriptions and argumentative books. Such has been my own experience."[47]

And finally, it might be concluded that Legge's insight—gravely conservative and founded upon a deeply held, even simple, faith derived from his Scottish background in both nonconformity and common sense philosophy—was paradoxically more lasting and even more radical than that of Giles. The latter, for all the sharp and historical scriptural criticism of the introduction to his *Travels of Fa-hsien*, regarded the work as little more than an example of literature, and his translation presents it as such—almost bearing comparisons with eighteenth-century English picaresque novels like Tobias Smollett's *Humphry Clinker* or Henry Fielding's *Joseph Andrews*. Scripture takes its place in world literature, but something is lost thereby—that mysterious quality of sacredness without a sense of which, as T. S. Eliot was to observe many years later, Scripture quickly perishes even as literature.[48] The more ponderous and precise, even old fashioned, translation of Legge is an acknowledgment that in the sacred books of the East may be found a mystery and a truth that, for Legge, is finally the truth in Christ. But the implications for the universal and comparative study of religions are clear. To this the massive undertaking, under the charismatic guidance of Max Müller, of the series of volumes published by Oxford University Press titled *The Sacred Books of the East*, to which Legge made such an enormous contribution, stands as a late Victorian monument to the comparative spirit, outdated even in their own time, but with a wisdom and a generosity that has outlasted the more brittle and more modern scholarship of the "always pugnacious" Herbert Giles.

Part III

TRANSLATION AS DISLOCATION

9

POETICALLY TRANSLATING CHINESE TEXTS INTO THE WEST

Ezra Pound's Translation of Chinese Poetry and Confucian Classics

GENG Youzhuang

> *My work has been that of translator who found all the heavy work done for him and who has had but the pleasure of arranging beauty into the words.*
>
> Ezra Pound[1]

> *The blossoms of the apricot*[2]
> *blow from the east to the west,*
> *And I have tried to keep them from falling.*
>
> Ezra Pound[3]

John Dryden, in his "Preface to the Translation of Ovid's Epistles," once said, "No man is capable of translating poetry, who, besides a genius to that art, is not a master both of his author's language, and his own."[4] According to those standards, American poet Ezra Pound is not a qualified translator. He is surely a genius of the poetic art and a master of the English language (and other Western languages), but he is not a master of his authors' language—that is, the Chinese language used by ancient Chinese poets and philosophers. However, of the great number of translations of Chinese texts by Western missionaries, sinologists, and writers in the past several centuries, Pound's contribution is truly unique and worthy of discussion. One reason is that Pound's translation of Chinese texts, unlike other translations by Westerners, consists of three parts: his translation of ancient Chinese poetry, his translation of Confucian classics, and his "translation" of Confucian ideas into his own poetic works. In all those translations, there exist numerous mistakes of understanding and interpretation; yet Pound's translation of ancient Chinese poetry did successfully bring the ancient Chinese poetics into the Western literary scene, and his translation of Confucian classics truly resulted in the successful employment of Confucian ideas in his own poetic works. Ultimately, the three parts are closely linked in Pound's works and, brought together, call into question what it means to translate *literally* versus *poetically.*

Pound did not know the Chinese language at all when, early on, he translated fourteen ancient Chinese poems, based on the notebooks left by the late American sinologist Ernest Fenollosa, to be published as *Cathay* in 1915. After he developed a better but still inaccurate and incomplete knowledge of the Chinese language and culture, he translated Confucian classics *Da Xue* (大学, *The Great Learning, The Unwobbling Pivot* in Pound's translation), *Zhong Yong* (中庸, *The Doctrine of the Mean, The Great Digest* in Pound's translation), *Analects* (论语), and *Mencius* (孟子, unfinished), based mainly on French sinologist Guillaume Pauthier's *Les Quartre Lives de Philosophie Morale Et Politique de La Chine* (1841)—a French translation of the Four Books—and the Scottish missionary and sinologist James Legge's *Chinese Classics.* Pound's last translation of a Chinese text was *Shi Jing* (诗经, *The Book of Songs*) with the assistance of a Chinese-American Ph.D. student, Veronica Sun, which was published with the title *The Classical Anthology Defined by Confucius* in 1954. Pound was able to do these translations without a deep comprehension of the Chinese language partly due to the invention of his famous (or notorious) "ideogrammic method," which he employed in his creation and translation following the first publication of Fenollosa's essay "The Chinese Written Character as a Medium for Poetry" (edited by Pound) in *The Little Review* (September–December 1919). As we know, some people believe the result to be prodigious, and others disastrous. Consequently, Pound's translations of Chinese texts have long been disputed by scholars both in the West and in China since, on the one hand, most of them are actually a sort of adaption or rewrite of the previous translations, while, on the other hand, the unique strategy employed in his translation and creation—the ideogrammic method—produces at once the most creative and beautiful and the most arbitrary and absurd rendering of ancient Chinese poetry and philosophy.

Of his translation works, it is *Cathay* that received the most praise and was widely hailed by both poets and scholars in America and Europe immediately after it was published and by some Chinese poets and scholars many years later. As it is well known, the appearance of *Cathay* gave rise to a little vogue of imitating the Chinese among European and American poets in the late 1910s and early 1920s. T. S. Eliot, talking about Pound's translations of Chinese poems and the impact of his translation upon the literati in the West, even said that "Chinese poetry, as we know it today, is something invented by Ezra Pound."[5] At the same time, the misreadings and mistranslations by Pound of Chinese characters and words, in effect of Chinese language and culture, have been strongly criticized, including the question of whether or in what degree the poems in *Cathay* can be thought of as works of translation, though, as we know, Pound himself claimed the poems in *Cathay* to be such, placing his name on the title page ("Translations by Ezra Pound"). It is certainly true that numerous misreadings and mistranslations occur in Pound's *Cathay*. For instance, 《青青河畔草》 is translated wrongly as "The Beautiful Toilet," and the lines in this poem "今为荡子妇。荡子行不归" are translated as "And she has married a sot, / who now goes drunkenly out"[6] with 荡子 (a wanderer or prodigal) mistranslated as "a sot" (酒鬼). Even in the most accepted poem, "The River Merchant's Wife: A Letter," there are some mistranslations. For instance, toward the beginning of the poem, the lines read: "郎骑竹马来, 绕床弄青梅。同居长干里, 两小无嫌猜。" Pound's translation is:

> You came by on bamboo stilts, playing horse,
> You walked about my seat, playing with blue plums.
> And we went on living in the village of Chogan:
> Two small people, without dislike or suspicion.[7]

Here, "bamboo pole" (竹马) and "blue plums" (青梅) are parts of a Chinese idiom used by Li Po in the first two lines of the original, 青梅竹马, to refer to childhood sweethearts; Pound, however, does not know this idiom and, thus, mistranslates "bamboo pole" as "bamboo stilts." Nevertheless, the following two lines are accurate, creative, and beautiful translations. Compared to Witter Bynner's translation—"Both of us young and happy-hearted"[8]—Pound's translation is more poetic with a straightforward expression and a humorous tone. Moreover, here we can see clearly the strategy adopted by Pound: to seek not a faithful and literal copy of the original and a "word by word" translation, but rather to aspire to a truthful rendering of a pervasive feeling of the original with concise expressions and distinctive images. This strategy was learned by Pound from ancient Chinese poetry and poetics through his reading of early sinologists' and orientalists' translations and introductions—of them the most important ones are Herbert Giles' *A History of Chinese Literature* and Arthur Waley's *A Hundred and Seventy Chinese Poems*.

In recent studies on the reception of Pound's *Cathay* in the West, two essays collected in *Ezra Pound and China*, an anthology edited by the Chinese-American scholar Zhaoming Qian (钱兆明), are worth noting. The first one, titled "*Cathay*: What Sort of Translation?" by Barry Ahearn, discusses some of Pound's strategies or treatments in his translation of Chinese poetry. For Ahearn, Pound "adopts a divided stance: the Chinese poems are like Western ones, and the Chinese poems are in many respects alien. One result of this division is the reader's frequent perception of these poems as simultaneously familiar and strange."[9] His conclusion is that "many readers [in the West] considered *Cathay* [a] faithful rendering of Chinese poetry, not realizing that it seemed so accurate because it mirrored Western conceptions of China."[10] What is insightful in Ahearn's essay, from my point of view, is not that *Cathay* simply mirrored something like a Western conception of China but rather that *Cathay* enabled the reader to have the mixed perception—that is, simultaneously familiar and strange. This is, moreover, true not only for the Western reader but also for the Chinese reader.

The second essay, titled "The Beauties of Mistranslation: On Pound's English after *Cathay*" by Christine Froula, employs a much broader view on translation theories to understand Pound's mistranslations in *Cathay*. For Froula,

> Ezra Pound's long adventure with Chinese poetry marks another linguistic and cultural crossroads, an encounter—some Sinologists say, a violent, scandalous collision—between a twentieth-century American poet's cosmopolitan English and the ancient written language of classical Chinese poetry. . . . How does Pound's decades-long encounter with ancient Chinese poetry and culture participate in the future of English, that borderless, exploratory, accretive, imperial, colonizing

> language whose twentieth-century advance toward a global destiny Fenollosa foresaw?[11]

That is to say, English and Chinese are different languages, in which different traditions in linguistic, literary, economic, ideological, and political forms are embodied; and, therefore, in the process of translation, both languages in fact have to change. According to Froula, this is what Walter Benjamin meant when he suggested that the value of a translation is not in its concrete utterance but in its power toward "coming to terms with the foreignness of language." Thus, "Benjamin's translator seeks to produce not a simulacrum of the original's 'meaning' but a peculiar 'echo' of its language such that both languages seem 'fragments' of a third, 'greater language.'"[12] That is why in *Cathay* (and in *The Cantos*) a "self-foreignizing" English language can be seen, in which some fragments of the original Chinese language are reflected.

It should be noted that both Ahearn and Froula built on some ideas from Lawrence Venuti's translation theory, especially the concept of "foreignizing translation" that, in contrast to the dominant traditional translation theory of "domesticating translation," seeks not a "fluent translation" or transparent translation but rather emphasizes "the difference of the foreign text" and provides a kind of "otherness." Eventually, a new global language is coming with all the beauties of mistranslation through the collision between languages, and that is what Fenollosa foresaw in theory and Pound created in practice. Therefore, *Cathay* becomes not only a good translation of ancient Chinese poetry but also a telling example of postmodern translation theory.

What, then, about the Chinese response to Pound's creation and translation? In fact, the reception of Pound's poetry and poetics in China has a long and complicated history. The school of Imagism was introduced into China very early, through the essay "The Movement of New Poetry in America" by a Chinese scholar named Liu Yanlin (刘延陵) in 1922. However, Pound's translation of ancient Chinese poetry did not receive any attention in China until 1934 when the Chinese poet and critic Xu Chi (徐迟) published two essays titled "Seven Imagist Poets" and "Ezra Pound and His Associates" that described Pound as being the most important poet of the Imagist movement. Before that, it was Amy Lowell, rather than Ezra Pound, who occupied this position of preeminence in Chinese academia. It was Xu Chi, in his essays, who discussed the relationship between Pound and ancient Chinese poetry for the first time in China. He wrote that Pound translated many ancient Chinese poems into English, and his translation of "The River Merchant's Wife: A Letter" by Li Po (Li Bai) was very popular in the West. At that same time, six poems by Pound were being translated into Chinese. However, from the 1920s and 1930s until the later 1970s and early 1980s, few studies on Pound, especially on his translation of ancient Chinese poetry, occurred due to the wars and social and political changes in China. One influential criticism did come during this time period from Qian Zhongshu (钱钟书), a well-known scholar in the field of comparative literature. In 1945 Qian criticized Pound's superficial understanding and arbitrary reading of the Chinese language and culture, saying, "Pound is constructing Chinese rather than reading it, and, as far as Chinese literature is concerned, his A.B.C. of Reading betrays him as an elementary reader of merely A.B.C."[13] When "Pound studies" were finally renewed in China in the 1980s, more than fifty poems by Pound were translated into Chinese in that decade, compared to the six during the 1920s and 1930s. And in the most recent two decades, Pound's popularity has only increased, led by younger generations of Chinese scholars and poets, with a focus on the relationship between Pound and Chinese language and culture. Recently, according to incomplete statistics, more than one hundred articles on or related to Pound have been published, and several monographs have appeared in mainland China—exploring different aspects of Pound's life, creation, translation, and ideas.

It must be pointed out that, despite the relative dearth of interest in Pound prior to the 1980s by Chinese scholars in China, a great number of overseas Chinese scholars (that is, those Chinese living, teaching, or doing research in Western countries) did play an important role throughout that period in supporting Pound studies and the reception of Pound in China. Among them are those who met and worked directly with Pound, including, for instance, Achilles Fang (方志彤), who met Pound in the early 1950s and kept frequent correspondence with Pound over many years, and whose unpublished dissertation on *The Cantos* is one of the most important references to *The Cantos* studies; Angela Chih-ying Jung (荣之颖), who also met Pound during the 1950s and used Pound as the subject of her dissertation, published later as *Ezra Pound and China*; and Veronica Sun (the Ph.D. student previously mentioned), who assisted Pound in translating *Shi Jing* in the same time frame. It is very interesting that all those Chinese-American scholars were very much aware of Pound's mistranslation of Chinese texts and misreading of Chinese culture and, in different ways, were attempting to correct him; but they all ultimately failed.

If the previously mentioned overseas Chinese scholars of the older generations could be grouped collectively by their careers in exclusively Western institutions and Western academia, it is not that easy to classify those in the younger generations. Do they belong to the West or to China? This is unclear, and this precise ability to straddle Western and Eastern academia enables the overseas Chinese scholars in younger generations to examine Pound's creation and translation with a much broader perspective. I am going to mention only three of them: Wai-Lim Yip (叶维廉), Zhaoming Qian, and Ming Xie (谢明). Wai-Lim Yip, a Chinese-American poet and scholar originally from Hong Kong, has been very influential in both the West and China through his 1969 dissertation, titled *Ezra Pound's Cathay*, and has exerted a great influence on Pound studies through numerous additional works on Pound's poetic theory, creation, and translation. Recently, Jonathan Stalling, an American scholar, highly praised Wai-Lim Yip's achievements, saying that, unlike the older generation of sinologists such as Chang Chung-yuan (张钟元),

> Yip converts this "Daoist" description of ancient Chinese poetry into a vibrant living poetics and critical methodology. . . . Writing prior to Edward Said's *Orientalism*, Yip claimed to have found a way to both acknowledge and challenge universal claims made by Western structures of knowledge, and he applied these critiques to translation practices decades before Lawrence Venuti or Tejaswini Niranjana's postcolonial translation theories, which raise similar concerns regarding translation's imperialist distortions.[14]

For Zhaoming Qian, now considered the most important overseas Chinese scholar in Pound studies, several works on Pound, including *Orientalism and Modernism: The Legacy of China in Pound and Williams* (1995), *The Modernist Response to Chinese Art: Pound, Moore, and Stevens* (2003), and *Ezra Pound's Chinese Friends: Stories in Letters* (ed., 2008), have garnered for him the reputation as an influential Pound scholar, and none of his works should be ignored in this field. Among those works, *Ezra Pound's Chinese Friends* contributed significantly to

Pound studies by collecting 162 letters between Pound and his Chinese friends, of which 85 letters are published for the first time. Especially, the letters between Pound and Achilles Fang show clearly that Pound became increasingly aware in his later years that sound is just as crucial as visual form in Chinese language. As Zhaoming Qian said, this book may change our ideas of the relationships between Pound and China, and modernism and China.[15] Ming Xie, another young overseas Chinese scholar, published his *Ezra Pound and the Appropriation of Chinese Poetry: Cathay, Translation, and Imagism* in 1999, which is a further important work by a Chinese scholar on Pound's translation theory and practice and has been widely cited since it was published. As Ira B. Nadel says, "Ming Xie investigates Pound's abilities as a translator and his treatment of language in the establishment of a set of new texts based on primary forms, admitting that Pound's new English versions often substitute for the originals. But translation strengthened his own poetic innovations which, in turn, guided his translations."[16]

For most Chinese scholars and poets of the younger generations, Pound's translations of ancient Chinese poetry—including not just *Cathay* but other Chinese poems, especially some found in *The Cantos*—are creative and beautiful, even with the evident misreadings and mistranslations. Instead of simply pointing out Pound's misunderstanding and misinterpretation of Chinese characters and words—which the older overseas Chinese-American scholars tended to focus on—the younger generations pay much more attention to the significance of Pound's translation of ancient Chinese poetry as a whole. For them, the cultural influence of Pound's translation of Chinese poetry is a great achievement, and his literary misreading and mistranslation of Chinese characters and words is less important when seen in this light.

Nonetheless, we must be aware of Pound's mistranslations of Chinese poetry. Numerous examples have been discussed in previous studies, and a few have already been mentioned in this essay. Let us see one more example, a poem by Liu Che (an emperor of the Han dynasty) that has been discussed by many scholars in both the West and China, through a helpful comparison between Giles' and Pound's translations:

刘彻《落叶哀蝉曲》
罗袂兮无声，玉墀兮尘生。
虚房冷而寂寞，落叶依于重扃。
望彼美之女兮，安得感余心之未宁？

The sound of rustling silk is stilled,
With dust the marble courtyard filled;
No footfalls echo on the floor,
Fallen leaves in heaps block up the door. . . .
For she, my pride, my lovely one, is lost,
And I am left, in hopeless anguish tossed.

(Giles)

The rustling of the silk is discontinued,
Dust drifts over the court-yard,
There is no sound of foot-fall, and the leaves
Scurry into heaps and lie still,
And she the rejoicer of the heart is beneath them:
A wet leaf that clings to the threshold.

(Pound)

Scholars generally agree that the main difference between the two translations is the last line, in which Pound's translation of this poem has been thought very successful and considered—in fact—as better than Giles' translation. For some Western scholars, where the last sentence or image in Pound's translation comes from is not very clear. For instance, Hugh Kenner believed that "no wet leaf clings in the Chinese, and there is no indication that Pound supposed one did; he simply knew what his poem needed." But Kenner rightly claims, "A wet leaf clings to the threshold simply applies Imagist canons, the mind's creative leap fetching some token of the gone woman into the poem's system."[17] However, a Chinese reader who is familiar with the original will know immediately the last line of Pound's translation is a rewrite of the fourth line in the original. In fact, Sanehide Kodama (儿玉英实), a Japanese scholar, has pointed this out. And Qian rightly adds that Pound's line is simply derived from Giles' "Fallen leaves in heaps block up the door." What Pound has done is to turn some of Giles' words into a better image: Giles' plural "Fallen leaves" to his singular "A wet leaf"; Giles' colorless "block up" to his emotionally vivid "clings to"; and Giles' general "door" to his concrete "threshold." Qian is certainly right to point out those details and explains the difference in poetic diction of the two translations.[18] However, Qian seems not to see, or at least not to emphasize, the different attitudes toward translation reflected in the two versions—that of translating factually and of translating poetically. From my point of view, Giles' translation is also beautiful, and his "Fallen leaves" is more faithful to the original noun (落叶) than Pound's "A wet leaf." However, "A wet leaf" much more accurately conveys the sad feelings in the original, and the verb "clings to" is also more powerful, possessing a sense of heaviness, rather than Giles' "block up," even though the latter is closer to the original verb (依于). More important, Pound moved the fourth line in the original and in Giles' translation to the last line in his translation and, thus, creatively rendered the feelings and atmosphere of the original poem's integrity as a whole with an extraordinarily distinctive and powerful image.

If Pound's translation of ancient Chinese poetry can be justified based on the poetic and creative rendering of the original, what about his translation of Confucian classics? Can Chinese texts of philosophy be translated poetically and creatively? This remains a question. As we know, Pound struggled to learn the Chinese language for most of his life, and, in translating Confucian classics, he relied heavily on previous translations. However, Pound thought that all previous English translations of Confucian classics (including *Chinese Classics* by James Legge, whom he called "old Legge"[19] in his *The Cantos*) were not satisfactory. That is one of the reasons why Pound translates Confucian classics himself and, in doing so, employs his "ideogrammic method," which can be seen clearly from the "Terminology" included in his *Confucius* published in 1969, in which he explained some Chinese characters by this method. For instance, 明 (light, bright), according to him, means "the sun and moon, the total light process, the radiation, reception and reflection of light; hence, the intelligence. Bright, brightness, shining. Refer to Scotus Erigens, Grossetests and the notes in light in my *Cavalcanti*."[20] Another reason why Pound translateds Confucian classics himself is that he loved Chinese culture, and he sought especially to uncover new resources from Confucianism to deal with the problems and crises in the West during his time. Last, but certainly not least, Pound also attempted to find his ultimate self through his translation of Chinese texts and his appreciation of Confucian ethics, though he probably failed in that ambition.

In contrast to his translation of ancient Chinese poetry, however, which overall tends to gain positive responses from Chinese academia, Pound's translation of Confucian classics seems to not be accepted in

China. It is true that Pound's restricted knowledge of Chinese language and culture limited the value of his translation of Confucian classics much more than his translation of ancient Chinese poetry in China. But many scholars seem to forget that Pound is, first and foremost, a poet rather than a philologist or sinologist and that, more importantly, his translation of Confucian classics cannot thus be separated from his translation of Chinese poetry or from his own creation of poetry. This does not simply indicate that the language used in his translation of Confucian classics is also poetic and beautiful, though some scholars in both China and the West continue trying to demonstrate this point, but also indicates that Confucian ideas were translated or transposed into his own poetic works. As Ming Xie says, on the one hand, "in Pound's *oeuvre*, it is often difficult to distinguish between what is translation or adaption and what is original composition. For Pound there seems to be no fundamental distinction between the two."[21] On the other hand, "Pound's concern with the paradigmatic frame of an entire culture [in *Cathay*] was to be fully evident in his later translation of the *Shih Ching* anthology. Such an understanding also paved the way for his increasing engagement with Confucian thought."[22]

On the former point, the Chinese scholar Wu Qiyao (吴其尧), in his *Pound and Chinese Culture*, compared, for instance, two translations of a sentence in *Zhong Yong* by Legge and Pound:

> 道之不行也, 我知之矣: 知者过之, 愚者不及也。
>
> I know how it is that the path of the Mean is not walked in:
> The knowing go beyond it, and the stupid do not come up to it.
>
> (Legge)[23]
>
> Those who know how, exceed. (The intelligentsia goes to extremes).
> The monkey-minded do not get started.
>
> (Pound)[24]

According to Wu, the translation by Legge is decent and loyal to the Chinese original but too rigid and scholarly, while the one by Pound is more creative and poetic. He even thinks that the expression and tone of Confucius are more vividly rendered in Pound's translation.[25] This might be true, though I personally still prefer Legge's translation since the first requirement in translating academic work is faithfulness to the original.

In the case of Pound, poetically translating Confucian classics is revealed fully more in the Confucian ideas that are translated or transposed successfully into his own major poetic work, *The Cantos.* Especially in the *Kung Canto* (Canto 13), the *Seven Lakes Canto* (Canto 49), the *Chinese History Cantos* (Cantos 53–61), the *Pisan Cantos* (Cantos 72–84), the *Rock Drill Cantos* (Cantos 85–95), the *Thrones Cantos* (Cantos 96–109), and *Drafts and Fragments* (Cantos 110–17), Chinese history and philosophy, particularly Confucianism, repeatedly appear along with some written Chinese characters. As we know, the Canto 52 is almost a translation or rewrite of chapters 6 and 7 of *Li Ji* (礼记, *The Book of Rites*); in the *Pisan Cantos*, *Da Xue* is quoted or mentioned twice, *Zhong Yong* four times, *Analects* twenty-one times, and *Mencius* nine times. Thus, the influence of Chinese language, philosophy, and culture are almost ubiquitous in *The Cantos.* A contemporary Chinese poet Yang Lian (杨炼) even thinks that "the *Cantos* are complete only in their Chinese translation."[26] Many scholars have pointed out that *Zheng Ming* (正名, "right naming," or "rectification of names," which Pound inaccurately translates as "using words precisely"; Pound's translation of "名不正, 则言不顺" is "if words are not precise, they cannot be followed out," similar to his translation of *Cheng Yi* [诚意] as "sought precise verbal definition of their articulate thoughts") is a link between Pound's poetic writing and his translation of Confucian classics, while the Confucian ideal of *Xiushen*, *Qijia*, *Zhiguo*, *Pingtianxia* (修身, 齐家, 治国, 平天下, meaning: "rectifying the mind," "regulating the family," "managing the country," and "bringing peace to the world") becomes a principle that runs through *The Cantos.*

In the past several decades, the *Seven Lakes Canto* (Canto 49) has attracted many scholars' attention, since it is the only one based on paintings—specifically on the *Eight Views of Xiao Xiang*—and, therefore, enables discussions focused on the interrelationship between verbal art and visual art. That is especially true from the perspectives of Chinese scholars because the *Seven Lakes Canto* is an outcome of Pound's encounter with Chinese art and poetry in the later 1910s and the 1920s. As Wai-Lim Yip has pointed out, in his *Pound and the Eight Views of Xiao Xiang*, "Most Chinese readers, in their first encounter with 'Canto 49,' would be struck by a certain vibrant familiarity in the poem with both the poetic feeling and syntactical structures often found in classical Chinese poetry. In many ways, 'Canto 49' is one of Pound's most beautiful, and perhaps 'most Chinese' creations, aside from the fact that it is, according to his daughter Mary de Rachewiltz, his most favored in the entire Cantos."[27] In fact, according to Pound himself, "Canto 49 . . . presented a glimpse of paradiso."[28]

We know now from previous studies the background and the related cultural exchanges behind the writing of this beautiful poem. In 1928 Pound received from his parents an album with eight ink paintings that had eight poems in Chinese (and eight poems in Japanese) inscribed in them, which was a reproduction of a Tang dynasty painting, *Eight Scenes of the T'ung T'ing Lake Region*, by a Japanese artist. Pound loved those paintings but did not know the meaning of those poems written on them. It was only when, later in the same year, Pound met a Chinese lady in Italy named Miss Zeng, whom Pound called a "descendant of Confucius," that he began to understand those poems through Miss Zeng's translation. Later on, Angela Chih-ying Jung discovered that this Miss Zeng was in fact Tseng Pao-shun (曾宝荪), whose grandfather was the famous general statesman and the great Confucian Zeng Kuo-fang (曾国藩). And as we know, the Zeng family came from the T'ung T'ing Lake region. Pound, then, retranslated or rewrote those poems based on Miss Zeng's translation, and these translations formed much of the *Seven Lakes Canto* (lines 1–32). Since Canto 49 was first published in 1937, many discussions on, and especially comparisons between, Miss Zeng's translation and Pound's have been made. And all scholars have agreed that Pound's translation is more poetic. This can be seen clearly from a comparison of the first several lines of the two translations:

> Rain, empty river,
> Place for soul to travel
>   (or room to travel)
> Frozen cloud, fire, rain damp twilight.
> One lantern inside boat cover (i.e., sort of shelter, not awning on
>   small boat)
> Throws reflection on bamboo branch,
>   Causes tears
>
> (Zeng)

[For the seven lakes, and by no man these verses:]
Rain; empty river; a voyage,
Fire from frozen cloud, heavy rain in the twilight
Under the cabin roof was one lantern.
The reeds are heavy; bent;
and the bamboos speak as if weeping.

(Pound)

However, much less attention has been paid to the two ancient Chinese songs before the end of Canto 49: *Qing yun ge* (卿云歌) and *Ji rang ge* (击壤歌), supposedly from the sage rulers Shun (舜) and Yao (尧) respectively. The first one was given in Japanese phonetic symbols, and the second in English, and both of them were found by Pound from Fenollosa's notebook. The first one reads:

KEI MEN RAN KEI
KIU MAN MAN KEI
JITSU GETSU KO KWA
TAN FUKU TAN KA

Neither Fenollosa nor Pound translated this song; Legge's translation is as follows:

Splendid are the clouds and bright
All aglow with various light
Grand the sun and moon move on
Daily down succeeds to dawn.[29]

卿云烂兮
纠缦缦兮
日月出兮
旦复旦兮

The second one translated by Fenollosa reads as follows:

Sun up, work
Sundown, to rest
Dig well and drink of the water
Dig field, eat of grain
Imperial power is? And to us what is it?[30]

日出而作，
日落而息。
凿井而饮，
耕田而食。
帝力于我何有哉？

Different from lines 1–32 (based on Miss Zeng's translations, which Pound took great pains to retranslate or rewrite to make them more poetic), This song was simply incorporated by Pound (and the first one in Japanese sound) from Fenollosa's notebook into the Canto. The reason might be that Pound thought Fenollosa's translation to be excellent because it, with simple words and colloquial language, effectively and accurately "copies" the simplicity of language and the innocence of life in the times of the legendary Emperors Yao and Shun as depicted in the original folk song. In addition, the last line of the translation is unusually complicated compared to the original, which enables the might of the imperial power to be rendered powerfully and poetically, but, at the same time, a strong ironic tone can be easily perceived. It is interesting to note that, through this poem, after a beautiful rendering of the so-called *Eight Views of Xiao Xiang*, Pound did not stop at the artistic conception of Chan (Zen) aroused by the ink paintings, but rather he began to think of the ideal society of ancient China he perceived in old folk song. The poet, as Zhaoming Qian says, "becomes a Westerner seeking a way out of political chaos"[31] in his own times using that idea of the "ideal society" based on Confucianism.

This is the main reason why Pound took great pains to poetically translate Confucian classics; this is most evident in his *Chinese History Cantos* and *Pisan Cantos*. The *Chinese History Cantos* (53–61) is, as the title indicates, devoted to China. As previously mentioned, Canto 52 (immediately preceding the *Chinese History Cantos*) is almost a translation or rewrite of chapters 6 and 7 of *Li Ji* (*The Book of Rites*), which deals with the Confucian ideas of management. The *Chinese History Cantos* are based on the eighteenth-century French missionary de Mailla's *Histoire general de la Chine*. De Mailla's monumental work (in twelve volumes) is actually part of the adaption of the Manchu script *History* (通鉴纲目, *Tongjian Gangmu*) by Zhu Xi (朱熹), a famous Confucian scholar in the South Song dynasty, which records a history of about five thousands years (3000 BC–AD 1900). It is worth noticing that Chinese ideograms are inserted repeatedly in Canto 53, which indicates that the ideogammic method is employed in Pound's poetic writing. Let us see an example. The following lines come from *Li Ji·Da Xue* (礼记·大学: "汤之《盘铭》曰: 苟日新, 日日新, 又日新。"):

> Tching prayed on the mountain and
>   wrote MAKE IT NEW
> on his bath tub
>   Day by day make it new
> cut underbrush,
> pile the logs
> keep it growing
> [Besides those lines are written Chinese characters: 新, 日日新][32]
>
> 成汤在山上祈祷并且
> 写下"日日新"
> 在他的浴盘上
> 每日求新
> 砍去矮树丛
> 堆起木柴
> 让树生长。
> (赵毅衡译)

Pound's understanding in the first half of this paragraph is basically right in relation to those Chinese characters, but the second half of it is inexplicably and significantly inflated. This is because the character 新 (new) is understood by Pound, through his ideogrammic method, as cutting wood (the bottom part of 亲 is 木, "wood") with an axe (斤). Moreover, in the eyes of Pound, 新 is same as 薪 (firewood), and therefore the last three lines are fabricated. This reminds us of his translation of the *Analects*. In Book 5, Confucius, talking about his idea about a failed process, says:

> The process is not acted upon [*old style: "the way is not trodden"*], I will get onto a raft and float at sea and . . . eh . . . Yu will follow me. Tsze-lu (Yu) was pleased to hear this. Confucius said: Yu likes audacity more than I do, he wouldn't bother to get the logs (to make his raft).[33]

> 子曰: "道不行, 乘桴浮于海。从我者, 其由也?" 子路闻之喜。子曰: "由也好勇过我, 无所取材。"

Here "无所取材" (*wu suo qu cai*) indicates someone who cannot undertake the due obligations since he does not know how to fashion himself, so Legge's translation reads rightly as follows:

> The Master said, "My doctrines make no way. I will get upon a raft, and float about on the sea. He that will accompany me will be Yu, I dare to say." Tsze-Lu hearing this was glad, upon which the Master said, "Yu is fonder of daring than I am. He does not exercise his judgment upon matter."[34]

Pound's translation, however, likely comes out of his staring at the character 材 and finding from it "one and a half trees," so he translated it as "logs."

Mistranslations like this are seen frequently in Pound's translation of Confucian classics, but at the same time his homage paid to Confucius' personality and ideas are also seen throughout his *The Cantos*. For instance, in the *Kung Canto*, Pound described Confucius like this:

> Kung walked
> by the dynastic temple
> and into the cedar grove,
> and then out by the lower river
> And with him Khien, Tchi, and Tian the low speaking.[35]

By those lines, the image of Confucius, who was travelling around in pursuit of his social and political ideal, undaunted by repeated setbacks, is vividly rendered. In the *Pisan Cantos*, he praised Confucius' noble and unsullied personality highly and said, quoting from *Mencius*, "To this whiteness, Tseng said / 'What shall add to this whiteness?' "[36] Concerning the ideas of managing the state, he wrote that "better gift can no man make to a nation / than the sense of Kung fu Tseu."[37]

In conclusion, although there are misreadings, mistranslations, and misinterpretations in Pound's translation of Confucian classics, Confucian ideas are successfully translated or transposed into his *The Cantos* and other poetic works through the poetic and creative use of English language. At the end of *The Cantos*, Pound wrote:

> That I lost my center
> fighting the world / the dreams clash
> and are shattered—
> and that I tried to make a paradise
> terrestre.[38]

This might include his quest for the ideal social system through Confucian ideas. In his later years, Pound became increasingly unwilling to speak, but he insisted, "I did not enter into silence; silence captured me."[39] Nevertheless, his translation of Chinese texts will continue to be part of the process of cultural exchanges—after all, as he wrote in *The Cantos*:

> The wind is part of the process
> The rain is part of the process.[40]

10

THE POWER OF POWERLESSNESS

Rediscovering the Radicality of Wu Wei *in Daoism through Blanchot*

WANG Hai

> *The most submissive thing in the world can ride roughshod over the hardest in the world—that which is without substance entering that which has no crevices.*
>
> *That is why I know the benefit of resorting to* non-action. *There are few in the world who attain to the teaching without words, and the advantage arising from* non-action.
>
> Laozi[1]

> *Now you have this big tree and you're distressed because it's useless. Why don't you plant it in Not Even-Anything Village, or the field of Broad-and-Boundless, relax and* do nothing *by its side, or lie down for a free and easy sleep under it?*
>
> Zhuangzi[2]

> *The ultimate goal . . . is to affirm the rupture. . . . The rupture with the powers that be, thus with the notion of power, thus all places where power predominates. . . . This decision of refusal is not a power, nor a power to negate, nor negation in relation to an always already posed affirmation. This decision is what we name when we inject spontaneity into the "revolutionary" process, with the proviso that this notion of spontaneity is subject to caution.*
>
> Maurice Blanchot[3]

The radicality of the Daoist school of thought was noticed by its reviewers and opponents from its very early days. "Radicality" here involves two related aspects of "being radical": (1) going to the root or origin; and (2) being thoroughgoing or extreme, especially regarding change from accepted or traditional forms, or, in other words, unconventional and revolutionary. Daoism and its radicality emerged in the period of "Contention of a Hundred Schools of Thought" (百家争鸣) or, more exactly, the late years of the Spring and Autumn period and the Warring States period of ancient China, from about the sixth century to 221 BC—within the Axial Age, in the German philosopher Karl Jaspers' term. Legalist Han Fei (ca. 280–233 BC) condemned the Daoist school implicitly but no less fiercely. He listed his accusations: first, "office and ranks are means to encourage people," but Daoist thinkers famously refuse to take any interest in pursuing any office,[4] and by doing so they in fact "act contrary to the masses, practice their own creed, and prefer differences from the others";[5] second, they pursue the philosophy of being indifferent to fame and gain (恬淡之学), which is totally useless; third, their speech is full of ambiguities and illusions (恍惚之言), which is lawless.[6]

More than one hundred years later, the radicality of Daoism is also highlighted in *Records of the Grand Historian* by Sima Qian (ca. 145 or 135–86 BC). The father of Chinese historiography and a sympathizer with Daoism, Sima, in his description of Daoist thinkers, remarked on the Daoist radical refusal to cooperate with the powerful and its refusal to be useful and totally transparent in our understanding. He rightly concluded that "Laozi's rhetoric and terminology were abstruse and difficult to understand,"[7] and "Zhuangzi's words billowed and swirled without restraint, to please himself[;] and so from kings and dukes down, the great men could not utilize him."[8]

However, it seems that in modern times the significance of Daoist radicality is not only underestimated but also even forgotten, when we are in need of it perhaps more than at any other time. One reason for this is that today to a large extent we see Daoism through the eyes of Confucianism (though without realizing it), which was the official ideology for most of the dynastic history of China after 135 BC.[9]

One example is the widespread argument that Confucianism and Daoism complement each other, in that one is active and the other is passive—one engaging with, the other withdrawing from, worldly affairs.[10] This schema turns Confucianism and Daoism into a binary and harmonious opposition, finally a unity. It is perhaps easily accepted by the scholars from mainland China who are familiar with Hegel-Marx dialectics and Mao Zedong's *On Contradiction*,[11] and the scholars both domestic and abroad who believe in something called "Chineseness," or the essence of being "Eastern" or "Western," and are eager to pin it down during an era of anxiety over identity in a globalized world still built on nation-states.

However, this dialectical picture not only smoothes over the incommensurable differences and disagreements between Daoism and Confucianism but also neglects a very important historical fact. With many other schools of thought, Daoism, especially its radical elements and its critique of Confucianism, has been largely marginalized and repressed in the interests of Confucianism, to the extent that after the Tang dynasty (618–907) no more significant philosophical developments or thinkers of Daoism have emerged.[12] In fact, after Neo-Confucianism (a much more rationalist and secular understanding of Confucianism) is promoted as the state ideology in 1241 and begins to permeate people's everyday life in almost every aspect, we can hardly find any independent Daoist intellectual within the *shidafu* (士大夫, scholar-officials).[13] Daoism has been transformed into an assistant to and as complementary to Confucianism; and it is needed only when an intellectual person encounters setbacks in his or her political career, for Daoism is supposed to be able to comfort by teaching one how to accept and let go of these setbacks. This limited role of Daoism is in fact still under the guidance of one of Mencius' mottos, a principle of Confucianism—that is, 穷则独善其身, 达则兼善天下 (If poor, they attended to their own virtue in solitude; if advanced to dignity, they made the whole kingdom virtuous as well [ch. 9, Jinxin I, Mencius]). The radical side of philosophical Daoism, however, has been repressed in the unconscious of Confucian intellectuals, and it is only allowed to emerge in a disguised way when channeled into such intellectuals' artistic activities, such as painting, poetry and novel writing, and . Today, to a large extent, we are still under the influence of this history, and our understanding of Daoism as a complement to Confucianism is perhaps just one proof that we more or less still see Daoism through Confucian eyes.

The passivity of Daoism, or more precisely the passive role played by Daoism in this binary oppositional system, has incurred many attacks from modern Chinese intellectuals. For example, Liu Xiaofeng in his

Salvation and Wandering accused the passivity of Daoism of being merely pessimism and escapism.[14]

However, I will argue that through examining *wu wei* (无为), one core idea of Daoism, we may find that the passivity of Daoism has a very positive significance. The key is that we should rediscover and revive the radicality of Daoist passivity (radicality in the sense of being primal, affirmative, and rebellious) outside the dialectical relation governed by Confucianism, outside this closed system that predetermines the position and the meaning of anyone even before one enters into it. There happens to be a thinker, whose thought is described as the thought from outside,[15] and whose preoccupation is also radical passivity.[16] He is the twentieth-century French writer and thinker Maurice Blanchot (1907–2003).

Blanchot has never written a single word on Daoism, and so far no clear proof has been found that he has been ever influenced by it; but we will find in extraordinary ways that there are many resonances between his thought and the Daoist thinkers Laozi and Zhuangzi, or rather between their texts. Blanchot creatively reinterpreted the concept of passivity in a very positive way, and, like Laozi and Zhuangzi, he promoted the idea of weakness, powerlessness, and very importantly *désoeuvrement* (idleness, worklessness).

This is not, however, a comparative study. It is an act of *translation* and *conversation*, if these two words really mean what they mean; that is, etymologically "translation" means "to bring over, carry over (from one place to another)," and "conversation" means "to live with, keep company with." The distance between Blanchot and Laozi and Zhuangzi, temporally and spatially, perhaps only indicates the necessity and exigency of this conversation.

Wu wei (无为) is one of the most fundamental ideas of Daoist philosophy. *Wu* (无) can be translated as "not have" or "without," and *wei* can be translated as "do," "act," "serve as," "govern," or "effort." So *wu wei* literally means "not doing," "doing nothing," or "non-action." But its exact meaning is far from clear, for first of all the word *wu wei* always appears in a paradoxical way in the texts of *Laozi* and *Zuangzi*.

For example in *Laozi*,

是以圣人处无为之事，行不言之教。

> Therefore the sage keeps to the deed that consists in taking *no action* and practices the teaching that uses no words. (ch. 2)

为无为，事无事，味无味。

> Do that which consists in taking no action; pursue that which is not meddlesome; savour that which has no flavour. (ch. 63)[17]

To solve this paradox, many interpretations of *wu wei* are suggested. Probably the most common one is this: *wu wei* is action that is natural, or, to put it another way, "taking no action that is contrary to Nature—in other words, letting Nature take its own course."[18] But the problem is this: What is natural, and what is not? In the natural world, a wolf preys on a hare, but does that make it natural in a human society for the strong to prey on the weak? Some behavior or custom is regarded as natural in one society but probably not at all in another society. We all know the saying "One man's meat is another man's poison."

Another interpretation of *wu wei* is this: "Action does not involve struggle or excessive effort." But this will mean that if one can just follow the majority, thw given rules, or the dominant ideology of a society, then one is practicing *wu wei*. It will also imply that if you practice one skill well enough, you can attain to the stage of *wu wei*. Actually one scholar claims that Confucians also pursue *wu wei*, and Confucius himself is a perfect example of it, though in a Confucian way, for Book 10 of the *Analects* says, "Every nuance of his expression, body language, and speech is portrayed as perfectly and effortlessly harmonizing the demands of the situation with the standards of ritual propriety."[19]

However, perhaps all these interpretations strive too hard to decipher the meaning of *wu wei* to take notice of a no less important issue, the "form" of it, more precisely the way the notion of *wu wei* is presented—as a paradox! Both Laozi and Zhuangzi are notorious for loving paradoxes and contradictions. We have shown some examples from *Laozi*, and now here are some from *Zhuangzi*:

> Great Benevolence is not benevolent; Great Modesty is not humble; Great Daring does not attack. If the Dao is made clear, it is not the Dao. . . . [U]nderstanding that rests in what it does not understand is the finest. Who can understand discriminations that are not spoken, the Dao that is not a Dao?
>
> (ch. 5, bk. 2)

Blanchot loved using paradoxes too, as his critic Tzvetan Todorov complained, "The oxymoron is indeed Blanchot's very favorite rhetorical figure. At random, I have gleaned in *The Book to Come* the following examples: 'empty plenitude'; 'always yet to come, always already gone by'; . . . 'these works of the spirit, originating in an absence of spirit.' "[20] Language tends to be linear, having a definitive direction, and it is especially so when the speech wants to teach, to lead, and to influence. This teaching speech appears to be representational, claiming it only represents what it is. In Blanchot's words, it is "a language where language itself would not be at stake."[21] Another problem with language, as Blanchot's friend Roland Barthes pointed out, is that power permeates language all the time, through conceptualization, classification, and the authority of assertion and the gregariousness of repetition in the speech.[22] Blanchot kept a vigilant watch against these risks.

Laozi and Zhuangzi are wary of language too. The opening line of *Laozi*, 道可道非常道, 名可名非常名 (The way that can be spoke of is not the constant way; the name that can be named is not the constant name[23]), recognizes the limitation of language. It can be taken as an act of confession of the inadequacy of the text itself and also as an act of self-deconstruction, therefore an act dismissing the power that the text will attract and accumulate. On the other hand, the text's confession of its inadequacy indicates that something always remains beyond language and knowledge. And this something ineffable is called the Nonknowledge in Bataille and the Outside in Blanchot.[24]

Perhaps we can say first of all that *wu wei* is a paradox that shall not and cannot be solved. And this paradoxical status keeps *wu wei* as a performative act—a generator of infinite conversations among different meanings, hence a generator of infinite potentialities—and keeps it from falling into a concept or a dogma, which can be followed and mastered. So being paradoxical is the first level of the radicality of *wu wei*.

Let us go back to the word *wu wei* itself again. Is *wu wei*, or non-action, an action? Hegel said the secret of all action is its power of negation, negating the given reality.[25] The character *wu* (无) means "non," "without" (i.e., a negative). In this sense perhaps *wu wei* can be seen as the most radical action, the most radical negation, for it has nothing to negate except the negating power of human action. It is "negativity without employ"[26] or suspension of negativity. But it does not lead to the opposite of negation—that is, affirmation of the given. It goes outside the circle of dialectics of negation and affirmation. It is Bartleby's saying, "I would prefer not to," in Herman Melville's *Bartleby, the Scrivener.*

As Liu Xiaogan has pointed out, actually *Laozi* and *Zhuangzi* are scattered with many words bearing a negative, such as 不言 (to use no words), 不恃 (to exact no gratitude), 弗居 (to claim no merit), 不仁 (not to be benevolent), 不争 (not to argue), 不有 (not to possess), and 不宰 (no authority).[27] They are full of the passion of *pas* (no) in Blanchot's word, forming a constellation, a spectrum of negatives with *wu wei* as their representative. Altogether they constitute an act of refusal and critique primarily of power. However, their negation or the negation of *wu wei* has an essential difference from Hegelian negation, which renders wu *wei* more radical and more extreme. In Hegel, action is negating; but since *wu wei* is meant to be the renunciation of action, then *wu wei* will be the renunciation of the power of negativity. If you oppose power with will directly and fiercely, your action of opposition will gather power around you instead, thanks to the hegemonic circle of dialectics. As Barthes argued, "Make a revolution to destroy it, power will immediately revive and flourish again in the new state of affairs."[28]

So the second level of the radicality of *wu wei* is its radical negativity, its radical refusal of power and domination.

If action corresponds to death in Hegel, then we can say *wu wei* or non-action corresponds to the idea of dying in Blanchot. Blanchot used the word "dying" to refer to the other side of death, the death without end, the restless negativity even negating itself. For Heidegger, death is one's utmost possibility; in other words, death is one's own death, but Blanchot reminds us of the other side of death, the more profound one, the impossible and anonymous side, or, so to speak, the death belonging to no one. No one can either plan or appropriate it. In this sense *wu wei* is an impossible action for one to pursue and execute intentionally with will. Actually *wu wei* is a process of losing the "I," the subject. It is one of the three ideals that Zhuangzi thought a perfect human being would achieve: "The Perfect Man has no self; the Holy Man has no merit; the

Sage has no fame" (至人无已, 神人无功, 圣人无名).[29] Zhuangzi called this process 吾丧我 (I lose myself) and described the scene when his fictional ideal Taoist model, Tzu-Ch'i, underwent it:

> Tzu-Ch'i of South Wall sat leaning on his armrest, staring up at the sky and breathing—vacant and far away, as though he'd lost his counterpart. Yen Ch'eng Tzu-yu, who was standing by his side in attendance, said, "What is this? Can you really make the body like a withered tree and the mind like dead ashes? The man leaning on the armrest now is not the one who leaned on it before!"
>
> Tzu-Ch'i said, "You do well to ask the question, Yen. Now I have lost myself."[30]

This means *wu wei* is an anonymous action. And without the positing of a subject, there will be no object. Zhuangzi described this entailed phenomenon as 丧其耦 (losing his counterpart), as we have read above.[31] Hence *wu wei* is a non-dual action, which dismisses the dichotomy of subject and object and the distinction between agent and action as such. Therefore the third level of the radicality of *wu wei* is the deconstruction of the subject.

The fourth level of the radicality of *wu wei* is its refusal to be useful, which is especially emphasized in the *Zhuangzi*. In Laozi there is still a trace of dialectics to the extent that one might suspect *wu wei* (doing nothing) is only for the purpose of *you wei* (doing something); in other words, *wu wei* is in fact the means serving the end of doing something. For example,

> 为无为, 则无不治。
>
> Do that which consists in taking no action, and order will prevail. (ch. 3)
>
> 道常无为而无不为。
>
> The way (Dao) never acts yet nothing is left undone. (ch. 37)

The above translation is from D. C. Lau (刘殿爵, 1921–2010), a Chinese scholar who taught Chinese language and philosophy in the School of Oriental and African Studies between 1950 and 1978, and after that in the Chinese University of Hong Kong. James Legge's translation of the above sentence is interestingly different from Lau's:

> The Tao in its regular course does nothing (for the sake of doing it), and so there is nothing which it does not do.[32]

He highlighted a means-end relation or dialectical relation between *wu wei* and *you wei* by adding his explanation "for the sake of it" after *wu wei*. In another place, when he translated *wu wei*, he added "with a purpose" after it. Like many other readers, Legge regarded *wu wei* in Laozi as a strategy, a means.

However, in Zhuangzi *wu wei* reveals its total radicality, for it is ontological, it has no purpose but itself, or, say, it is means without end. When Zhuangzi's friend Huishi condemned his words as "big and useless," Zhuangzi replied in a humorous way by mentioning *wu wei*: "Now you have this big tree and you're distressed because it's useless. Why don't you plant it in Not-Even-Anything Village, or the field of Broad-and-Boundless, relax and *do nothing* by its side, or lie down for a free and easy sleep under it? Axes will never shorten its life, nothing can ever harm it. If there's no use for it, how can it come to grief or pain?"[33] This uselessness of *wu wei* corresponds to dying or death without end in Blanchot.

Through Blanchot, we are able to perhaps not only rediscover *wu wei*'s radicality but also revive it as a contemporary idea with much more explanatory power dealing with the crisis of modernity and our contemporary issues.

11

WHAT IS LOST IN THE CHINESE TRANSLATIONS OF *THE MERCHANT OF VENICE*?

A Comparative Reading of the Texts

YANG Huilin

In a discussion of the classics, Shakespeare's dialogue in *A Midsummer Night's Dream* deserves further contemplation:

> O Bottom, thou art changed! What do I see on thee?
> What do you see? You see an ass-head of your own, do you?
> Bless thee, Bottom! Bless thee! Thou art translated.[1]

In the Chinese translation, the implied meaning in the phrase "thou art translated" is all but absent, and the phrase is expressed in much the same terms as "thou art changed."[2]

From "translated" to "changed into another form," what has been erased or blurred is just the hidden, or secondary, meaning of the words themselves; but if we take into consideration the text and the cultural context behind the words, a similar erasure and ambiguity here leaves a profound "absence" or "emptiness." In the process of the translation and the circulation of a work, different understandings, receptions, and rewriting will become manifest.

Put another way, in the face of this persistent tension between "cultural unconsciousness" and "pre-understanding," the comparative reading of text and context is perhaps precisely the discovery of subtle "absences" and a highlighting of the "emptiness" of meaning, or the *reductione* of some "irreducible" hidden meaning. The trajectory of the classic in this way might not just add new meaning for the alien culture but also strengthen meaning in its original context. In this, *The Merchant of Venice* (hereafter *Merchant of Venice*) provides a model case study.

Ever since Nevill Coghill published his essay "The Basis of Shakespearean Comedy,"[3] it has been generally accepted that "Shylock and Antonio embody the theological conflicts and historical interrelationships of Old Law and New."[4] Yet Coghill also contends that even for later generations of Western readers, a kind of "reduction" is the norm: "The . . . age that has produced *The Faerie Queene* felt more at home in allegory than we do. Thinking in allegory is to us an unaccustomed habit of mind, but to those in a medieval tradition, second nature. . . . Ceasing to think of them, we lose the faculty to do so and at last deny that such a faculty can have had genuine part in a poetry which we think can be well enough understood without it."[5]

On this basis, Coghill discusses the "Trial Scene" in *Merchant of Venice*:

> The principle here mainly adumbrated in Shylock is justice, in Portia, mercy. He stands, and says he stands, for the Law, for the notion that a man must be as good as his bond. It is the Old Law. . . . Before Shylock's uncompromising demand for justice, mercy is in the posture of a suppliant refused. Thrice his money is offered him and rejected. He is begged to supply a surgeon at his own cost. But no, it is not in the bond. From the technical point of view the scene is constructed on a sudden reversal of situation, a traditional dramatic dodge to create surprise and denouement. The verbal trick played by Portia is not a part of her "character," but a device to turn the tables and show justice in the posture of a suppliant before mercy. . . . Once this aspect of the Trial scene is perceived, the Fifth Act becomes an intelligible extension of the allegory; for we return to Belmont to find Lorenzo and Jessica in each other's arms. Christian and Jew, New Law and Old, are visibly united in love.[6]

Roy Battenhouse also argues that

> central to this play is the test of the three caskets, a parable about the Christian paradox of losing things worldly to gain things heavenly. . . .

> If law and grace need not be mutually exclusive, neither are justice and mercy, or the letter of the law and the spirit hidden behind the letter. . . . It is therefore not by mere quibbling or trickery, as some critics of the play would suppose, that Portia defeats Shylock, but rather by revealing the heart of the law within its literal demands.[7]

Those proposing a similar point of view also include John R. Cooper and Joan Ozark Holmer, among others.[8] And so, even though Shakespeare provided many powerful soliloquies for Shylock, the accusations of the Jew are destined to be in vain; although the outcome of Shylock seems wretched for many modern audiences, the play is destined to be a comedy. For Coghill, Shylock's loss of his family fortune and his daughter's elopement do not affect the "surprise and denouement" at the end of the play, and the music that accompanies the dialogue remains as the "symbol of harmony." For Battenhouse, this is still to "return good for evil," and indeed to "offer brotherhood to a neighbor he formerly treated as an outsider." But for the Chinese readers who are alien to this "allegorical" context, or even for later Western readers, is it still possible to understand *Merchant of Venice* in this way?

In the early twentieth century, there were several Chinese versions of *Merchant of Venice.*[9] Although the rhetoric of mercy over law and the pedagogical teaching in the test of three caskets were consistent in all translations, and although Portia's wisdom has always been praised and Shylock's appeal always laughed at, meriting little sympathy, the deeper conflicts between the Old Law and the New, and between Judaism and Christianity, have been all but obliterated. As a result, Shylock becomes a figure like Molière's *L'Avare*, no longer representing any difference between the Old and New. *Merchant of Venice* in the West has likewise been staged in many different forms and versions, with the Shylock of some even a hero striving for ethnic rights, garnering warm applause for his eloquent speeches in Act I, Scene III and Act IV, Scene I. How can the same story elicit such different responses? And how can a Chinese audience, who might not relate to the religious conflicts in the play or understand the historic humiliation of the Jews, maintain these primary images?

In 1903 the Shanghai Dawen Bookstore published the earliest Chinese translations of Shakespeare's work, *Xie wai qi tan* (澥外奇谈), a translation of *Tales from Shakespeare* edited by Charles and Mary Lamb, in which *Merchant of Venice* is translated literally as "*Yan Dunli*

[Shylock's Chinese name] *Lends Money and Makes a Bond of Flesh*." In 1904 Lin Shu and Wei Yi translated and published the same *Tales* under the title *Yin bian yan yu* (吟边燕语), with *Merchant of Venice* translated as "Bond of Flesh" (肉券). In 1911 Bao Tianxiao translated and edited the same play and published it in the journal *Female Students* under the title "A Female Lawyer" (女律师). In 1913 director Zheng Zhengqiu directed the play "Bond of Flesh," probably based on Lin Shu and Wei Yi's translation. A most interesting case is that of American missionary Laura M. White, who translated this play as "A Tale of Cutting off Flesh" (剜肉记) and serialized it in the daily newspaper *Nü Duo bao* (女铎, *The Woman's Messenger*).

From these translations of the title, we can see that "cutting off flesh" or "the bond of flesh" has been the key to the understanding of this play, even in the version by White. As a Christian missionary, White could scarcely ignore the religious elements in *Merchant of Venice*, nor was she likely to jettison the aim of converting and educating through the text.[10] Perhaps it was precisely because she wanted to educate and convert Chinese people that she adapted to the reading habits and tastes of Chinese readers, and she had to dilute the original context and the religious ideas hidden in the text of *Merchant of Venice* when introducing Christian ethics. In White's version it is already difficult to sense "the theological conflicts and historical interrelationships of the Old Law and New." Perhaps this is also why Coghill thinks that later Western readers need some form of "reduction."

The "absence" or "dilution" in White's version is generally accompanied by "addition," in order for Chinese readers better to accept and understand the play. For instance, when Antonio enters, the translator has him greet the audience in Chinese fashion: "My family name is An, and my given name is Duoli [meaning "with many reasons"]. I am an Italian." When his two friends enter, they also engage in Chinese pleasantries. "Ha, ha. . . . You two came in at the right time. We have not seen each other for quite a long time. Sit down, sit down, please." The two guests also answer likewise, "We are sitting, we're sitting. How are you Mr. An?" At Act I, Scene II, when Shylock enters, a similar accommodation to Chinese style is made.

There are other "absences" and "additions" in the translation, which are also related to the translator's understanding of Chinese cultural characteristics. For example, in the opening scene Shakespeare uses the words "signiors and rich burghers" to describe the grandeur of Antonio's merchant vessel,[11] and Fang Ping, a modern translator, faithfully translates these words as "wealthy and powerful landlords and rich men." White meanwhile uses "a majestic high-ranking official" and replaced Shakespeare's "petty traffickers" with "low-ranking officials" in her version: "Look at the merchant ships on the sea, . . . just like a majestic high-ranking official, whose power drives the other small boats, like the low-ranking officials, to retreat most respectfully to the side ways." In a similar manner, Portia, who has inherited a great fortune, is detached from the fortune in White's version and becomes a "girl from high official family" with "good talents and virtue." Bassanio's courting of Portia is originally "to get clear of all the debts I owe,"[12] made very clear in Shakespeare's work and Fang's translation,[13] but White's version skates over this so rapidly as to turn the play into a pure love story with nothing to do with earthly fortune or money.

In order to adapt to the Chinese readers' reading context, White made many simplifications and popularizations in her translation. For instance, in Act II, Scene I, the Prince of Morocco speaks about his skin color in lyrical terms in the original: "The shadow'd livery of the burnish'd sun, / Bring me the fairest creature northward born, / Where Phoebus' fire scarce thaws the icicles, / And let us make incision for your love, / To prove whose blood is reddest, his or mine. . . . this aspect of mine / Hath fear'd the valiant . . . The best regarded virgins of our clime."[14] White's translation simply states: "My face is black because we Africans spend a lot of time basking in the sun. Although my face is black, my blood is the reddest, even the white people cannot be compared with me, and this is the proof of my courage and bravery."

In Act I, Scene I, Antonio's friend utters the witticism "you are sad, / Because you are not merry . . . / you are merry, / Because you are not sad."[15] White's emendation here seems a little strange: "I fear your worries are merely a matter of common cold, and that is why you are not happy." We do not know where this "cold" comes from. But thinking of the Chinese readers who might not understand Shakespeare's inverted chiasmus, it seems that at least we should appreciate the effort of White to put it in an easier way.

Various other complicated Western allusions are erased or abandoned by White, such as the reference to Portia as "Cato's daughter and Brutus' Portia" and to Portia's tresses as "a golden fleece" in Act

I, Scene I,[16] or such as a note to the Greek mythical hero Alcides and a howling Troy in Act III, Scene II,[17] all of which disappear in White's translation. Many biblical allusions are also excised by the translator, who presumably thought they would not aid in transmitting church doctrine, such as Shylock's use of the story of Jacob grazing for his uncle Laban in Act I, Scene III,[18] or the following in Act IV, Scene I, which is hard for Chinese to understand without a footnote: "In christening thou shalt have two godfathers; / Had I been judged, thou shouldst have had ten more, / To bring thee to the gallows, not the font."[19]

In White's version there are some quite profound erasures and additions that merit closer attention. In Act I, Scene II, for example, Portia says, "It is a good divine that follows his own instructions: I can easier teach twenty what were good to be done than be one of the twenty to follow mine own teaching."[20] White's "a good divine" becomes a "pastor," and "Pastors seldom practice what they preach" is not an unreasonable translation either, but the following section changes the meaning entirely: "For instance, if I teach twenty people to do what they should do, I can say whatever I like; but if I want to make one of the twenty really follow my teaching, I am not confident I can succeed." Who is the one who finds it difficult to put into practice what has been learnt or said? In Shakespeare's version it is "I," but in White's version it is the "other" whom "I" have taught. Perhaps White would rather avoid altogether confusing her new Chinese converts with Portia's words. Replacing the self-critical "It is hard for me to follow my own teaching" with "It is hard to make any of my converts really follow my teaching" will do little harm to pastors' teachings but may precisely alarm or caution believers.

Minor changes of words in White's version may also be related to her need to explain Christianity to her Chinese believers. When Bassanio picks up a note in the lead casket, the original reads: "Since this fortune falls to you, / Be content and seek no new. / If you be well pleased with this / And hold your fortune for your bliss, / Turn you where your lady is / And claim her with a loving kiss."[21] Fang's translation is a direct rendition of the original, but White changes "a loving kiss" into "a loving heart" and deliberately adds a further explanation to "be content": "As a human being you should be content." Not only does this add a layer of pastoral teaching, but a close reading also suggests a similar diction and style to the 1919 Chinese Union Version Bible passage: "Now you have such a wife, do not think of any woman in other men's homes. You should be content as a human being. Now this girl is your wife; you should treat her with a loving heart." In Act III, Scene II, Antonio writes a letter to Bassanio, hoping to "see you at my death" but at the same time claiming that "if your love do not persuade you to come, let not my letter." Fang translates this as, "if your love does not approve your presence here, please ignore this letter."[22] White seems to feel that "your love" is not strong enough, so she translates it in a more biblical manner: "If you come, do not come only for my letter, but for your loving heart."

Without close scrutiny, we might barely notice the above subtractions and additions where White erases or blurs the "theological conflict and historical entanglement" between Judaism and Christianity.[23] In the translation she published in *Nü Duo bao*, the story of Jessica and Lorenzo has been deleted completely, and so expressions such as Jessica's "I shall be saved by my husband; he hath made me a Christian"[24] are lost. Nor do we see Shylock's curses, such as "I have a daughter / Would any of the stock of Barabbas / Had been her husband rather than a Christian!"[25] or his complaint, "I'll not be made a soft and dull-eyed fool, / To shake the head, relent, and sign and yield / To Christian intercessors."[26]

More critical is the scene in Act IV, Scene I, when Portia declares judgment on "cutting off the flesh." In Shakespeare's text, the statement is clear: "But, in the cutting it, if thou dost shed / One drop of Christian blood, thy lands and goods / Are, by the laws of Venice, confiscate / Unto the state of Venice."[27] White's erasure is most thought-provoking here: she deletes the word "Christian" and translates the phrase as, "You had better be careful not to drop any blood. If one drop of blood be seen, all your belongings will be confiscated to the state of Venice according to the laws of Venice."

For a Christian missionary and a newspaper aimed at evangelism, the difference between "one drop of Christian blood" and "one drop of blood" is clear. On the other hand, it is even more clear that the spread and teaching of Christianity in China should operate in a non-Christian language sphere and context for the commoners where moral teaching is far more effective than denominational implications. And so it is better to reinforce the contrast between good and evil, lessen any conflicts between old and new or between different Christian traditions, and bypass the doctrinal differences between the Old and New Testament, a strategy that suits the basic aims of *yu jiao yu le* (寓教于乐, to educate through pleasurable activities) or *wen yi zai dao* (文以载道, to illustrate truth through writing). Occurrences of contemptuous terms like "Jew" in the original have been erased by White. When Shylock, for example, realizes that "cutting off the flesh" is not workable, he says:

> SHYLOCK: I take this offer then: pay the bond thrice,
> And let the Christian go.
> BASSANIO: Here is the money.
> PORTIA: Soft!
> The Jew shall have all justice; soft! no haste—
> He shall have nothing but the penalty.[28]

White erases "the Christian" and "the Jew" here. Later, when Portia suggests that Shylock beg the mercy of the Duke of Venice, the Duke says, "That thou shalt see that difference of our spirits, / I pardon thee thy life before thou ask it." Where modern translation may deliberately translate the "spirit" here as "Christian spirit"[29] in order to highlight the difference between Judaism and Christianity, White's translation, however, is: "Now you shall know the difference between you and me. I have forgiven you before you ask for it." Here the attention is the difference between two human beings, having nothing to do with any kind of religious difference.

Why would a Christian missionary deliberately erase in her translation of *Merchant of Venice* such words as "Christian," "Jew," "Christian blood," or "Christian spirit"? This can be due only to the needs of contextualization as White understood them. In her translation, the various additions and erasures seem to have greatly simplified Shakespeare's works, but, even more, they have preserved and highlighted basic moral teachings exhorting people to do good. If White believes these to be fundamental to educating and converting believers, why would she bother with complex threads of religious or Western conflicts, or allow excessively straightforward evangelical teachings to confuse or divert her audience? It is worth noticing that White's efforts at "contextualization" may have complemented the real experience of the acceptance of *Merchant of Venice* in China. Although later translators, unlike those earlier translators who reduced and deleted the text freely, have all tried to present in full the original content, these erasures or additions might have reflected in a more extreme manner the real reading patterns of the common readers, giving specific form to the collective unconsciousness of different language spheres.

For researchers, *Merchant of Venice* is indeed different from Molière's *L'Avare*. Hegel, in comparing Greek drama and Shakespeare's plays with the characters in Roman comedies and Molière's comedies, criticized those "comedies of intrigue" as "actually repulsive when downright evil."[30] From another perspective, the "Praise and Satire" (美刺) of ancient Chinese critical theory might have represented the oriental views on tragedy and comedy in an understanding quite different to that of Sir Edmund Chambers' definition of "medieval" comedy: "Comedy is a poem changing a sad beginning into a happy ending."[31] If "satire" is regarded as the function of comedy, Shylock has no way to laugh with us but could be only a character to be laughed at, which might make Shylock more or less similar to *L'Avare* in its acceptance in China. In this sense, the researcher's differentiation between Shakespeare and Molière, like the analysis on the theological conflict in *Merchant of Venice* by Coghill and others, seems not to have actually influenced the common readers' understanding. On the contrary, the journey of *Merchant of Venice* in this alien land of China may have identified Laura White's policy of inculturation.

The original intention and the "problem consciousness" of the translators when Shakespeare was first introduced to China may remain beyond our understanding today. For instance, when Lin Shu wrote the preface for *Yin bian yan yu* in May 1904 (still in the late Qing dynasty), he said explicitly that he wanted to use Shakespeare as an example to verify the controversial question whether China's "decline and weakness" was the result of "too much effort in imitating the ancient times and too much fear in facing the current challenges" (拟古骇今). Lin's conclusion was that "politics and morality had nothing to do with literature." Lin writes:

> The radical and ambitious young men in our country have been trying their best to renovate and renew the world. They look down upon their ancestors and give up their history. They only want to accept new things. . . . In comparison, the Westerners pay a lot of attention to politics and morality, making their country rich and strengthening their armies so that foreign forces will not have any chance to bully them. Then they start to use their spare time in literature to afford people pleasure. . . . Shakespeare's ideas are old-fashioned given the

> ghosts and gods in the plays. However, the civilized English men do not think his plays crazy or irrational. Rather, they accept his plays with pleasure. . . . The British are pursuing the new political system, and they did not abolish Shakespeare's works. Today I am translating Shakespeare. I hope this will not be rejected by the new scholars in our country.[32]

Lin's comment, "to use their spare time in literature to afford people pleasure," seems to be similar to John Dryden's defense of the "incomparable" Shakespeare and "English dramatic poetry" when these were criticized as "irregular" by French critics. Dryden says, "We, who are a more sullen people, come to be diverted at our Plays; they who are of an airy and gay temper come thither to make themselves more serious."[33] It may be true that any varied understanding of a text may "afford people pleasure," whereas comparative studies should go further to understand the contexts of the varied understandings.

In this case, turning to Lin's preface, we should recognize that "the unanimous consent of an audience is so powerful," in Dryden's phrase. And White's delicate and deliberate efforts in translating furnishes the exact proof that "politics and morality" have much to do with "literature" because only in a given context could we have true contact with a text. Therefore, the translated "donkey head" in White's translation is precisely the entrance for us to understand a transformed text as well as the context that transformed it.

12

TRANSLATION AS TRANS-LITERAL
Radical Formations in Contemporary Chinese Art

Andrew W. Hass

If the essence of translation is, as its linguistic roots indicate, a "bearing across," then the act of translation itself always bears two fundamental questions: How is the bearing achieved? and, What is born in the bearing? These are well-acknowledged questions in any formal consideration of translation, the former in relation to its practice, the latter to its theory. Less acknowledged is what is implicit in the "trans"—the divide that separates the two distinct realms from which and to which the bearing takes place. What is the precise nature of this divide? It is the traditional task of hermeneutics to sound the depths of this chasm, but the translator, herself a kind of hermeneut, is never without a sense of its existence, like the latent vertigo of a traveller skirting the canyon's edge. In what follows we want to bring the question of the divide to bear more fully on the task of bearing, particularly in relation to East-West constructions, and to contemporary Chinese visual art. For what meets the eye in this divide between East and West, or how we are to interpret the visual nature of seeing a language, Chinese and English in particular, is always more than what simple translation—translation reduced merely to semantic equivalence—can bear. Much more. And this "more" requires its own translation, or what we will call its own *trans-literation*, even if it leads us toward, ultimately, an untranslatability.

Divided Language

The cultural divide between China and the West remains obvious, despite all the so-called homogenizing forces of globalization, and even more the linguistic divide, which keeps apart two wholly disparate systems of speaking and writing. Yet we deceive ourselves if we think that these two systems—and for our concerns here, the Chinese script and the English script—can be described solely by an appeal to their respective linguistic and textual elements, radically different as they are. Of course, these elements are the chief concern of the translator as practitioner, the one whose principal goal is linguistico-textual correspondence. And here we reduce the practice to its syntactical and grammatical functions, in order that meaning might find its most unencumbered passage from the one side to the other. But the Chinese script carries another element, equally significant—the visual. And this visual interferes with the pragmatics of translation. For the visual, as pictogrammatic, pushes into view the dark chasm that splits the two systems, so that it no longer rests there in the shadows or outside our line of sight. We might insist that this does not happen literally, for the Chinese script, most would claim, does not visually depict to us a black abyss. But on the other hand, indeed, it does happen *literally*, for what the visual envisions for us is precisely the literal as abyss.

All signification, as semiotic, or as an intricate economy of signs, is, we might say, visual. But the translator is taught to ignore the imagistic nature of the sign and concentrate on signification: the transferring of meaning through the sign as signifier. This is to say that the translator must fixate on what is being born. Now what has been born is what has been carried, and this carrying takes place in a womb, so to speak, hidden from sight: meaning is something that gestates, and after, through labor and delivery, comes into the light of day from within a *chora* that is always beyond the image. We recall that Plato in the *Timaeus* tried to give this *chora*, as a receptacle that allows things to come into being, a certain image—a mother, for example, or gold, or fragrant ointment, or an imprint-bearer. But then he quickly rescinds these images: "For if it [the *chora*] resembled any of the things that enter it, it could not successfully copy their opposites or things of a totally different nature whenever it were to receive them. It would be showing its own face as well. This is why the thing that is to receive in itself all the elemental kinds *must be totally devoid of any characteristics*."[1] Meaning, then, does not emerge from the particularities of a fixed image, a fixed thing. Meaning floats above the specific image in any singularity; the receptacle in translation (the signifier as a visual thing) should be "devoid of any characteristics" (lit. "no form").

Now this void or lack, we know, is ultimately impossible, for the sign must present *something* to us. Unless, however, the something that we see is precisely a void. And here we mean "see" literally—see the void as a literal presentation. This is what the Chinese script opens up to us with its picto-, ideo-, or logographic forms and countless stylistic variations. It visualizes for us the divide, indeed the void, between the visual as the supposed physical receptacle and the meaning that is supposed to enter it but then float above it, move beyond it, situate itself outside it (though we never know quite where). By bringing the visual into view, Chinese script redraws the two sides of the divide, for it is no longer merely about a single signification that needs to find two equivalent linguistico-textual markers, and be borne from the one to the other, in a manner that leaves the chasm behind. It is about the marker, as a visual radical, itself carrying meaning by virtue of its visuality, so that the visual is also what is carried, and carried across the divide to a place—here the alphabetic Latin script—that traditionally has no space for it, no picto-grammatic or ideogrammatic function.

We can find this doubled nature, this internal contradiction, within the *contranym*, that signifier (also called the auto-antonym[2]) that moves in two opposing semantic directions at once. English has its fair share—cleave, fast, oversight, sanction, apology, throw out, radical, etc.—and we have already put one into service: the past participle of the verb "to bear." What is born is what is carried, transported, an existing thing raised and relocated; but what is born is also what has had no prior existence, and what *comes into existence*. The origin of being, therefore, has within the history of English a confusion, for being born must presume existence and at the same time must presume a coming into existence from nothing. This confusion was already present in Plato's discourse on *chora* and, as Derrida unveils, also in the name of *chora* itself as signifier. But in English it takes on a visible feature: to help distinguish the two, an "e" is sometimes added to the former ("borne," as "being carried," "sustained"). It is as if the trouble, the confusion, was too much to bear, and a visual difference had to be introduced.[3]

How does one properly translate a contranym? And how does one translate in or across two opposing directions that are not merely semantic—a single meaning and its contradiction—but also modal—the grammatical and the visual?

The Task of Abandonment

Walter Benjamin's influential essay "Die Aufgabe des Übersetzers" (The Task of the Translator) provides us with a model.[4] The German term *Aufgabe* in the title has contranymic force, as it means either "task" (something that is taken up—a job, a responsibility) or "abandonment," "surrender" (lit. a "giving up").[5] How then to translate this title? If we look to the essay itself for an answer, we see not only that both meanings possible but that both should be retained, simultaneously. As a preface ostensibly to his own translation of Baudelaire's *Tableaux Parisiens*, the essay does not once mention either *Tableaux Parisiens* or its author. Instead, the "task" seems to be toward not the translation of any one specific source language into a designated target language but rather a "translatability" (*Übersetzbarkeit*) that transcends the specificities of any singular linguistic system and strives, even yearns, for a "pure language." This pure language is a community of all languages, languages bound together by some kind of original kinship, or movement,[6] but now available only through a certain renunciation (surrender) of the original specific tongue or script. French theory would call this a surrender of *parole* for the sake of an abiding *langue*, but now a *langue* with no structural (or structuralist) basis because it remains at the level of a translatability, the *in potentia* of a shared and unifying knowledge that nevertheless remains unexpressed and inexpressible, rather than at the level of determinate meaning in any given form or linguistic/grammatical system. Such translatability (*Übersetzbarkeit*), itself a term with virtually no clear or suitable translation, carries us into the realm of the mystical—a Jewish mysticism for Benjamin, as informed by Gershom Scholem and the Kabbalah, but ultimately, if we are following the logic of Benjamin's "task," a mysticism that exceeds and abandons all specificities, even religious ones. To "translate" in this highly indeterminate manner, where ultimately there is no referent for the signifier, where "language as such" is an immediacy beyond any mediating signification, is to bring any specific language to its own unravelling and into an ineffable purity that is at once its own untranslation. For language "to survive suspended precisely over this abyss is its task/abandonment [*Aufgabe*]," Benjamin had written several years earlier.[7]

So the *Aufgabe* goes both ways: it is the translator's task to abandon the pursuit of the fixed and stable meaning through linguistic structure and equivalence, in order that the text, the work of art, might be released, and in turn might release us, into an *immediate* realm of language, a realm that supplies no mediation through word, through sign, or through expression, and therefore a realm that is inexpressible (*Ausdrucklosen*). William Franke insists that this *Aufgabe* is therefore a kind of apophasis:

> The unsayable in language—pure language—is thereby exalted in the most unmistakable manner. Pure language emerges from the act of translation because it is what cannot be expressed directly by any single language alone. Hence translation works as a foregrounding and an apotheosis of an inexpressible layer, a sort of superstratum of pure language. In translation, language signifies a higher language than itself and thereby estranges itself from and even violates its own historical and semantic content. . . . As such, it is revealed as pure—and expressionless. Pure language erases all that is sayable and said: that is how it is manifest—as the "Non-communicable" (*das Nicht-Mitteilbares*) in all languages.[8]

Such a mystical hermeneutics, whereby meaning surrenders itself to an abyss, an inexpressible purity of original divine potency or unutterable Creation beyond human subjectivity, reasoning, and abstraction, nevertheless operates, for Benjamin, from within the linguistic context of historical languages and the written text. Even if the "translation" it manifests is one outside the expressible, a bearing not *across* a divide but *into* that divide as *Abgrund*, as abyss, still, it is possible only through the broken ("fallen," in Benjamin's theology) mediations that make up our many specific languages (*die Sprache des Menschen* versus *die Sprache überhaupt* or "language as such"). Thus Benjamin writes: "It is the task of the translator to release in his own language that pure language which is under the spell of another, to liberate the language imprisoned in a work in his re-creation of that work. For the sake of pure language he breaks through decayed barriers of his own language."[9] To do so requires a certain "free translation," one that frees itself (through *Aufgabe*) from both source and target. This is why, at the end of his essay on "Die Aufgabe," he puts the sacred text forward as the most "unconditionally translatable," for in the truth of the sacred there lies no split between language and revelation; and therefore all meaning is surpassed (as immediate), and what translations might follow should be merely attempts to get us to move "between the lines" of the original and the language into which it is translated. The most effective human translation is thus the interlinear version, Benjamin concludes, since it retains the gap, the divide, the open abyss between the two sides, while uniting "literalness and freedom." "The interlinear version of the Scriptures is the prototype or ideal of all translation," he claims.[10] For it inscribes the *Abgrund*, and it does this literally, which is to say, *visually*, in the empty space that separates the two interlinear systems of signification.[11]

The interlinear presentation is thus a special form of transliteration. In the transliteral process, a visual shift is made across two writing or semiotic systems, whereby the original is retained in the significatory marks of another. This is a halfway house, a dwelling of the original in a graphological system foreign to it. But this process invokes yet another *semiosis*, a system of correspondence that eliminates meaning as the target of any corresponding and instead reduces equivalence to graphic signs and their phonetic associations. The semantic component is suspended (in a moment of *Aufgabe*) so that more visual criteria may proceed, as they are tied to the phonological. Χώρα becomes *chora*, or *khora*, or *khôra*, or *khōra*, for example. This semantic suspension is what is invoked in Benjamin's interlinearity: the central gap draws in both sides like a vortex, leaving the visual component foremost and centralized, yet pointing to nothing. The *trans*-literal enacts a going beyond the literal; the literal becomes visual in the graphemic unit flushed of meaning, if only in a temporary moment of abeyance, but a moment that harbors the very nothing of the pure language. In this sense, transliteration translates contranymically: signification empties itself of itself, signifying, in Macbeth's words, nothing—the nothing between the lines, the nothing of the blank or dead space.

In this transliteration therefore the entire wealth of signification—with all its pictographic, ideographic, logographic, phonologic, and symbolic transferences—comes into play and then recedes. In this recession, as *Aufgabe*, the visual asserts itself as a material force. This is why in the earlier essay "Über Sprache überhaupt und über die Sprache des Menschen," Benjamin can speak of language as coextensive with nature and the material world, for in receding from all meaning, pure language (language as such, *Sprache überhaupt*) divests itself of all mediation, except its own self-mediation, which in its absolute totality is a revelation of itself in its *immediacy*. In this immediacy is the "magical" revelation of the world as such, where name and thing are absolutely transparent to each other (no mediation).[12] The image—which we know is part of the prohibitory structure of Jewish theology—comes to life as a trans-literal event, signifying nothing. This event frustrates even Benjamin's notion of translatability, for the ability to be born across the divide that separates the visual and the nonvisual gives way to a transliterability, the ability to suspend meaning for the sake of the visual—but a visual that is purely self-revelatory, in that it reveals only its visuality, the seeing of semantic suspension. It is this transliterability that the later Heidegger touches upon in his own understanding of language that "speaks," of the thing that "things," of the work of art that "opens," of a truth that unconceals.[13] But what is born into the openness of the event is here, in Benjamin's *Aufgabe*, not even translatable into Being. The trans-literal is the suspension of translation, all translation, even the translation of Being. Or, it is translation *as* suspension, the task of renunciation. This is what the trans-literal allows us to see.

In the logographic features of the Chinese script, features that are complex and combine many variations (pictographs, ideographs, phono-semantic compounds, and manifold derivations), the script as image is not something that will let itself be wholly appropriated by or subsumed into the intangibilities of logocentric meaning. Unless, of course, the image comes back upon the text in an expansionary manner, to "grow" the original, as Benjamin describes it.[14] But this expansion would now carry us beyond the original linguistic parameters, for the pure, mystical language—should any there be—must now incorporate the visual and gestural as material embodiment, or, we might say, must now incorporate the trans-literal. And it is precisely this kind of expansion, this trans-literality between East and West, that certain contemporary Chinese artists have been suggesting, an expansion that is also a subversion, or a negation, or a move to the ineffable beyond all language—an untranslatability.

East-West Translation

Western art historians have long remarked on the distinctive cohabitation of painting and calligraphy in Chinese (and other Eastern) art. But this cohabitation has not always been understood as the confluence it more properly is. Chinese ink drawings are still often categorized within Western volumes as "landscapes" or "nature painting," as if the calligraphic features are mere addenda, philosophic or poetic enhancements of the visual. And this betrays a certain gap that has historically existed between the two traditions of painting, whereby the prestige of one was protected from the foreignness, the exoticism, even, in extremis, the barbarity of the other. An early figure as august as Matteo Ricci in the sixteenth century could say of Chinese artists only that, not knowing how to paint in oil or with shadows, their "paintings are dead and without life."[15] The relatively late contact of Chinese artists with Europe is most often cited as the chief reason for this mutual lack of comprehension and influence. Yet when this contact finally developed, thanks in large part to Jesuit activity at the beginnings of modernity or in the later Ming dynasty, it was the Western missionaries who had the greater initial impact. (Ricci had his portrait painted at least once by Chinese artists—*in oil*, as he impressed upon them.)[16]

But the cultural divide here goes beyond a question of contact: we know that the conception of Chinese ink art as "landscape" was formed chiefly by the *literati* of the Yuan dynasty, those for whom writing (as philosophy and poetry) was inseparable from the image, and who were themselves poet-artists.[17] The word as image was, calligraphically, central to their understanding of high art, and thus European painting stood far below the magisterial heights reached by the Eastern masters. The great six laws or canons of Xie He had long before established this centrality (in the sixth century): the second canon elevated brush technique to a spiritual expression of the individual artist consonant with the vitality of the life force (the first canon) operating between humans and nature, as embodied within Confucian and Daoist texts. The Western masters, for their part, had no logographic framework in which to place such laws, no semiotic principles in which to apprehend the reductions of brush and ink to the gestural strokes that unite the Chinese radicals with the depicted landscapes. Thus, within the "bone method" that is this second canon of the brush, "we have perhaps the most trying and difficult concept, the one that produces the greatest gulf between East and West in the judgment of Chinese painting."[18]

If Chinese artists gave way more readily to Western visual approaches during that modern period of increasing East-West contact—their interest in the nineteenth-century movement of "realism," for example, is now accepted art history—this is because the Western aesthetic was in no position to appreciate its Eastern counterpart until the entire question of representation was later problematized, first by Impressionism. There are unmistakable Chinese influences in those that come after Impressionism—Matisse, for example, as noted even during his career,[19] and certainly Kandinsky and Klee opened up a new relationship between the visual and (non-)representation that, in leading us toward the Abstract Expressionism of succeeding artists like Pollock, drew from an aesthetic that understood very differently how visuality might be rendered. In Klee's words, "Art does not reproduce the visible, rather it makes visible."[20] But if Michael Sullivan is correct, this is less a matter of Western adoption of Chinese philosophy and aesthetic theory than it is a shift in the West's own understanding of nature, as suggested by the revolutions in modern physics concerning the essential reality of material substance and the make-up of the universe, whereby space and time become infinite, so that "our knowledge of them can be but partial and relative" and what "the eye sees at any one point is ephemeral, and so illusory," truths long since maintained in the richness of Eastern (Hindu, Buddhist, Taoist) thought.[21]

But Sullivan might have also pointed to shifts in our understanding of language during this period: words had become no less ephemeral and illusory. If, as Nietzsche had taught, truth can be reduced to the operations of language—"a movable host of metaphors, metonymies, and anthropomorphisms: in short, a sum of human relations which have been poetically and rhetorically intensified, transferred, and embellished"[22]—then the art of language as much as the language of art trades on illusion. "Everything which is good and beautiful depends upon illusion," the young Nietzsche had averred, with requisite irony.[23] Benjamin's subsequent task is very much within this lineage.[24] What we are striving for is not something we can immediately translate into clear and stable truths. It is the ongoing making of translation's possibility through the mythic transformation of language as such. "Translation passes through a continua of transformation, not abstract areas of identity and similarity," Benjamin wrote.[25] This ongoing metamorphosis, this movable host, carries us through the so-called permanence of the "Word" and the "Name." "TAO called TAO is not TAO," begins the *Tao Te Ching*. "Names can name no lasting name."[26] Or in Paul Carus' translation: "The name [*yiu ming*] that can be named is not the eternal Name [*Ming*] / The Unnameable [*wu ming*] is of heaven and earth the beginning," the two, the *yui ming* and the *wu ming*, being "the same in source but different in name."[27] The movement from the one to the other—the Tao is *the way*—bears us to a place *between* all linguistic manifestations, the *between* of interlinearity, the gap in the middle that engulfs us like the sea.[28] From the twentieth century onward, this gap—an increasingly blank space of unsayability or untranslatability, the mysterious sameness of Name and Unnameable, of task and renunciation, of not-Tao and Tao[29]—appears as a gap both dividing and connecting the East (with its linguistic and aesthetic traditions) and the West (with its linguistic and aesthetic traditions).

Radical Language

Contemporary Chinese artists are increasingly occupying this space and doing so in the manner of Benjamin's "expansion": the widening of the interlinear gap between both cultures encroaches on either side equally. This expansion acts upon the two specific languages, Chinese and English, altering both; but it also acts upon the two expressions of the visual and the written. If in the Chinese radical both the visual and the written are "the same in source but different in name," then the idea of a graphic poetics, which Ezra Pound had already begun to develop through imagism—nature is not, pace Hegel, "logical" in its processes, and therefore the Chinese character is better suited to poetry and its concreteness—becomes an intriguing idea for Western thought and art. But the intrigue is also a subversion, a negation, since it shifts us away from a phonocentrism and its corresponding logocentrism, whereby speech is part of self-formation,[30] and moves us instead toward a more concrete rendering of the "illusion" at the core of language's/languages' identity, and indeed our identity as self.

The work of Wenda Gu (b. 1955, Shanghai) is here exemplary.[31] Shortly before his crossing of the seas to the United States in 1987, Gu introduced a series titled *Mythos of Lost Dynasties* into the Chinese art world. The term "mythos" here we must invest with meaning derived from a Western context, in its contrasting relationship with "logos." Influenced by his reading of many Western philosophical texts that had just become available in translation, including Nietzsche, Freud, and Wittgenstein, Gu began what has been called "conceptual ink art," a term that might be misleading, since the revolution Gu helped to launch in fact moves us away from the conceptual nature of language in its traditional linguistic form and purpose. Gu has said:

> My work is concerned with Chinese calligraphy or Chinese words. This interest began in 1982. The first seal I carved consisted of two fake characters. At this time, I was studying the language of philosophy from Russell and Wittgenstein. This coincided with my study of seal script. Seal script is an ancient form of writing that isn't used today; you can't understand it at all. So I thought of the seal script as a fake language. I became really interested in Wittgenstein's theory of the mystery of the universe that cannot be described by language.[32]

In the triptych, or three hanging scrolls, from the *Mythos* series titled *Negative and Positive Characters* (1984–1985), Gu shows us how the calligraphic nature of the Chinese script begins to frustrate conventional linguistic expression and conceptualization:[33]

12.1 Wenda Gu, Mythos *series, work 1*

In the center scroll, we find two Chinese characters, transliterated *zheng* (正) and *fan* (反). When brought together, they can denote either "correct" or "contrary," either "proper" or "improper," either "orthodox" or "unorthodox," either "front" or "back."[34] Such juxtaposition, such expansion, goes well beyond most English contranymic phrases. But Gu does not leave the two characters to interact, and subvert, merely on the linguistic level. On either side are scrolls in which the characters are inverted and then obscured by what appears to be dark human-like figures. The left figure, with what looks like a right hand extended, enfolds the two characters *zheng* and *fan* within the drapery of its form, and perhaps even the radical for "female" (*nü*, 女) around the head;[35] the right figure appears to be a side profile of a human figure walking, though rendered in a manner all too similar to Francis Bacon's contorted or misshapen figures. But if in Bacon "the visible movements of the Figures are subordinated to the invisible forces exerted upon them,"[36] in Gu the forces at work are those that operate between or across the dipolarity of the scripted characters' meaning as much as between or across the dipolarity of the linguistic and the figural, the semantic and the visible. In Gu, the figures fully embody the script itself; they are infused by the script, as if the black ink of the central panel has been siphoned into the forms, drained of their inky color, to de-form both script and human body accordingly. If Bacon's geometry always gives way to the curvature of corporeality, Gu's materiality retains a scripturality, for the geometry of the Chinese characters—never of course a strict geometry, despite the central scroll's rendering—is always materially gestural, as the arms and hands of both forms imply. The yin and the yang of Gu's title (negative and positive) are not so much a cosmic principle, then, as they are the coming together of the modalities of the linguistic script and the gestural body, in order to efface both while at the same time to retain both (negative and positive). In their boldness, both become, we might say contranymically, transparent.

There is, however, a greater mysticism at work in Gu. If Wittgenstein's later understanding of the silence at the heart of our logical, and logocentric, systems of language has informed Gu's understanding of his own language, and indeed of any language, even in the Benjaminian sense of a "pure" language, then the script, as a material, bodily gesture, in the very intercalation between the physical world and the abstraction of semantics, is a portal to something beyond language altogether.

We can see this from another of Gu's scroll pieces in the same *Mythos* series, *Tranquillity Comes from Meditation*. Here again the title, always returning us to the conventions of textual hermeneutics, points us toward something well beyond the linguistic. In this case, we have five large original scrolls (all over nine feet tall) in which Chinese characters frame or hang suspended over a landscape or a cloudscape. Figure 12.2 shows three from that original ink pentad:

12.2 Wenda Gu, Mythos *series, work 2*

The traditions of Chinese landscape painting are clearly visible here, as are the scriptural insertions in those traditions. And the title suggests a deeply religious sense: tranquillity through meditation. But we also have something different from the traditional, for the characters in the paintings are not real Chinese characters. They are pseudo-script. In the center scroll above, titled *Synthesized Words*, the three ideographs hanging in midair are invented characters. "To me," Gu says, "illegible script is more creative, more illusionary and imaginative than normal script. I felt so free when working with illegible words. I thought, 'There must be a meaning, I just don't understand it yet.' "[37] But the striking central element, when combined with the character on its left, has a striking resemblance to the Chinese *shen*, the character for "God," "spirit," "deity," "supernatural," "magic," and so forth within Chinese religion, philosophy, and mythology:

Gu has admitted as much, suggesting that the three cursive-script components might be interpreted for both *shen* and "unobstructed" (*chang*, 畅), the divine spirit as unbound and free.[38] Now there is certainly a political way to read this freedom, and we might even read sexual imagery into the composition (since Gu was reading Freud at the time, and admitted sexual imagery into his work).[39] But a more striking correlation can be made with a twentieth-century artist deeply influenced by Freud, Salvador Dalí, and Dalí's picture *Christ of St. John of the Cross*, itself an expression of mysticism:[40]

12.3 Dalí, Christ of St. John of the Cross

12.4 Wenda Gu, Mythos *series work (middle panel)*

The visual similarities are unmistakable. What makes Dalí's crucifixion so unorthodox, of course, is its mystical location. The cross is suspended in midair, not rooted in the soil of the earth. In fact, that soil is barely visible in the picture, overtaken by water, and clouds, and the dark night sky. The cross hangs in between worlds (just as the boat, at its base, is suspended between dry land and sea). But Jesus is still on that cross, as if the death of the Savior, in being elevated, still remains a death, a death that is not yet a resurrection, but a death that is more than an earthly event: the death of God as a mystical suspension. Moreover, our own perspective is from on high: we look down upon the crucified Christ as though we were situated in the heavens ourselves, casting divine light upon the figure so finely detailed in its human flesh (but not, significantly, in blood). If this is a deity, a *shen* in the Chinese terms of a spirit or supernatural being, it is one whose iconography is disturbed by a radical resituating of the Christ figure and of ourselves who look upon him. We know we are not divine—the human figures at the bottom of the picture remind us of our position—but we nevertheless take up a god-like perspective, as if in union with the divine light. Our path, visually, is not unlike the dark night of the soul described by the mystic Carmelite, the titular St. John of the Cross in his sixteenth-century writings, as we travel from the mundane activities of the earth through the glow of the horizon and into the dark night of the sky, only to emerge, through the body of Christ, into the heavenly light. And yet this passage does not allow us fully to escape its suspended nature. Whatever our mystical transports, we remain bound to that suspended body, whose face and eyes we cannot see. We remain in the darkness that is light, in the light that is darkness.

Ink painting exaggerates this spectral contrast, as the black ink presents itself as nothing other than black, set against the lighter shades of gray and the oppositional white. In Gu's *Synthesized Words*, "God" too is suspended in midair, like the "Word made flesh" of Dalí. But it is *shen* that is pure black, not the night in which it is suspended. And this *shen* is also not *shen*, not the pure character or script, only a spectral image of what it could be. Scripturally, it is between an ideograph and its linguistic referent. Unlike Dalí, whose "vision" assumes the already transferred "Word" into the mystical night that is light, Gu's "Words" remain script, but a script that has no referent that can itself be enscripted. The "synthesis" is—if we affix a Hegelian sense to this term (and Gu has read his Hegel, he acknowledges)[41]—a sublation, an *Aufhebung*, literally a "lifting up" out of its oppositional framework that nevertheless preserves the oppositions: the written and the thought, the visual and the invisible, or, contranymically, the *spectral*.

The juxtaposition here between two competing worlds, their interlinear placement that becomes their trans-literal suspension, necessarily encompasses the two worlds of the East and West. Gu has made it very clear that his understanding of Chinese religion/philosophy, such as the Tao and perhaps even here *shen*, comes through the prism of the West. This is the case for most of his generation, as Western texts, and Western artists, become more available through conventional translation. "Without Nietzsche, without other Western thinkers who look at Asian things, I would probably never have looked into the Chinese tradition and philosophy," Gu has admitted.[42] What then is a suspension in visual and conceptual terms becomes a suspension also in cultural terms. One becomes more Chinese by seeing its traditions through Western lenses; one is more Western by seeing its traditions through Chinese creativity, even Chinese script.

The same dialectical phenomenon is in operation within the works of Gu's contemporary, the renowned Xu Bing (also b. 1955). In his now famous (or infamous) *Book from the Sky* (*Tianshu*) installation (1987–1991), Bing constructs long draping sheets suspended from the ceiling on which is printed a countless number of Chinese characters printed from the old hand-carved printing woodblocks used in traditional publications. On the ground are open books with similar characters, and on the surrounding walls are printed sheets with the same:

12.5 Xu Bing, Book from the Sky *Installation*

One enters the room overwhelmed by the dazzling ubiquity of script and by the sheer contrast of black on white. But when the realization hits that none of the characters are true Chinese characters, that they are all invented ideographs, and that the sheets, the books, the scrolls, the walls, all in fact say nothing intelligible at all, one's initial sensation—which is not dissimilar to Gilles Deleuze's use of the term "sensation" in relation to Bacon ("acting immediately upon the nervous system, which is the flesh")[43]—this sensation turns away from the physical and toward the hermeneutical: How does one interpret this scriptural presentation, so stark in its material expression?

A strong political reading of this work remains customary, more than twenty-five years after its first exhibition, as supported by Bing's firsthand experience of the Cultural Revolution and the oppressive restraints place upon his parents, both university professionals. In evoking canonical writings through homage to traditional printing and its veneration of the written word, Bing seems to suggest that the old traditions of the past are no longer accessible or decipherable.[44] Words from on high give the illusion of truth, but ultimately they obscure the past and leave one bereft of a future. That authorities shut down a Beijing exhibition of this work in 1989 a few months before the Tiananmen Square protests, only to officially condemn it afterward, indicates the far-reaching effects of a subversive interpretation.

Yet the title *Tianshu* is a composite of *Tian* (天)—meaning "heaven" or "sky," or, in religious/philosophical contexts, even "god"—and *shu* (书), meaning "book," "document," "writing," or even "calligraphy." We thus enter similar territory to that of Gu's *Mythos* series, as the unintelligible or illegible script points, in its very illegibility, to something beyond any and all words. The deeply political gives way to something more than subversion, something that enters the mystical, the Benjaminian purity: the pseudo-script invokes a divine language that, in infusing everything (wood, ink, earth, sky, deity), exceeds our ability to grasp it with any regime (grammatical or political), any system, any symbolics, any dogma, any theology.[45]

Bing's move to the United States in 1990 drew him to reflect further on the nature of the Chinese script and its interpretation through non-Eastern eyes. If *Tianshu* took Chinese script outside of its immediate context, through the irony of a "false" return to its traditional context, then his "square word calligraphy" went much further in crossing East with West (see fig. 12.7).

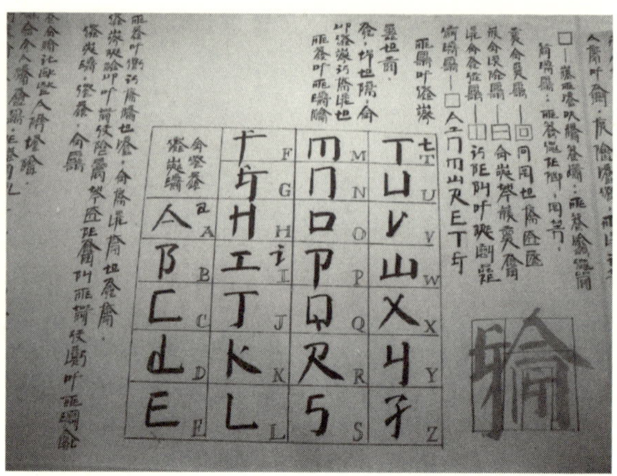

12.6 Xu Bing, Square Word Calligraphy

Here Bing devised a system, a script that put the English alphabet, redrawn with Chinese strokes, into imaginary squares similar to those of Chinese characters. This was both a heuristic exercise and an art, for in helping English readers to orient themselves to the Chinese system, with its traditions of brush, ink, gestural application, and vertical arrangement, it also placed the question of language *between* the distinctions of either culture. This is transliteration taken to its extreme: a fusion of two graphological systems that suspends the suspension of meaning; yet in that very suspension (as negation of negation), meaning is further dispelled, as the system itself, the trans-literal, the literal as visual (the appearance of English as Chinese), becomes the focus, or the *force*, of the work of art. Square word calligraphy thus goes beyond the transference of language across two distinct scripts, and thus two distinct cultural histories—the *Aufgabe* as the narrow determinations of human enterprise, human *task*. As a work of art (Benjamin's abiding concern—*Art des Meinens*[46]), it brings us, by means of the visual, to abandon both language systems altogether for the *Tianshu* of "pure language" that resides in the background space of each square.

In both Gu and Bing, language becomes both a barrier and an opening, both an obfuscation and a clarity, both a validation and a subversion. It is this contranymic feature of language as a whole that suggests a "translatability" exceeding all translation, and that brings us into the purview of a mysticism, whereby presence and absence coexist (the presence of a script that is not a script, of a language that is not a language, of a translation that is not a translation, of a transliteration that is not a transliteration, etc.).

Other contemporary Chinese artists try to exploit this contranymic force, but not with the language of deconstruction, or apophaticism, or even necessarily mysticism, all of which, in the West, rely on a logocentrism (where the *logos* is at root conceptual—the *Logos* of the Greeks). Instead, like the above artists, they utilize the material nature of ink writing and calligraphy, and its stark contrasts between the black strokes and the white surface. In *Writing the "Orchid Pavilion Preface" One Thousand Times* by Qui Zhijie (b. 1969), for example, the artist rewrites over the period of five years (1990–1995) an ancient calligraphy text by the poet Wang Xizhi (303–361). Written for the Orchid Pavilion Gathering in 353, the text became a hallmark of running-cursive calligraphy, which every calligrapher has since aspired to emulate, even though the original was lost soon after its spontaneous composition. Qui, in honoring this tradition, also complicates it, by repeating the lines over and over on the same sheet until the text, and indeed the sheet, is obliterated by an inky over-layering:

12.7 Qui Zhijie, Writing the Orchid

Writing the text, rather than the text as a *fait accompli*, becomes a form of meditative practice, according to Qui, a "written meditation," with Confucian and Buddhist notions of self-cultivation and enlightenment informing the exercise.[47] But any such enlightenment comes with increasing obscuration.

A Mystical Sense

What all these works suggest is that the physical and material nature of language does not merely act as a vehicle or agent for the nonphysical and immaterial sense and meaning that the written script, in all its symbological variations, points us toward. Rather, its very physicality and materiality, in all its gestural manifestations, is part of what is being conveyed in the "sense" of the word, phrase, sentence, character, or text. For we know that, in any hermeneutical context, the English word "sense" too is a contranym, affixed both to the physical and sensate faculties and to the intangible meaning behind that which we perceive with those faculties. Deleuze has tried to capture this *coincidentia oppositorum* in connection to Bacon's art: the *logic* of sensation (making visible the forces of the invisible). Jean-Luc Nancy has worked this out, especially in relation to Hegel's concept of negation, to suggest that we are constantly moving in between these two senses of "sense" and that the very passage between the two is what is "sense" in all its truth, even if it must negate itself in that very movement: "Sense passes between the two, from the one to the other absence of sense, from the one to the other truth." In true Hegelian fashion, "it is sense insofar as it dissolves itself in its operation."[48] The above examples of Chinese art visualize this same phenomenon, the sense of the text retreating in the very sense (and sensation) of its material expression. But in the ink art tradition, the polarization of the senses in play, the contrarieties of black and white, the reduction of the spectrum to its outer spectral extremes, allow for a more emphatic showing of this paradox and, along with this paradox, a more emphatic gesture toward the mystical, that is to say, of the abandonment of all language in the name of a language—in the name of a Word, a *shen*.

Inevitably, such emphasis leads to abstraction. Even divine abstraction. But the abstraction is still material. Consider two examples from either extreme of the spectrum. The work of Qui Shihua (b. 1940), under the influence of a Taoist understanding, commonly features the contrasts of white and black, light and dark, presence and absence, fullness and emptiness, distinction and indistinction. In three untitled works (dated 1996, 2001, and 2002—their lack of title not without significance), Qui first painted three traditional landscape scenes in black: a steep-rising mountain, a lakeside grove of trees, and an expanse of water shimmering in the sun. He then applied thin layers of white paint over and over again, so that the original scenes become all but obliterated, as if a dense fog had rolled in.

Though the effects are easily lost in reproduction, standing before these minimalist canvases produces a remarkable sensation. One begins to sense—in Nancy's sense—the luminosity of the whiteness lose its singularity and uniformity, and the serenity of the blank canvas begin to come alive, as the veiled landscape emerges in its spectral darkness, which remains a transparency, and the silence of the scene takes on a certain resonation. These are not abstract expressionist paintings, in the manner of a Barnett Newman or Mark Rothko, though they may first appear so. Rather, the heightened whiteness against the black both orients and disorients, both obfuscates and opens up, and the sense of another world, spectral and mystical at once, begins to shine forth. This is a veiling that is a profound unveiling.

At the other extreme, the artist Yang Jeichang (b. 1956), also a student of Taoist (and Chan) philosophy, began a series in 1989 commissioned by the Centre Georges Pompidou in Paris, along with other Western and Eastern artists, in which he daily added a fresh layer of ink to the same sheets of paper over an extended period. The result, *100 Layers of Ink*, repeated thrice in 1994, produced the opposite effect to Qui's work above:

12.8 Yang Jeichang, 100 Layers of Ink

The buildup of ink upon ink, of black upon black, creates a highly textured surface, which, though not scriptural in any form, nevertheless develops its own rhythmic contours, its own gestural lines. And like Qui's three pieces, the layering of one extreme eventually leads to the other: the sculptural lines, in their relief, begin to reflect the surrounding light, so that amid all the pitch of darkness there nevertheless emerges its very opposite. The yin and yang duality is no doubt standing behind Yang's approach; but the duality does not stop with the extremes of coloration. The very substance, ink, despite its material application, tacitly points to the language that is in no way rendered here but remains present in association, so that the *sense* of the work is, as Nancy suggests, in the passage between, on the one hand, the ink as an extreme material, layered upon itself to combine two aesthetic modes (sculpted color), and, on the other hand, ink as the progenitor, we might say, of language as script and semiotic transference. To engage with these works is to move in that passage; we make "sense" by being caught up and then tarrying, in its movement, *between* the two worlds, *beyond* the two worlds.

This interlinear passage, between and beyond, is what we might also call an active negation. What is lost, obfuscated, deconstructed, erased, is also, in the process, the very source of creativity that engenders new possibilities out of the abyss. How we read these "texts," then, must be in such a way as to let this active negation abide as a constant force, as it lends its passage to the unknown between and beyond ourselves and our experience.

This negation operates on the origin, as original. This all translators know: to translate is to obliterate the origin, as original, and to set it anew within a possibility it was unaware it had. This newness is what Benjamin meant by translatability, the capacity of a work to usher in its foundational power in a manner that will necessarily alter it, expand it, even negate it, and perhaps go so far as to require that it remain untranslated.[49] But the origin is not solely the source language. As we have seen, it is also the culture that produced it and the medium by which it is produced. In all the works explored above, the origin is sublated. The "East" does not remain East, despite the author's ethnicity or birth place. Neither does the "West" remain West. In the coming together of the scriptural and the visual, and in their mutually active negation of themselves and each other, neither the one nor the other remains original. Both are expanded, as they are contracted within the work. And this expansion, as contraction, leads to plural possibilities and to multiple originations. Hence we might speak of *translatabilities*: not the power of a single, universal ur-source, but manifold potentialities that agitate between and beyond every sense we might give our written and spoken words, every transliteration as translation, whatever their original context and whatever their form of expression.

Our task, then, our *Aufgabe*, is toward *both* a submission and a renunciation of translation's ability, of interpretation's possibility, of transliteration's visuality. This is the task, the radical task, called upon by these contemporary works, beyond the East/West spectrum. For to follow this task is to allow the work and its language, in whatever form, or formation, or de-formation, to live more and to live better, beyond the means of the author, or the medium, or the cultural source.[50] And to allow this is to let the work call us to the potentialities for which we have no name whatsoever. We might call these, provisionally, "mystical." Or we might elicit the Tao. But these names too we must renounce, for the sake of a still greater translation, which bears an all-important silence.

NOTES

INTRODUCTION

1 The phrase is taken from Jonathan D. Spence, *The Chan's Great Continent: China in Western Minds* (New York: W. W. Norton, 1998), 62–80.
2 See Spence, *Chan's Great Continent*, 85.
3 Spence takes the examples of Kafka's short story "The Great Wall of China," Jorge Luis Borges' "The Garden of Forking Paths," and Italo Calvino's visionary return to the China of Marco Polo and Kublai Khan, *Invisible Cities*.
4 Jorge Luis Borges, "The Garden of Forking Paths," in *Labyrinths: Selected Stories and Other Writings*, ed. Donald A. Yates and James E. Irby (Harmondsworth: Penguin, 1970), 49.
5 See ch. 2 below.
6 Borges, "Garden of Forking Paths," 48.
7 See ch. 12 below.
8 See ch. 1 below.
9 Norman J. Girardot, *The Victorian Translation of China: James Legge's Oriental Pilgrimage* (Berkeley: University of California Press, 2002), 495; and David Jasper, ch. 8 below.
10 See further, Peter J. Kitson, *Forging Romantic China: Sino-British Cultural Exchange, 1760–1840* (Cambridge: Cambridge University Press, 2013).
11 See ch. 7 below.
12 Achilles Fang, "Introduction" to *The Confucian Odes* by Ezra Pound (New York: New Directions, 1954), xiii.

1. JEFFREY: POETIC DESIRE AND THE LAWS OF HEAVEN

1 Foreword to Joseph R. Allen, ed., *The Book of Songs: The Ancient Chinese Classic of Poetry* (New York: Grove Press, 1996), xiv. I am further indebted to my graduate assistant Yan Mengyao for assistance with aspects of Chinese philology beyond my ken.

2 James Legge, *The Chinese Classics, with a Translation, Critical and Exegetical Notes, Prolegomena, and Copious Indexes*, vol. 4, *The She-King* (1871; repr., Hong Kong: Hong Kong University Press, 1960). Hereafter cited as Legge, *Odes*.

3 Bernhard Karlgren, *The Book of Odes* (Stockholm: Museum of Far Eastern Antiquities, 1974).

4 Owen Barfield, *Poetic Diction: A Study in Meaning* (Middletown, Conn.: Wesleyan University Press, 1973), 41.

5 Legge, *Odes*, app. 1, pp. 34ff. The interposition of the verbal adjective is Legge's.

6 Legge, *Odes*, app. 1, pp. 34ff.

7 William Wordsworth, Preface to *Lyrical Ballads* (1800).

8 "As the hart panteth after the water brooks / so panteth my soul after thee, O God" (Ps 42:1 KJV).

9 Legge, *Odes*, app. 1, pp. 34ff.

10 Robert Alter, *The Art of Biblical Poetry* (New York: Basic Books, 1985).

11 E.g., *Shi-jing* I.11.3 and 4; also III.3.7; cf. Karlgren's note on *Kiang yu si*, in *Book of Odes*, 13.

12 Barfield, *Poetic Diction*, 29. Cf. Confucius, *Analects* 7.17; 8.7; 9.

13 Barfield, *Poetic Diction*, 28.

14 Max Müller, "On the Enormous Antiquity of the East," *Nineteenth Century* 29 (1891): 808; also in his address to open the Ninth International Congress of Orientalists, London, September 5, 1892, in which he expressed his bewilderment at the unfathomableness of oriental antiquity.

15 Max Müller, Preface to *Sacred Books of the East, Translated, with Introductions and Notes, by Various Oriental Scholars, and Edited by F. Max Müller* (Oxford: Oxford University Press, 1877–1908), 1:xxvi–xxxvii.

16 In James Legge, *Chinese Classics*, vol. 2, *The Works of Mencius* (1861).

17 Norman J. Girardot, *The Victorian Translation of China: James Legge's Oriental Pilgrimage* (Berkeley: University of California Press, 2002), 361. See also John B. Henderson, *Scripture, Canon and Commentary: A Comparison of Confucian and Western Exegesis* (Princeton, N.J.: Princeton University Press, 1991), a work comparable in erudition and insight to Girardot's own volume, and on which he draws (689ff., nn. 63–68).

18 Girardot, *Victorian Translation of China*, 362.

19 S. Robert Ramsey, *The Languages of China* (Princeton, N.J.: Princeton University Press, 1987), 125; cf. Legge, *Odes*, 111. Jerry Norman argues that prior to the late medieval Fukienese scholar Chén Di (1541–1617), "the Chinese lacked any notion of historical change in language; when they encountered discrepancies in the rhymes of verse from different historical eras, they attributed it to the rhyming laxity of ancient poets, or, to put it in another way, they attributed changes in rhyming practice to a gradual development of more strict prosodic standards,

rather than to a change in the language itself." Norman, *Chinese* (Cambridge: Cambridge University Press, 1988), 42. For a guide to the evolution of the characters, see Zhou Youguang, *The Historical Evolution of Chinese Languages and Script*, trans. Zhang Liqing (Columbus: Ohio State University, National East Asian Languages Resource Center, 2003).

20 書= 聿曰, in James Legge, *Chinese Classics*, vol. 3, *The Shoo King* (1865; repr., Hong Kong: Hong Kong University Press, 1960), prolegomena, 1.

21 Legge, *Odes*, 12.

22 Legge, *Odes*, 112.

23 See Bernhard Kalgren, *Philology and Ancient China* (Oslo: Instituttet for Sammenlignende Kulturforskning, 1926), 17.

24 Kalgren, *Philology*, 43, 80. More recently, advances in linguistic recovery have tended to confirm Legge's intuitions; indispensable for the Western student is the work of W. A. C. H. Dobson, *Early Archaic Chinese: A Descriptive Grammar* (Toronto: University of Toronto Press, 1962); and his *Late Archaic Chinese: A Grammatical Study* (Toronto: University of Toronto Press, 1959).

25 Norman, *Chinese*, 57; cf. Legge, *Odes*, 100–102.

26 Legge, *Odes*, 5; prolegomena, 102; cf. Norman, *Chinese*, 42.

27 Legge, *Odes*, 93n; cf. Norman, *Chinese*, 14.

28 Legge, *Odes*, 185n; other examples of Legge's reflection on the evolution of meaning are found throughout his text, but see, e.g., his remarkable notes to the first of the Odes of Chow (*Odes*, 4nn, 5nn).

29 Kalgren, *Philology*, 44. See the first canon of "The Great Preface," cited above, and n. 5.

30 As Lauren F. Pfister notes correctly, "Neither the broader nuances nor the metaphysical implications of the term could be in any way communicated to a Chinese audience by this particular rendering." Pfister, *Striving for "The Whole Duty of Man": James Legge and the Scottish Protestant Encounter with China*, 2 vols. (Frankfurt am Main: Peter Lang, 2004), 1:172. Although *Dao* (道) is not unproblematic as an analogue for *logos* in John, it carries much more of the force of "universal, animating principle." Robert Morrison brought out from 1815–1823 his *A Dictionary of the Chinese Language*, in three parts (Macao: East India Company Press), which was then reprinted in 1865 in Shanghai by the London Mission Press. Of great value to the missionaries, it had severe limitations as a guide to the ancient Chinese classics.

31 Girardot, *Victorian Translation of China*, 26.

32 Fredrick Fyvie Bruce, in a lecture for Regent College, Vancouver, June 1969, at which I was pleased to be present.

33 Girardot, *Victorian Translation of China*, 10 and notes.

34 Girardot, *Victorian Translation of China*, 355.

35 Robert Alter, "The Question of Eloquence in the King James Bible," in *The King James Bible and the World It Made*, ed. David Lyle Jeffrey (Waco, Tex.: Baylor University Press, 2011), 135–48; and, in the same volume, David W. Bebbington, "The King James Bible in Britain from the Late Eighteenth Century," 49–70.

36 Owen quoted in Girardot, *Victorian Translation of China*, 41, 58, 58n100.

37 Legge, "Introduction to the Shi-king," in *Odes* (1871), 23–33.

38 James Legge, *The Religions of China: Confucianism and Taoism Described and Compared with Christianity* (London: Chatto & Windus, 1880); quoted by Girardot, *Victorian Translation of China*, 298.

39 Deborah Shuger, *The Renaissance Bible: Scholarship, Sacrifice and Subjectivity* (Berkeley: University of California Press, 1994; 1998; repr., Waco, Tex.: Baylor University Press, 2012), 5, 26–27.

40 Owen, foreword to Allen, *Book of Songs*, xxiv. The best available study of the poems of love-longing from the *Shi-jing*, in which they are compared to the Hebrew *Shir ha-Shirim* or "Song of Songs," is by Marian Galik, in his *Influence, Translation and Parallels: Selected Studies on the Bible in China* (Sankt Augustin, Germany: Collectanea Serica, 2004), 165–93. See also Zhang Longxi, "The Letter or the Spirit: The *Song of Songs*, Allegoresis, and the *Book of Poetry*," *Comparative Literature* 39, no. 3 (1987): 193–217.

41 Legge was aware of the close parallels between the Genesis account of a universal flood, as well as other archetypal narratives, and the similar account in the *Shoo King*, yet, unlike some of his fellow missionaries, he resists making much of it (*Shoo King*, prolegomena, 74–76). One wonders what he might have made of the recent discovery in a Beijing dialect of words with the same sound and meaning as words in Hebrew (e.g., *yadar* [young girl]; cf. Hebrew *yaldah*, *deba* [murmuring]; cf. Hebrew *dabar*, *duwr* [settlement/small village]; cf. Hebrew *dur*, *dura*, etc.). See the fascinating book by Shi Xuhao (石旭浩), *Shiloh, Jehu Emperor and His Nationality* [石勒皇帝与羯胡人之谜] (Beijing: China Social Press [中国社会出版社], 2011), which traces these and other terms to a nomadic north Chinese people living along the border of Inner Mongolia north of the capital. See http://book.ifeng.com/shuxun/detail_2011_10/09/9703340_0.shtml.

42 E.g., I.3.V.3; Legge, *Odes*, 94.

43 Legge, *Religions of China*, 10–11.

44 Legge, *Odes*, prolegomena, 117.

45 Legge, *Odes*, 452, note to Ode III.1.VII.4.

46 A similar idea is advanced by Yang Huilin in *China, Christianity and the Question of Culture* (Waco, Tex.: Baylor University Press, 2014), 156–57.

47 Preface to the Y-King, in *Sacred Books of the East*, vol. 26 (1882); quoted in Girardot, *Victorian Translation of China*, 336; cf. Yang, *China, Christianity*, 56.

48 Girardot, *Victorian Translation of China*, 34. Throughout this book, unless otherwise notes, all emphasis is in the original.

49 Girardot, *Victorian Translation of China*, 35.

50 II.iv.VIII.4.

51 Legge, *Odes*, 160, 131.

52 James Legge, *Confucianism in Relation to Christianity: A Paper Read before the Missionary Conference in Shanghai, on May 11th, 1877* (Shanghai: Kelly & Walsh, 1877; London: Trübner, 1877), 10. He also thought the ancient Chinese, on these philological grounds, to have been monotheists; see his *Religions of China*, 16–17.

53 For an apt example of what he means, see the poem *Ching min*, III.3.6; Legge, *Odes*, 541.

54 A good reprise may be found in Henrietta Harrison, *The Missionary's Curse and Other Tales from a Chinese Catholic Village* (Berkeley: University of California Press, 2013).

55 Not without some warrant. In 1976 Thomas McClatchie translated the Yi-Qing and, as Girardot unsparingly quotes him, discovered there a Shang-di who was "a filthy hermaphroditic monad" fit only to be compared with the likes of Baal, Jupiter, and Priapus. Giradot, *Victorian Translation of China*, 220.

56 Girardot gives a much more extensive discussion in *Victorian Translation of China*, 44, 278–81; 215ff. In the Chinese Union Version, "God" is translated into *shen* (神). In order to distinguish "God" from pre-Christian gods, the translation puts a space before 神. Interestingly, however, the Chinese Contemporary Version translates "God" into *Shang di* (上帝), thus vindicating Legge's opinion. For another review of Legge's developing convictions, see Wong Man Kong, *A Pioneer at Crossroads of East and West* (Hong Kong: Hong Kong Educational Publishing, 1996), 99–113.

57 *Records of the General Conference of the Protestant Missionaries of China, Held at Shanghai, May 10–14, 1877* (repr., Tapei: Cheng Wen Publishing, 1973), 419. All subsequent citations are taken from this edition. On the similar problem facing Anglo-Saxon as well as modern translators of the Bible, see David Lyle Jeffrey, "Bible Translation and the Future of Spiritual Interpretation," *Modern Theology* 28, no. 4 (2012): 687–706.

58 *Records of the General Conference*, 420.

59 *Records of the General Conference*, 421.

60 *Records of the General Conference*, 423.

61 *Records of the General Conference*, 425.

62 *Records of the General Conference*, 427.

63 Pfister, *Whole Duty of Man*, 2:158. On Legge's exclusion from the published proceedings, see the discussion by Girardot, *Victorian Translation of China*, 218–25; also Lauren Pfister, "Clues to the Academic Achievements of One of the Most Famous Nineteenth Century European Sinologists," *Journal of the Hong Kong Branch of the Royal Asiatic Society* 36 (1993): 180–218.

64 Pfister notes that the Missionary Society was so exercised on hearing Legge's paper read by another member (he was absent) that "they voted in a sub-committee to delete Legge's contribution from the published proceedings" ("Clues to the Academic Achievement," 181), but friends of Legge subsequently voted funds for it to be published in London (see n. 26). The publication consists of only twelve pages of text.

65 Girardot likewise takes this more balanced view. *Victorian Translation of China*, 303.

66 Legge, *Shoo King*, prolegomena, 200.

67 Pfister, "Clues to the Academic Achievement," 194. For a richly informed consideration of the "chasm" itself, see Wei-ming Tu, "Confucian Encounter with the Enlightenment Mentality of the Modern West," *Oriens Extremus* 49 (2010): 249–308; a seminal study.

68 Pfister, "Clues to the Academic Achievement," 188, 201.

69 Pfister, "Clues to the Academic Achievement," 199.

70 Pfister, "Clues to the Academic Achievement," 199.
71 Owen Barfield, *Saving the Appearances: A Study in Idolatry* (New York: Harcourt, Brace & World, 1965), 30–31.
72 Barfield, *Saving the Appearances*, 32.
73 Barfield, *Saving the Appearances*, 33.
74 Barfield, *Saving the Appearances*, 42.
75 Barfield, *Saving the Appearances*, 43.
76 Barfield, *Saving the Appearances*, 57–58.
77 Barfield, *Saving the Appearances*, 89.

2. ZIOLKOWSKI: THE TALE WITHIN A TALE AS UNIVERSAL THEME

1 Étiemble, *Comparaison n'est pas raison: La crise de la littérature comparée* (Paris: Gallimard, 1963), 98–99; Eng.: *Crisis in Comparative Literature* (East Lansing: Michigan State University Press, 1966), 53.
2 Claudio Guillén, "Some Observations on Parallel Poetic Forms," *Tamkang Review* (double issue) 2, no. 2 & 3, no. 1 (1971–1972): 395.
3 Anthony C. Yu, "Problems and Prospects in Chinese-Western Literary Relations" (1974), in idem, *Comparative Journeys: Essays on Literature and Religion East and West* (New York: Columbia University Press, 2009), 96.
4 Bryan Boyd, *On the Origin of Stories: Evolution, Cognition, and Fiction* (Cambridge, Mass.: Belknap Press of Harvard University Press, 2009), 209.
5 Boyd, *On the Origin of Stories*, 208: "[Storytelling] helps us to understand ourselves, to think—emotionally, imaginatively, reflectively—about human behavior, and to step outside the immediate pressures and the automatic reactions of the moment. From pretend play and jokes to Homer, Murasaki, or James Joyce, fiction taps into the swift efficiency of our understanding of agents and actions."
6 Anthony C. Yu, "Introduction" to *The Journey to the West*, trans. and ed. Anthony C. Yu, 4 vols. (1977–1983; 2nd rev. ed., Chicago: University of Chicago Press, 2012), 5; hereafter *JW*.
7 On questions of the *Journey*'s textual history and authorship, see Yu, Introduction to *JW* 17–31.
8 See James Fitzmaurice-Kelly, "Cervantes and Shakespeare" (1916), *Proceedings of the British Academy 1915–1916* (London: Humphrey Milford, Oxford University Press, 1916), 297–317.
9 Anthony C. Yu, *Rereading the Stone: Desire and the Making of Fiction in "Dream of the Red Chamber"* (Princeton, N.J.: Princeton University Press, 1997), xi.
10 C. T. Hsia, *The Classic Chinese Novel: A Critical Introduction* (New York: Columbia University Press, 1968), 116. Nor does Hsia note how closely together in time the *Journey* and the *Quixote* were written. Likening the two works as "satiric fantas[ies] grounded in realistic observation and philosophy," he limits his comparison to noting that they feature equally "memorable . . . pair[s] of complementary characters": Monkey and Pigsy in the one, Don Quixote and Sancho in the other. Hsia's references to Cervantes, Chaucer, and Rabelais in his chapter on the *Journey* are cited by Yu as examples of Hsia's pioneering comparative approach to the Chinese novel; see Athony C. Yu, "Heroic Verse and Heroic Mission:

Dimensions of the Epic in the *Hsi-yu chi*," *Journal of Asian Studies* 31, no. 4 (1972): 879–97; see 881. Yu, incidentally, describes the *Journey*'s Chu Pachieh as "a sort of Falstaff, Don Quixote, and Sancho Panza all rolled into one." Yu, "Religion and Literature in China: The 'Obscure Way' of *The Journey to the West*," in *Tradition and Creativity: Essays on East Asian Civilization: Proceedings of the Lecture Series on East Asian Civilization*, ed. Ching-I Tu (New Brunswick, N.J.: Transaction Books, 1987), 109–54; see 135.

11 André Gide, *Journal, 1889–1939* (Paris: Gallimard, 1951), 41 (translation mine).

12 Lucien Dällenbach, *Le récit spéculaire: Essai sur la mise en abyme* (Paris: Seuil, 1977), 16; Eng.: *The Mirror in the Text*, trans. Jeremy Whiteley with Emma Hughes (Chicago: University of Chicago Press, 1989), 8.

13 Anthony C. Yu refers to this episode as an example of the avenging-ghost-type narrative in his "'Rest, Rest, Perturbed Spirit!' Ghosts in Traditional Chinese Prose Fiction," *Harvard Journal of Asiatic Studies* 47, no. 2 (1987): 397–434; see 415.

14 See *JW* 2:201–2; *Hamlet* 3.2.

15 In Jorge Luis Borges, *Ficciones* (1944), in idem, *Prosa completa*, 2 vols. (Bruguera: Narradas de Hoy, 1980), 1:425–33.

16 See *The Ramayana: A Modern Translation*, Ramesh Menon (San Jose: Writers Club Press, 2001), bk. 7, ch. 38, pp. 681–86.

17 Jorge Luis Borges, "Magias parciales del 'Quijote,'" in idem, *Otras inquisiciones* (1952), in idem, *Prosa completa*, 2:174; Eng.: "Partial Enchantments of the *Quixote*," in idem, *Other Inquisitions 1937–1952*, trans. Ruth L. C. Simms (Austin: University of Texas Press, 1964), 45. As Evelyn Fishburn notes, this passage "continues to baffle" readers, many of whom—including me—have been led by Borges' citation of "night DCII [*la noche*]" to search fruitlessly for this tale in any number of the many different editions of the *Arabian Nights* in various languages. Fishburn, "Readings and Re-readings of Night 602," *Variaciones Borges* 18 (2004): 35–42; quotes on 35–36. Through the typically Borgesian labyrinth of allusions to this tale in a number of essays and stories by Borges, as well as his poem "Metáforas de las mil y una noches," Fishburn traces "Night 602" back to certain editions of the *Arabian Nights* discussed by him: e.g., in the rare edition, Sir Richard Francis Burton, *A Plain and Literal Translation of the Arabian Nights: Entertainments and Supplemental Nights to the Book of the Thousand Nights and a Night*, 17 vols. [12 vols. of the *Nights* + 7 vols. *Supplemental Nights*] (Boston[?]: Burton Club, ca. 1919; a.k.a. "the Luristan Edition"); see the Introduction in vol. 1, pp. 10–12, of the *Nights*, and its repetition in the story "Shahrazad and Shahryar" in vol. 2 (*sic*), pp. 257–72, of the *Supplemental Nights*, esp. 269, where the sultan's epiphany occurs: "By Allah, this story is my story and this case is my case . . . !"; quoted by Fishburn, "Readings and Re-readings," 41; see also Fishburn's "Traces of the *Thousand and One Nights* in Borges," *Variaciones Borges* 17 (2004): 143–58. I am grateful to Daniel Balderston for informing me of Dr. Fishburn's articles on this subject, and to Dr. Fishburn for notifying me afterward that "vol. 2" of the *Supplemental Nights* is inadvertently miscited as "vol. 6" in her "Readings and Re-readings." The latter essay, with the corrected citation, is included in a volume of her essays forthcoming under the title *Hidden Pleasures in Borges's Fictions*.

18 Borges, "Magias parciales del 'Quijote,'" 2:175; "Partial Enchantments," 46.

19 Nathan A. Scott Jr., "Tillich's Legacy and the New Scene in Literature," in *The Thought of Paul Tillich*, ed. James Luther Adams, Wilhelm Puck, and Roger L. Shinn (New York: Harper & Row, 1985), 137–55.

20 *As You Like It* 2.7.139–40.

21 Borges, "Magias parciales del 'Quijote,'" 1:175; "Partial Enchantments," 46. The allusion is most likely to Carlyle's essay "Count Cagliostro" (1833), where, in the voice of his fictive German alter-ego "Sauerteig," Carlyle speaks of "the grand sacred Epos, or Bible of World-History" and "Grand Bible of Universal History." *The Works of Thomas Carlyle*, centenary ed., ed. Henry Duff Traill, 30 vols. (London: Chapman & Hall, 1896–1899), 28:250, 318; see also 250–52. Compare Carlyle's allusions elsewhere to "this 'Bible of Universal History'" (*Past and Present*, in *Works*, 10:240); to "Man's History" as "a perpetual Evangel" (*Sartor Resartus: The Life and Opinions of Herr Teufelsdröckh* [1833–1834], 3.7, in *Works* 1:202); and to history as "a real Prophetic Manuscript" ("On History" [1830], in *Works*, 27:90). Borges elaborates upon this theme, again referencing Carlyle, in his "Del culto de los libros" (1951), in *Otras inquisiciones*, in *Prosa completa*, 2:233; Eng.: "On the Cult of Books," in *Other Inquisitions*, 120.

22 See n. 21.

23 Charles Hartshorne, "Time, Death, and Everlasting Life" (1952), in idem, *The Logic of Perfection* (La Salle, Ill.: Open Court, 1962), 245–62; see esp. 250–53.

24 *JW* 1:141, 159.

25 Friedrich Wilhelm Joseph von Schelling, *System des transzendentalen Idealismus (1800)*, in idem, *Werke*, 3 vols. (Leipzig: Fritz Eckardt, 1907), 2:276; Eng.: *System of Transcendental Idealism*, trans. Peter Lauclan Heath (Charlottesville: University Press of Virginia, 1978), 210. This idea struck Søren Kierkegaard, whose pseudonym Judge William invokes it in Kierkegaard's *Either/Or*, ed. and trans. Howard V. Hong and Edna H. Hong, 2 vols. (Princeton, N.J.: Princeton University Press, 1987), 2:137.

26 G. W. F. Hegel, *Vorlesungen über die Philosophie der Geschichte*, in *Georg Wilhelm Friedrich Hegel's Werke*, ed. Eduard Gans, 18 vols. (Berlin: Dunker & Humblot, 1832–1845), 9:20; Eng.: *Lectures on the Philosophy of History*, trans. J. Sibree (London: George Bell, 1890; repr., 1902), 17. See also, e.g., his references to "Spirit; which has the History of the World for its Theatre [*Schauplatz*]," and "the real theatre of History" (*das wirkliche Theater der Weltgeschichte*), in *Vorlesungen über die Philosophie der Geschichte*, in *Werke*, 52, 97; *Lectures on the Philosophy of History*, 57, 103–4. These and other similar quotations of Hegel's use of the *theatrum mundi* (theater of the world) topos are found in Howard Pickett, "Beyond the Mask: Kierkegaard's Postscript as Anti-theatrical, Anti-Hegelian Drama," in my edited book manuscript, *Kierkegaard, Literature, and the Arts* (forthcoming).

27 See my discussion of this theme in Carlyle, in Eric Ziolkowski, *The Literary Kierkegaard* (Evanston, Ill.: Northwestern University Press, 2011), 137, 215–16, 219.

28 John Calvin, *Institutes of the Christian Religion*, ed. John T. McNeill, trans. Ford Lewis Battles, 2 vols., The Library of Christian Classics 20–21 (Louisville: Westminster John Knox, 1960), 1:61 (1.5.8). Cf. *Institutes*, 1:72 (1.6.2): "this most glorious theater"; 1:179 (1.14.20): "this most beautiful theater"; 1:341 (2.6.1): "[t]his magnificent theater"; and in other works of Calvin.

29 *The Works of John Donne*, ed. Henry Alford, 6 vols. (London: John W. Parker, 1839), 4:538: "Our whole life is but a parenthesis, our receiving of our soul, and delivering it back again, makes up the perfect sentence"; quoted by James Wood, "Why? The Fictions of Life and Death," *New Yorker*, December 9, 2013, 34–39. I am grateful to Anthony Yu for calling my attention to this article in another connection.

30 *The Koran Interpreted*, trans. Arthur J. Arberry (New York: Macmillan, 1955), 239 (emphasis added). Cf. the rendering in Sahih International: "All is in a clear register."

31 33:33; 48:26 (Sahih International).

32 Augustine, *Contra Faustum Manichaeum* 32.20, in *Patrologiae Cursus Completes, Series Latina*, ed. J.-P. Migne, 222 vols. (Paris: Migne, 1844–1864), 42:509.

33 David Damrosch, *The Buried Book: The Loss and Rediscovery of the Great Epic of Gilgamesh* (New York: Henry Holt, 2007), 168.

34 Jean Bottéro, "The Birth of Astrology," in idem et al., *Everyday Life in Ancient Mesopotamia*, trans. Antonia Nevill (Baltimore: Johns Hopkins University Press, 1992), 189; quoted by Damrosch, *Buried Book*, 168.

35 "To Shamash," lines 3–6; in Benjamin R. Foster, ed., *Before the Muses: An Anthology of Akkadian Literature*, 3rd ed. (Bethesda, Md.: CDL Press, 2005), 827 (brackets in text); quoted (without brackets) by Damrosh, *Buried Book*, 168.

36 Scholars have shown little restraint in trying to ensure *Gilgamesh* chronological primacy in the history of secular literature, while at the same time acknowledging the epic's distinctly "modern"-seeming qualities. "For the first time in the history of the world," claimed James B. Pritchard, "a profound experience on such a heroic scale has found expression in a noble style." Pritchard, ed., *The Ancient Near East*, vol. 1, *An Anthology of Texts and Pictures* (Princeton, N.J.: Princeton University Press, 1958), 40. For Nikki Sandars, "[i]f Gilgamesh is not the first human hero, he is the first tragic hero of whom anything is known." Introduction to *The Epic of Gilgamesh*, trans. N. K. Sandars (1960; rev. ed., Harmondsworth: Penguin, 1972), 7. Yet he also seems timeless, "an unsuccessful shaman"—in the late Ioan Couliano's words—"whose deeds . . . fit very well into the Faustian spirit of Western civilization." Couliano, *Out of This World: Otherworldly Journeys from Gilgamesh to Albert Einstein* (Boston: Shambhala, 1991), 52. According to Sabatino Moscati, "The elevated tone of this expression of human misery gives the poem of Gilgamesh a vitality which we could regard as almost modern." Moscati, *The Face of the Ancient Orient: A Panorama of Near Eastern Civilization in Pre-classical Times*, trans. (anon.) (Garden City, N.Y.: Anchor, 1962), 83.

37 Standard Babylonian X 1, in A. R. George, *The Babylonian Gilgamesh Epic: Introduction, Critical Edition and Cuneiform Texts*, 2 vols. (Oxford: Oxford University Press, 2003), 1:679. Hereafter all citations, by tablet (Roman numeral) and verse (Arabic numeral), are of the Standard Babylonian (SB) version of the text as established and translated by George.

38 This famous speech—found in the translated editions by Pritchard (in his *Ancient Near East*, 64), Sandars (*Epic of Gilgamesh*, 102), and Benjamin R. Foster (*The Gilgamesh Epic*, Norton Critical Edition [New York: Norton, 2001], 75)—is from an Old Babylonian version but is not found in SB.

39 SB X 28, trans. George, *Babylonian Gilgamesh*, 1:679: "[. . .] let me learn of [your . . .]."

40 SB X 30–34, 56–57, 62, trans. George, *Babylonian Gilgamesh*, 1:679. Gilgamesh's whole recounting of his adventures encompasses vv. 31–71.

41 SB VIII 52–55, trans. George, *Babylonian Gilgamesh*, 1:655.

42 SB X 113–48 // 213–48, trans. George, *Babylonian Gilgamesh*, 1:685–87, 691–93.

43 Homer, *Odyssey* 8.75–82, 499–520; 9.1–12.453.

44 *Beowulf* 883–914. Seamus Heaney calls attention to this last case of a poem within a poem in his introduction to *Beowulf: A New Verse Translation* (New York: Farrar, Straus & Giroux, 2000), xiii.

45 Vladimir Nabokov, *King, Queen, Knave: A Novel* [*Korol', Dama, Valet* (1928] trans. Dmitri Nabokov in collaboration with the author (New York: McGraw-Hill, 1968), 20–21; quoted by John J. Allen, *Don Quixote: Hero or Fool? A Study in Narrative Technique* (Gainesville: University of Florida Press, 1969), 67.

46 See Anthony C. Yu, "The Quest of Brother Amor: Buddhist Intimations in *The Story of the Stone*," *Harvard Journal of Asiatic Studies* 49, no. 1 (1989): 55–92, esp. 79–81; idem, *Rereading the Stone*, esp. 138–39.

47 See, e.g., Borges, "La muralla y los libros" (1950), in *Prosa completa*, 2:131–33; Eng.: "The Wall and the Books," in *Other Inquisitions*, 3–5.

48 See Borges, "Nueva refutación del tiempo," in *Otras inquisiciones*, in *Prosa completa*, 2:297–98; Eng.: "New Refutation of Time," in *Other Inquisitions*, 184–85; and idem, "Avatares de la tortuga," in *Discusión* (1932), in *Prosa completa*, 1:201n1; Eng.: "Avatars of the Tortoise," in *Other Inquisitions*, 111n2. This last essay does not appear in the Spanish edition of *Otras inquisiciones*.

49 Carlos Fuentes, *Don Quixote, or the Critique of Reading* (Austin: University of Texas Press, 1976), 12; for elaboration see pp. 37–42. On a first level, as in his study at the novel's start, Don Quixote is the master of his reading of chivalry books. On a second level, throughout most of pt. 1, he transforms reality in accordance with that reading (by perceiving windmills as giants, sheep-flocks as armies, etc.) and becomes an actor in his own adventures. On a third level, in pt. 2, ch. 2, he learns of the existence of a book called *Don Quixote* (i.e., the *Quixote*'s first part) and thus, as reader, becomes *read*. On a fourth level, following that discovery, he transforms the real world in accordance not with the reading of chivalry books but with the reading of his own history. On a fifth and final level, the incarnation of his fantasies in reality robs him of his imagination, so that by the time he arrives at the ducal castle, he can *see* that it really is a castle; whereas formerly he could *imagine* that any country inn he chanced to come across was a castle.

50 John J. Allen, "Coping with *Don Quixote*," in *Approaches to Teaching Cervantes' Don Quixote*, ed. Richard Bjornson (New York: Modern Language Association of America, 1984), 45–49; here 47.

51 Allen, "Coping with *Don Quixote*," in Bjornson, *Approaches*. Cf. Allen, *Don Quixote: Hero or Fool?* passim.

52 Américo Castro, "Incarnation in Don Quijote," in *An Idea of History: Selected Essays of Américo Castro*, trans. and ed. Stephen Gilman and Edmund L. King (Columbus: Ohio State University Press, 1977), 23, 26.

53 Castro, "Incarnation in Don Quijote," in Gilman and King, *Idea of History*, 26–27.

54 Castro, "Incarnation in Don Quijote," in Gilman and King, *Idea of History*, 42.
55 Castro, "Incarnation in Don Quijote," in Gilman and King, *Idea of History*, 43.
56 Miguel de Cervantes, *Don Quijote de la Mancha*, new ed., ed. Martín de Riquer, 2 vols. (1959; Barcelona: Juventud, 1979), 1:19. Hereafter *DQ*, from which all translations are mine.
57 Cao Xueqin, *The Story of the Stone: A Chinese Novel*, trans. David Hawkes, 5 vols. (Harmondsworth: Penguin, 1973–1986), 1:47.
58 *DQ* 1:37 (pt. 1, ch. 2). Quoted in Spanish by Yu, *Rereading the Stone*, 172.
59 Yu, "Quest of Brother Amor," 57.
60 Anthony C. Yu, trans., "Liu I-ming on How to Read the *Hsi-yu chi* (*The Journey to the West*)," in *How to Read the Chinese Novel*, ed. David L. Rolston (Princeton, N.J.: Princeton University Press, 1990), 303.
61 *JW* 1:129 (ch. 2):

> "The year I left you all," Wukong said, "I drifted with the waves across the Great Eastern Ocean and reached the West Aparagodānīya Continent. I then arrived at the South Jambūdvīpa Continent, where I learned human ways, wearing this garment and these shoes. I swaggered along with the clouds for eight years, but I had yet to learn the Great Art. I then crossed the Great Western Ocean and reached the West Aparagodānīya Continent. After searching for a long time, I had the good fortune to discover an Old Patriarch, who imparted to me the formula for enjoying the same age as Heaven, the secret of immortality."

62 *JW* 1:179.
63 *JW* 1:192.
64 Anthony C. Yu, "Narrative Structure and the Problem of Chapter Nine in the 'Hsi-Yu Chi,'" *Journal of Asian Studies* 34, no. 2 (1975): 295–311; here 310.
65 See Yu, "Narrative Structure," 295.
66 According to the critic Huang Su-ch'iu, as noted by Yu, "Narrative Structure," 296.
67 *JW* 1:275.
68 The biography of Monkey, initially narrated in *JW*, chs. 1–7, is rehearsed, e.g., in chs. 17, 52, 63, 70, 71, 86, and 94; that of Zhu Bajie, initially narrated in ch. 8, is rehearsed, e.g., in chs. 19, 85, 94; and that of Sha Wujing, likewise initially narrated in ch. 8, is rehearsed in chs. 22, 85, and 94. See also Yu, "Narrative Structure," 296, 308–10.
69 *JW* 2:200–201.
70 *JW* 3:59–60.
71 *JW* 4:358–61.
72 *JW* 4:355–56.
73 *JW* 4:356–57; quote on 357. As Yu points out, this "harmonizing numerical symbolism in the text" is achieved by "reduc[ing] the length of the [actual] pilgrimage [from seventeen years] to fourteen years, making the number of days on the journey 5,048 (i.e., 360 x 14)." *JW* 1:497n129. See also Yu's discussion elsewhere of the popular tradition that "ascribes 5,048 *juan* . . . of Buddhist scriptures to the famous Kaiyuan Catalogue." *JW* 4:396n7.
74 *JW* 1:291.

75 As Guanyin announces to Xuanzang: "I have in my possession Tripitaka, three collections of the Great Vehicle Laws of Buddha." *JW* 1:287 (ch. 12).
76 *JW* 1:390.
77 *JW* 1:293; cf. 1:290.
78 *JW* 4:381.
79 *DQ* 2:1066.
80 Both episodes revolve around the doppelganger device, though the religio-philosophic implications of the accompanying Buddhistic notion of "Two Minds" in the *Journey to the West* episode (*JW* 3:104 [ch. 58]) are of course absent from the *Quixote* episode. Nonetheless, compare the Jade Emperor's unsuccessful attempt to distinguish the two monkeys from one another by means of "the imp-reflecting mirror" (3:107) with the images of reflection invoked by the title of Sansón Carrasco here as Knight of the White Moon and also earlier as Knight of the Mirrors (*el Caballero de los Espejos*; see *DQ*, pt. 2, chs. 12–15)—images "that suggest his aim of forcing Don Quixote to confront his true identity (as an object reflected in a mirror, or sunlight upon the moon), and to give up his illusory self-conception as a knight." Eric Ziolkowski, *The Sanctification of Don Quixote: From Hidalgo to Priest* (University Park: Pennsylvania State University Press, 1991), 165.
81 *DQ* 2:1067.
82 *JW* 1:115.
83 This same point was noted by the Buddha of the Past, Dīpaṁkara, as he overheard Ānanda and Kāśyapa pulling off this prank; see *JW* 4:351–52 (ch. 98).
84 *JW* 4:366.
85 *DQ* 1:6–7.
86 Here I am playing upon Karl Jaspers' famous concept of the ancient Axial Age, on which see Eric Ziolkowski, "Axial Age Theorising and the Comparative Study of Religion and Literature," *Literature and Theology* 28, no. 2 (2014): 129–50; published also in Chinese as "轴心时代的理论化及宗教与文学 的比较研究," trans. Zhang Jing, *Journal for the Study of Christian Culture* (Beijing) 31 (2014): 152–83.
87 See Ziolkowski, *Literary Kierkegaard*, 202–11.
88 Gene Fendt, *Is* Hamlet *a Religious Drama? An Essay on a Question in Kierkegaard* (Milwaukee: Marquette University Press, 1998), 197.
89 Fendt, *Is* Hamlet *a Religious Drama*, 222.
90 See Ziolkowski, *Sanctification of Don Quixote*, 172–83.
91 Ziolkowski, *Literary Kierkegaard*, 127–81; here 167.
92 Yu, "Liu I-ming on How to Read the *Hsi-yu chi*," in Rolston, *How to Read*, 299, 300, 301.
93 Published by the Christian Literature Society, Shanghai.
94 Anthony C. Yu, "Readability: Religion and the Reception of Translation" (1998), in *Comparative Journeys*, 304.

3. LAI: PILGRIMAGE TO HEAVEN

1 David Limon, "Translators as Cultural Mediators: Wish or Reality? A Question for Translation Studies," in *Why Translation Studies Matters*, ed. Daniel Gile, Gyde Hansen, and Nike K. Pokorn (Amsterdam: John Benjamins, 2010), 29.

2 *The Journey to the West* narrates the legendary pilgrimage of Xuanzang (玄奘), a Tang dynasty Buddhist monk, who travels to the "Western Heaven" (India) to fetch true scriptures (Buddhist sūtras), with the superhuman assistance of three disciples, namely Sun Wukong (孫悟空 the Monkey), Zhu Wuneng (豬悟能 the Pig), and Sha Wujing (沙悟淨 Sha Monk), together with the Dragon Horse. For a succinct discussion of its major characters and themes, see William H. Nienhauser Jr., ed., *The Indiana Companion to Traditional Chinese Literature* (Bloomington: Indiana University Press, 1986), 413–17. For the purpose of textual comparison, this paper will refer to Wu Cheng'en (吳承恩), *Xiyou ji* (西遊記) (Hong Kong: Zhonghua shuju, 2007), which is based on the Ming dynasty Shide Tang (世德堂) edition; Huang Zhouxing (黃周星) annotated, *Xiyou ji* (Beijing: Zhonghua shuju, 2009), which is based on the Qing dynasty *Xiyou zhengdao shu* (西遊證道書); and Anthony Yu's authoritative four-volume English translation *The Journey to the West* (Chicago: University of Chicago Press, 1977–1983). For the discussion of the source texts for *Mission to Heaven*, see Hu Chunyan (胡淳艷) and Wang Hui (王慧), "佛耶之間——李提摩太《天國之行》的翻譯傳播" [Between Buddhism and Christianity: The Translation and Distribution of Timothy Richard's *Mission to Heaven*], *Journal of Ming-Qing Fiction Studies* 4 (2012): 238–41. In the use of romanization for Chinese terms in this paper, the standard *hanyu pinyin* is generally adopted, but Timothy Richard's romanization will be followed for discussing specific terms related to *Mission to Heaven*.

3 The other three works are *The Dream of the Red Chamber* (*Honglou meng*, 紅樓夢), *Romance of the Three Kingdoms* (*Sanguo yanyi*, 三國演義), and *Water Margin* (*Shuihu zhuan*, 水滸傳). See Andrew H. Plaks, *The Four Masterworks of the Ming Novel* (Princeton, N.J.: Princeton University Press, 1987).

4 Timothy Richard was instrumental in the reform movement and modernization of China in the late nineteenth and early twentieth centuries. For twenty-five years the secretary of the Christian Literature Society (廣學會, Guangxue hui) in Shanghai, Timothy Richard made great advancements in its publication operations, with a distinct publication strategy targeting literati and officials. Richard influenced the Hundred Days Reform (1898) by his voluminous publications, for which the Chinese literati had an enormous demand. His most influential and widely circulated work was a translation of Robert Mackenzie's *The 19th Century: A History*, titled *Taixi xinshi lanyao* (泰西新史攬要, 1894). The book was submitted by Kang Youwei (康有為, 1858–1927) to the Guangxu emperor, who studied it with care and was very impressed. Required reading for the Changsha literary examination, it was even pirated repeatedly to satisfy the huge social demand, and some one million copies were sold in total. For the life and work of Richard, see Timothy Richard, *Forty-Five Years in China: Reminiscences by Timothy Richard* (London: T. Fisher Unwin, 1916); Timothy Richard, *Conversion by the Million in China: Being Biographies and Articles*, 2 vols. (Shanghai: Christian Literature Society, 1907); William Edward Soothill, *Timothy Richard of China: Seer, Statesman, Missionary and the Most Distinguished Adviser to China* (London: Seeley Service, 1926); Paul R. Bohr, *Famine in China and the Missionary: Timothy Richard as Relief Administrator and Advocate of National Reform, 1876–1884* (Cambridge, Mass.: East Asian Research Center, Harvard University, 1972);

Patrick Hanan, *Chinese Fiction of the Nineteenth and Early Twentieth Centuries* (New York: Columbia University Press, 2004), 76–77.

5 Richard provides a fairly detailed translation of the first seven chapters (depicting the havocs in Heaven that the Monkey caused, the sins he committed, and the punishment he received) and the last three chapters (describing how the pilgrims arrived at the Western Heaven, brought back the scriptures, and finally got canonized). The rest of the novel is heavily abridged. See Timothy Richard, trans., *A Mission to Heaven: A Great Chinese Epic and Allegory* (Shanghai: Christian Literature Society, 1913). An adapted version of *Mission to Heaven* was published titled *Journey to the West: The Monkey King's Amazing Adventures* (North Clarendon, Vt.: Tuttle, 2008). It should be noted that the novel has been abridged from one hundred chapters to twenty-six, while Richard's introduction, most of the translator notes, and special terms embedded with Christian implication were removed.

6 Timothy Richard, trans., *A Mission to Heaven*, "Advertisement: Standard Books on Buddhism."

7 Anthony C. Yu, "Two Literary Examples of Religious Pilgrimage: The *Commedia* and *The Journey to the West*," in *Comparative Journeys: Essays on Literature and Religion East and West*, ed. Anthony C. Yu (New York: Columbia University Press, 2009), 140.

8 Richard, *Mission to Heaven*, xxvii. Richard further elaborates the transformation of individual characters, "turning the proud, masterful monkey to repentance and a right use of his intellectual gifts, converting the low, selfish tastes of the pig into desires for high self-sacrifice, changing the conceit of the dolphin into humility and the stupidity of the dragon into usefulness, so that after all have led lives of service for the salvation of men, they are received into heaven where God rewards them with immortal glory." See Richard, *Forty-Five Years in China*, 343–44.

9 Richard, *Forty-Five Years in China*, 343.

10 Richard, *Forty-Five Years in China*, 344.

11 The first known English translation is Samuel I. Woodbridge, trans., *The Golden-Horned Dragon King; or, The Emperor's Visits to the Spirit World* (Shanghai: North-China Herald Office, 1895), which is the translation of chs. 10 and 11. Herbert Giles translated parts of chs. 7 and 98 for his *A History of Chinese Literature* (New York: D. Appleton, 1901), 282–87. In the mid-twentieth century, a popular abridged translation known as *Monkey* was produced by Arthur Waley. See Arthur Waley, trans., *Monkey* (New York: Grove Press, 1958).

12 See Yu Huaijin (于懷瑾), "論李提摩太對《西遊記》的詮譯" [Timothy Richard's Interpretation and Translation of *The Journey to the West*] (master's thesis, Capital Normal University, China, 2007); Hu Chunyan and Wang Hui, "Between Buddhism and Christianity," 236–51; Li Hui (李暉), "永生' 的寓喻敘事：淺析李提摩太對《西遊記》的翻譯理解方案" [An Allegory of Christian Immortality: Timothy Richard's Scheme of Understanding in His Translation of *Xiyouji*], *Journal of Beijing International Studies University* 8 (2013): 28–35. *Mission to Heaven* was also briefly discussed in Samuel Couling, *The Encyclopaedia Sinica* (Shanghai: Kelly & Walsh, 1917), 241–42, 484; Lin Yutang, *My Country and My People* (New York: Reynal & Hitchcock, 1935), 276.

13 Richard maintained that "the Epic assumes most clearly some of the early fundamentals of the Great Religion (Mahayana Christianity) in pre-Nestorian and post-Nestorian times." See Richard, *Mission to Heaven*, xx. For a recent study of Mahayana Christian theology, see Lai Pan-chiu (賴品超), *Dacheng Jidujiao shenxue: Hanyu shenxue de sixiang shiyan* [大乘基督教神學: 漢語神學的思想實驗, Mahayana Christian Theology: Thought Experiments of Sino-Christian Theology] (Hong Kong: Daofeng shushe, 2011).

14 For the missionary study of Chinese Buddhism, see Joseph Edkins, *Chinese Buddhism: A Volume of Sketches, Historical, Descriptive, and Critical* (London: Trübner, 1880); Ernest J. Eitel, *Handbook of Chinese Buddhism* (London: Trübner, 1888). See also Li Xinde (李新德), "晚清新教傳教士的中國佛教觀" [Late-Qing Protestant Missionaries' Views on Chinese Buddhism], *Religious Studies* 1 (2007): 115–21.

15 With the acquisition of the Buddhist work *The Awakening of Faith* (大乘起信論, *Dacheng qixin lun*), Richard insisted that the book was Christian, though his Buddhist friend Yang Wen Hui contended, "You are reading your own thoughts into the book." See Timothy Richard, *New Testament of Higher Buddhism* (Edinburgh: T&T Clark, 1910), 44–45. In search for a vocabulary of religious terms intelligible to the Chinese, Richard read various Buddhist scriptures, notably spending about an hour a day on studying and copying *The Diamond Sutra* (*Jingang jing*, 金剛經). He also visited a Buddhist Monastery in Wu Tai Shan and recorded in musical notes about the Buddhist rituals. See Richard, *Forty-Five Years in China*, 86, 169.

16 Richard, *New Testament of Higher Buddhism*, 2.

17 Richard, *New Testament of Higher Buddhism*, 39.

18 "With regard to the doctrine of Immortality taught in the New Testament to Western nations—we find that in the Far East, there is what might be called a Fifth Gospel, or 'Lotus Gospel,' which for fifteen centuries has shone throughout the Buddhist world in China, Korea, and Japan with such brilliancy, that countless millions trust to its light alone, for their hope of Immortal Life." Richard, *New Testament of Higher Buddhism*, 134.

19 Richard, *New Testament of Higher Buddhism*, 12–13.

20 Richard, *New Testament of Higher Buddhism*, 15–16.

21 William Edward Soothill, comp., *A Dictionary of Chinese Buddhist Terms* (New York: Paragon Book Gallery, 1976), 210.

22 Richard, *Mission to Heaven*, xxxv–xxxvi.

23 Richard, *New Testament of Higher Buddhism*, 52.

24 Richard, *New Testament of Higher Buddhism*, 66.

25 Richard, *Mission to Heaven*, facing p. 242. A similar dove can be found above the head of Julai in the illustration facing p. 105, depicting "Buddha Provides Sacred Scriptures for the Salvation of Men."

26 Yu, *Journey to the West*, 1:184.

27 Richard, *Mission to Heaven*, 106.

28 Yu, *Journey to the West*, 1:186.

29 Richard, *Mission to Heaven*, 106.

30 Richard, *Mission to Heaven*, xxi.

31 Yu, *Journey to the West*, 1:171–72.

32 The expression "Namah Amitabha" is the formula of faith of the Pure-land sect, representing the believing heart of all beings and Amitabha's power and will to save; people who recite "Amitabha" by the time of dying will be born in the Land of Ultimate Bliss with the reception by Amitabha.

33 Richard, *Mission to Heaven*, 96.

34 Richard, *Mission to Heaven*, 360n. In *New Testament of Higher Buddhism*, ch. 11 ("God's Dwelling Place"), when the name Sâkyamuni appeared in the passage, Richard added the footnote, "Kern says he had not the slightest doubt that by 'Sâkyamuni' here is meant the Supreme Being, God of gods, Almighty and All-wise." *Sacred Books of the East*, vol. 21, Introduction, 28. See Richard, *New Testament of Higher Buddhism*, 190.

35 Richard, *Mission to Heaven*, Introduction, xxxv.

36 "I thank thee, O Father, Lord of heaven and earth, because thou hast hid these things from the wise and prudent, and hast revealed them unto babes" (Matt 11:25 KJV).

37 Richard, *Mission to Heaven*, xxxvi.

38 Richard, *Mission to Heaven*, 260.

39 Soothill, *Dictionary*, 456.

40 "Huge ears, jutting jaw, and a squarelike face; / Broad shoulders, large belly, and a stoutish frame. . . . First among those honored in paradise, / All hail to Maitreya, the laughing priest!" Yu, *Journey to the West*, 3:266.

41 Richard, *New Testament of Higher Buddhism*, 12–13.

42 Richard, *Mission to Heaven*, facing p. 133.

43 Richard, *Mission to Heaven*, xxxvi.

44 Lin Yutang, *My Country and My People* (New York: Reynal & Hitchcock, 1935), 276.

45 Richard, *Mission to Heaven*, 108. Anthony Yu translated the line into "I implore the Bodhisattva to show a little mercy and rescue old Monkey!" See Yu, *Journey to the West*, 1:195.

46 Richard, *Mission to Heaven*, 108. Anthony Yu translated the line into "I beg the Bodhisattva to save me." See Yu, *Journey to the West*, 1:194.

47 Richard, *Mission to Heaven*, 106. However, the importance of good works and merits is emphasized in the original text, "Why don't you come into my fold, take refuge in good works, and follow the scripture pilgrim as his disciple when he goes to the Western Heaven to ask Buddha for the scriptures? I'll order the flying sword to stop piercing you. At the time when you achieve merit, your sin will be expiated and you will be restored to your former position." Yu, *Journey to the West*, 1:190.

48 Richard, *New Testament of Higher Buddhism*, 25. Richard makes reference to the imagery of dry bones in Ezek 37:1-14.

49 Yu, *Journey to the West*, 1:232.

50 Richard, *Mission to Heaven*, 115.

51 According to the Nicene Creed, the Holy Spirit is referred to as "the Lord and Life-Giver." See Colin E. Gunton, ed., *The Cambridge Companion to Christian Doctrine* (Cambridge: Cambridge University Press, 1997), 280–85.

52 Richard, *Mission to Heaven*, xx–xxi.

53 Richard, *Mission to Heaven*, xxxvi. See also the illustration "The Master. Buddhist Monk. First followed Primitive Buddhism, Later converted to Higher Buddhism" (136–37).

54 Richard, *Mission to Heaven*, 359.

55 Richard, *Mission to Heaven*, 134.

56 See Yu Huaijin, "Timothy Richard's Interpretation," 42–44; Hu Chunyan and Wang Hui, "Between Buddhism and Christianity," 248.

57 Richard, *Mission to Heaven*, xxxvi.

58 Richard, *Forty-Five Years in China*, 343.

59 Richard, *Mission to Heaven*, xxxii. The introduction to *Mission to Heaven* has a separate section titled "Lost Nestorian Rediscovered" claiming that there was evidence in ch. 88 and p. 310 to show that *Mission to Heaven* was "not a Bible of Nestorianism but the Pilgrim's Progress of it." See Richard, *Mission to Heaven*, xxxi–xxxii. This section echoes Richard's encounter with a salt manufacturer who was called by Richard a "Lost Nestorian" in his ways of worship. See Richard, *Forty-Five Years in China*, 48–49.

60 Richard, *Mission to Heaven*, 359.

61 Christianity was first introduced to China with the arrival of the Nestorian missionary Allopen to Chang'an during the Tang dynasty in the seventh century. Nestorian Christianity in China was known as Jingjiao (景教). For the history of Nestorian Christianity in China, see Daniel H. Bays, *A New History of Christianity in China* (Malden, Mass.: Wiley Blackwell, 2012), 4–16. For the Protestant missionary study of Nestorianism in China, see James Legge, *The Nestorian Monument of Hsî-an Fû in Shen-hsî, China, Relating to the Diffusion of Christianity in China in the Seventh and Eighth Centuries with the Chinese Text of the Inscription, a Translation, and Notes, and a Lecture on the Monument* (London: Trübner, 1888).

62 Richard, *Mission to Heaven*, xxxii. It is noteworthy that Richard was not the first one to compare *Journey to the West* with *Pilgrim's Progress*. Herbert Giles pinpointed the possible connection between these two works with special reference to Xuanzang's crossing of the river prior to his arrival in the Western Heaven. See Giles, *History of Chinese Literature*, 284.

63 Richard, *Mission to Heaven*, Advertisement: Standard Books on Buddhism. Richard asserted that *Mission to Heaven* was authored by the Yuan dynasty Daoist master Chiu Ch'ang Ch'un (邱長春, a.k.a. 邱處機), who was regarded as a "Taoist Gamaliel who became a Nestorian Prophet and Advisor to the Chinese Court." See Richard, *Mission to Heaven*, title page.

64 Richard, *Mission to Heaven*, xxxii.

65 Richard, *Mission to Heaven*, 310.

66 Yu, *Journey to the West*, 4:223–24.

67 Soothill, *Dictionary*, 333.

68 Richard interpreted "Shen" as "Taoist Saint." See Richard, *Mission to Heaven*, index p. vi.

69 "And the Lord God formed man of the dust of the ground, and breathed into his nostrils the breath of life; and man became a living soul" (Gen 2:7).

70 According to the meditative schools of Daoism, *yuanshen* refers to the spiritual consciousness that exists already before birth and is part of the energy that pervades the whole of the universe. See Ingrid Fischer-Schreiber, *The Shambhala Dictionary of Taoism*, trans. Werner Wünsche (Boston: Shambhala, 1996), 136–37.

71 "Know ye not that ye are the temple of God, and that the Spirit of God dwelleth in you?" (1 Cor 3:16 KJV).

72 Richard, *Forty-Five Years in China*, 343.

73 Theo Hermans, "Translational Norms and Correct Translations," in *Translation Studies: The State of the Art; Proceedings of the First James S. Holmes Symposium on Translation Studies*, ed. Kitty M. van Leuven-Zwart and Ton Naaijkens (Amsterdam: Rodopi, 1991), 166.

74 Richard, *Mission to Heaven*, 309.

75 The lines in the Nestorian monument 真常之道, 妙而難名, 功用昭彰, 強稱景教 were translated as "It is difficult to find a name to express the excellence of the true and unchangeable doctrine; but as its meritorious operations are manifestly displayed, by accommodation it is named the illustrious Religion." See Alexander Wylie, *Chinese Researches* (Shanghai, 1897), pt. 2, p. 27.

76 The first two lines of the original poem 真禪景象不凡同, 大道緣由滿太空 were rendered by Anthony Yu into "The image of true Zen's no common view / The Great Way's causes the cosmos imbue." See Yu, *Journey to the West*, 4:218.

77 Dictionary Department, Institute of Linguistics, Chinese Academy of Social Science, comp., *The Contemporary Chinese Dictionary*, Chinese-English ed. (Beijing: Foreign Language Teaching and Research Press, 2002), 1029.

78 Richard, *Mission to Heaven*, 259. According to the original text, it was not Chin Wu's wife who swallowed a beam of light and gave birth to a child but Chin Wu's mother who swallowed a beam of light and gave birth to Chin Wu. Apparently Richard confused the ambiguous term *huanghou* (皇后), referring to either "queen" or "queen mother" in Chinese. "The august patriarch [Chin Wu] was the offspring of King Pure Joy and Queen Triumphant Virtue, who was conceived with child after she dreamed that she had swallowed the sun." See Yu, *Journey to the West*, 3:256.

79 Richard, *Mission to Heaven*, 259.

80 Theo Hermans, ed., *The Manipulation of Literature: Studies in Literary Translation* (London: Croom Helm, 1985), 11.

81 "And they sung as it were a new song before the throne, and before the four beasts, and the elders: and no man could learn that song but the hundred and forty and four thousand, which were redeemed from the earth" (Rev 14:3 KJV).

82 Richard, *Mission to Heaven*, xxxiii.

83 Some of Richard's translations are grossly far-fetched. E.g., 南無清淨大海眾菩薩 was rendered as "Mohammed of the Great Sea," compared with "Bodhisattvas of the Great Pure Ocean" by Anthony Yu; 摩尼幢佛 was translated as "Him with the Mani canopy," compared with Yu's "Buddha of Jeweled Banner." The term 摩尼 (*mani* in Sanskrit) means "a jewel, gem, precious stone" (esp. a pearl, bead, or other globular ornament). See Soothill, *Dictionary*, 435.

84 Richard, *Mission to Heaven*, xii.

85 Max Müller, ed., *Sacred Books of the East* (Oxford: Oxford University Press, 1879), 1:xxxvii.

86 A. A. Macdonnell, on Max Müller, in *A General Index to the Names and Subject-Matter of the Sacred Books of the East*, comp. M. Winternitz (Delhi: Motilal Banarsidass, 1966), Preface, viii.
87 Apart from studying Buddhist classics, Richard also showed a great enthusiasm in reading the Qur'an and other books on Islam. See Richard, *Forty-Five Years in China*, 86–89.
88 Richard, *Forty-Five Years in China*, 159.
89 Richard, *New Testament of Higher Buddhism*, 190.
90 See Eric J. Sharpe, *Comparative Religion: A History*, 2nd ed. (London: Duckworth, 1986), 35–46; Richard Hughes Seager, *The World's Parliament of Religion: The East / West Encounter, Chicago, 1893* (Bloomington: Indiana University Press, 1995), 67–72.
91 Richard, *New Testament of Higher Buddhism*, 35–36. Richard argued that what China needed was not confined to the spiritual realm but also required social and scientific modernization: "The problem before the missionary in China . . . was not only how to save the souls of a fourth of the human race, but also how to save their bodies . . . and to free their minds. . . . [I]f the nation were liberated from the bonds of ignorance and harmful custom, and were to receive the light of education—scientific, industrial, religious—it might become one of the most powerful nations on earth." Richard, *Forty-Five Years in China*, 7.
92 Lai Pan-chiu, "Timothy Richard's Buddhist-Christian Studies," *Buddhist-Christian Studies* 29 (2009): 34.
93 Richard, *New Testament of Higher Buddhism*, 35–36.
94 Richard, *New Testament of Higher Buddhism*, 138–39.
95 Maria Tymoczko, *Translation in a Postcolonial Context: Early Irish Literature in English Translation* (Manchester: St. Jerome, 1999), 282.
96 Li Hui, "An Allegory of Christian Immortality: Timothy Richard's Scheme of Understanding in His Translation of *Xiyouji*," *Journal of Beijing International Studies University* 8 (2013): 34.
97 Lai, "Timothy Richard's Buddhist-Christian Studies," 35–36.

4. HART: REVISITING THE MISSIONARY STANCE

1 George Steiner, *After Babel: Aspects of Language and Translation*, 2nd ed. (Oxford: Oxford University Press, 1992). See esp. ch. 1.
2 Cited in Steiner, *After Babel*, 181.
3 Steiner, *After Babel*, 264.
4 See further the discussion in Trevor Hart, *Between the Image and the Word: Theological Engagements with Imagination, Language and Literature* (Farnham: Ashgate, 2013), 97–117.
5 See Iris Murdoch, *Metaphysics as a Guide to Morals* (London: Vintage, 2003), 214–15. See, too, her accounts of "attention" and an "other-centred" conception of truth in "On 'God' and 'Good'" and "Against Dryness," in *Existentialists and Mystics* (London: Penguin, 1999), 287–95, 337–62.
6 It seems to me that there is a potential vulnerability here in Murdoch's language of curiosity, lest it seem to connote a mere titillation of the imaginative intellect,

or the gratification of an imaginative itch. Curiosity of the sort she has in mind is more morally robust than anything quite so self-serving.

7 Cited in Lindsay Ride, "Biographical Note," in *The Chinese Classics*, by James Legge (repr., Hong Kong: Hong Kong University Press, 1960), 1:21.

8 Cited in Ride, "Biographical Note," in Legge, *Chinese Classics*, 20.

9 Wang T'ao's tribute to James Legge, cited in Ride, "Biographical Note," in Legge, *Chinese Classics*, 17.

10 Cited in Ride, "Biographical Note," in Legge, *Chinese Classics*, 24.

11 Cited in Ride, "Biographical Note," in Legge, *Chinese Classics*, 9.

12 Cited in Ride, "Biographical Note," in Legge, *Chinese Classics*, 9.

13 Cited in Ride, "Biographical Note," in Legge, *Chinese Classics*, 23.

14 Legge, writing in Hong Kong in 1866. Cited in Ride, "Biographical Note," in Legge, *Chinese Classics*, 1.

15 Tribute to Legge by Wang T'ao, cited in Ride, "Biographical Note," in Legge, *Chinese Classics*, 17.

16 Cf., for instance, Hendrik Kraemer, *Religion and the Christian Faith* (London: Lutterworth Press, 1956), passim.

17 Kraemer, *Religion and the Christian Faith*, 83.

18 James Legge, *The Religions of China: Confucianism and Taoism Described and Compared with Christianity* (London: Hodder & Stoughton, 1880).

19 The view taken by one commentator in *The China Review* VIII.i., p. 59. Cited in Legge, *Religions of China*, 5. Herbert A. Giles concurs with Legge's judgment in broad terms, but finally pulls his punches: "Confucius undoubtedly believed in a Power, unseen and eternal, whom he vaguely addressed as Heaven. . . . His greatest commentator, however, Chu Hsi, has explained that by 'Heaven' is meant 'Abstract Right,' and that interpretation is accepted by Confucianists at the present day." Giles, *A History of Chinese Literature* (London: William Heinemann, 1901), 33.

20 Legge, *Religions of China*, 11.

21 Legge notes, somewhat sniffily, that by comparison Christian worship, "certainly in Protestant circles," is free from "this depraving admixture of the worship of inferior spirits." Legge, *Religions of China*, 255. The qualificatory clause is, of course, rather a significant one.

22 Legge, *Religions of China*, 27.

23 Legge, *Religions of China*, 26–27.

24 Those cited are from 1538 CE, and taken from the Statutes of the Ming Dynasty.

25 Both of these examples are cited in Legge, *Religions of China*, 46–47.

26 See, e.g., William Brown, *The Ethos of the Cosmos: The Genesis of Moral Imagination in the Bible* (Grand Rapids: Eerdmans, 1999); Terrence Fretheim, *God and World in the Old Testament: A Relational Theology of Creation* (Nashville: Abingdon, 2005); Jon Levenson, *Creation and the Persistence of Evil: The Jewish Drama of Divine Omnipotence* (Princeton, N.J.: Princeton University Press, 1994); Michael Welker, *Creation and Reality* (Minneapolis: Augsburg Fortress, 1999).

27 Both of these examples are cited in Legge, *Religions of China*, 50–51.

28 *Shû* IV.iii.2. Cited in Legge, *Religions of China*, 98.

29 *Shû* II.ii.2. Cited in Legge, *Religions of China*, 102.

30 Cited in Giles, *History of Chinese Literature*, 37. Giles notes the view of the philosopher Hsün Tzû (3rd century BC): "By nature man is evil. If a man is good, that is an artificial result." This, though, Giles admits, is a maverick and "heretical" suggestion in terms of the pattern of Confucianism more widely. See Giles, *History of Chinese Literature*, 47.
31 Legge, *Religions of China*, 261.
32 Richard Kearney, *Strangers, Gods and Monsters: Interpreting Otherness* (London: Routledge, 2003), 79–80, esp. 79.
33 Legge, *Religions of China*, 242–43.
34 Kraemer, *Religion and the Christian Faith*, 85.
35 For a related account of the same point, see Charles Taylor's treatment of "metaphysical frameworks" in *Sources of the Self: The Making of Modern Identity* (Cambridge: Cambridge University Press, 1989).
36 Lesslie Newbigin, *The Open Secret: Sketches for a Missionary Theology* (Grand Rapids: Eerdmans, 1978), 184.
37 See, e.g., Michael Polanyi, *Personal Knowledge: Towards a Post-critical Philosophy* (London: Routledge & Kegan Paul, 1958), passim.
38 Kraemer, *Religion and the Christian Faith*, 60.
39 Kraemer, *Religion and the Christian Faith*, 83.
40 Kraemer, *Religion and the Christian Faith*, 80–81.
41 See Ride, "Biographical Note," in Legge, *Chinese Classics*, 10.
42 Cited in Ride, "Biographical Note," in Legge, *Chinese Classics*, 10.
43 Newbigin, *Open Secret*, 196–97.
44 Newbigin, *Open Secret*, 197.
45 Newbigin, *Open Secret*, 198.
46 Newbigin, *Open Secret*, 199.
47 Newbigin, *Open Secret*, 203.
48 Newbigin, *Open Secret*, 206.
49 Newbigin, *Open Secret*, 207.

5. ZHAO: A STUDY ON THE "PREFACE" AND "INTRODUCTION"

1 吴澄 [Wu Cheng], 《道德真经吴澄注》 [Wu Cheng's Commentary on *Daodejing*] (上海: 华东师范大学出版社 [Shanghai: ECNU Press], 2010), 页 15.
2 王韬 [Wang Tao], 《漫游随录》 [Manyousuilu] (长沙: 岳麓书社 [Changsha: Yuelu Press], 1985), 页 43.
3 理雅各 [James Legge],《中国经典》, 卷一至卷五 [The Chinese Classics, vols. 1–5] (上海: 华东师范大学出版社 [Shanghai: ECNU Press], 2011).
4 The prefaces of vols. 1, 2, and 4 are written by Lauren Pfister; those of vols. 3 and 5, by Liu Jiahe (刘家和).
5 James Legge, Preface and Introduction to *The Sacred Books of the East* (New York: Dover, 1961), 39:xi–xxii, 1–44.
6 杨慧林 [Yang Huilin], "读经之'辩'" ["Reasoning" in Reading of Scriptures], 载《基督教文化学刊》 [*Journal for the Study of Christian Culture*] 期 25 (2011): 页 4–5.

7 杨慧林 [Yang Huilin], "中西经文辩读的可能性及其价值" [On the Possibility and Values of Scriptural Reasoning between China and the West], 载《中国社会科学》 [Social Science of China] 期 1 (2011): 页193.

8 James Legge, *The Religions of China: Confuscianism and Taoism Compared with Christianity* (London: Hodder & Stoughton, 1880), 242–43.

9 杨慧林 [Yang Huilin], "读经之'辩' " ["Reasoning" in Reading of Scriptures], 页 6.

10 韦宁 [Ralph Weber], "'经'之局限与理性之局限" [Limits of Scripture and Limits of Reason: On Confucianism and the "Scriptural Reasoning"], 载《基督教文化学刊》 [*Journal for the Study of Christian Culture*] 期 26 (2011): 页 162.

11 Frederic Henry Balfour, trans. and ed., *Taoist Texts, Ethical Political and Speculative* (London: Trübner, 1884).

12 Legge, Introduction, 39.

13 Stanislas Julien, *Le livre des récompenseset des peines* (Paris: Oriental Translation Fund, 1835).

14 Legge, Preface, xi.

15 Legge, Preface, xi.

16 Legge, Preface, xii.

17 Legge, Preface, xii.

18 Legge, Preface, xx–xxi.

19 独与天地精神往来. Legge translated it as, "He chiefly cared to occupy himself with the spirit-like operation of heaven and earth." *The Texts of Taoism*, in *Sacred Books of the East*, 40:228.

20 Legge, Preface, xxii.

21 Cited from Legge, Preface, xv.

22 Legge, Preface, xvi.

23 吴澄 [Wu Cheng], 《道德真经吴澄注》 [Commentary on Daodejing], 页 115.

24 Legge, Preface, xvii.

25 吴澄 [Wu Cheng], 《道德真经吴澄注》 [Commentary on Daodejing], 页 1.

26 Legge, Introduction, 2. See also Legge, *Sacred Books of the East*, 39:61.

27 《孟子·万章上》: 故说诗者, 不以文害辞, 不以辞害志, 以意逆志, 是谓得之; Legge translated it as, "Those who explain the odes, may not insist on one term so as to do violence to a sentence, nor on a sentence so as to do violence to the general scope. They must try with their thoughts to meet that scope, and then we shall apprehend it." See James Legge, *The Chinese Classics* (Taipei: SMC Publishing, 1991), 2:353.

28 《孟子·公孙丑上》: 我知言, 我善养吾浩然之气; Legge translated it as, "I understand words. I am skillful in nourishing vast, flowing passion-nature." Legge, *Chinese Classics*, 2:189.

29 Jiao Hong claimed that "from the Emperor Jing of Han, *Laozi* was beginning to be named as a scripture (*jing*)." Legge accepted this questionable statement. See Legge, Introduction, 8.

30 Legge, Introduction, 18n1.

31 Legge, Introduction, 5n1.

32 See 司马迁 [Sima Qian], 《史记·老子韩非列传》 ["Laozi Han Fei liezhuan" in *Shiji*]. On the question of Laozi's identity, the earliest historical account by Qian already took an unsure voice.
33 See Legge, Introduction, 35.
34 Legge, Introduction, 5. See also Sima, "Laozi Han Fei liezhuan": 老子乃著上,下篇,言道,德之意五千余言而去 ("Then Laozi composed two pieces of work, that is, the upper chapter and the lower chapter, explaining the Tao and its attributes within five thousand characters. And he left").
35 Legge, Introduction, 35.
36 Legge, Introduction, 4.
37 Legge, Introduction, 6 and 8.
38 Norman Girardot, *The Victorian Translation of China: James Legge's Oriental Pilgrimage* (Berkeley: University of California Press, 2002), 430.
39 Girardot, *Victorian Translation of China*, 430.
40 Raper quoted in Legge, Introduction, 12.
41 Legge, Preface, xiii.
42 Rémusat quoted in Legge, Introduction, 12.
43 Stanislas Julien, *Le livre, de la voie et de la vertu* (Paris: l'Imprimerie Royal, 1842), viii–xii.
44 Legge, *Sacred Books of the East,* 39:58.
45 This "Nature" is often rendered into Chinese as 自然 (lit. "self-suchness"), which is also an important concept in *Daodejing* and in Taoism.
46 Legge, Introduction, 14.
47 Legge, *Sacred Books of the East,* 39:68.
48 Hardwick quoted in Legge, Introduction, 13.
49 Legge, Introduction, 41.
50 Legge, Introduction, 13–14.
51 The name "Seneca" seemed to Legge a Western "Laozi," which means "Old Gentleman" in Chinese. See Legge, Introduction, 35.
52 James Legge, *The Notions of the Chinese concerning God and Spirits* (Hong Kong: Hong Kong Register Office, 1852), 32.
53 麦克斯·缪勒 [Max Müller], 《宗教的起源与发展》 [The Origin and Development of Religions], 金泽译 [trans. Jinze] (上海: 上海人民出版社 [Shanghai: Shanghai Renmin Press], 2010), 页 21.
54 Legge, Introduction, 15.
55 Legge, Introduction, 18.
56 Legge, Introduction, 19–21.
57 按道家之术, 杂而多端。 马端临 [Ma Duanlin], 《文献通考》, 下卷 [Wenxiantongkao, vol. 2] (北京: 中华书局 [Beijing: Zhonghuashuju Press], 1986), 页 1729.
58 然则柱史之言, 曷尝有是乎? 盖愈远愈失其真矣。 Duanlin, *Wenxiantongkao*, 1729.
59 许地山 [Xu Dishan], 《道教史》 [The History of Taoism] (南京: 江苏文艺出版社 [Nanjing: Jiangsu Arts Press], 2008), 页 1.
60 Legge, *Religions of China*, 159–60.
61 Legge, *Sacred Books of the East*, 3:xxi.
62 Legge, Introduction, 2.

63 Legge, Introduction, 3.

64 《庄子·天下》: 皆原于一; Legge translated as "the origin of both is the One." See Legge, *Sacred Books of the East*, 40:214.

65 王辉 [Wang Hui], "理雅各的儒教一神论" [On the Confucian Monotheism of James Legge], 载 《世界宗教研究》 [Research of World Religions] 期 2 (2007): 页 134–43.

66 Legge, *Notions of the Chinese*, 23.

67 Legge, *Notions of the Chinese*.

68 Legge, *Notions of the Chinese*, 48.

69 Legge, *Notions of the Chinese*, 50.

70 Legge, *Religions of China*, 248.

71 Legge, *Sacred Books of the East*, 3:xv.

72 Legge, *Religions of China*, 164.

73 Legge, *Religions of China*, 247.

74 Legge, Introduction, 16.

75 Legge, Introduction, 17.

76 Legge, Introduction, 28

77 Legge, Introduction, 43.

78 Legge, Introduction, 44.

79 Girardot, *Victorian Translation of China*, 55.

80 缪勒 [Max Müller], 《宗教学导论》 [Introduction to Religious Studies], 陈观胜, 李培茱译 [trans. Chen Guansheng and Li Peizhu] (上海: 上海人民出版社 [Shanghai: Shanghai Renmin Press], 2010), 页 12.

81 Müller, *Introduction to Religious Studies*, 19.

82 Helen Edith Legge, *James Legge, Missionary and Scholar* (London: Religious Tract Society, 1905), 30.

83 Legge, *Notions of the Chinese*, 33.

84 Legge, Introduction, 29.

85 《论语·卫灵公》. See Legge, *Chinese Classics*, 1:305. In Legge's translation, 道 was rendered as "courses."

86 Legge, Introduction, 29–30.

87 Girardot, *Victorian Translation of China*, 438.

88 Legge, Introduction, 30.

89 鲁迅 [Lu Xun], 《鲁迅全集》, 第九卷 [Complete Works of Luxun, vol. 9] (北京: 人民文学出版社 [Beijing: Renmin Literature Press], 1958), 页 258.

90 Legge, Introduction, 26.

91 Legge, Introduction, 32.

92 Lauren Pfister, *Striving for "The Whole Duty of Man": James Legge and the Scottish Protestant Encounter with China* (Frankfurt am Main: Peter Lang, 2004), 2:229–35.

93 《论语·述而》: 信而好古. See Legge, *Chinese Classics*, 1:195.

94 《礼记·学记》: 一年视离经辨志. See James Legge, *The Sacred Books of the East: The Texts of Confucianism* (Oxford: Clarendon, 1885), 28:83.

6. McLEAN: THE HERMENEUTICS OF TRANSLATING CHRISTIAN THEOLOGY

1 Chloë Starr, "Reading Christian Scriptures: The Nineteenth-Century Context," in *Reading Christian Scriptures in China*, ed. Chloë Starr (London: T&T Clark, 2008), 32–48, esp. 32–33. John T. P. Lai's recent *Negotiating Religious Gaps: The Enterprise of Translating Christian Missionary Tracts by Protestant Missionaries in Nineteenth-Century China* (Sankt Augustin: Institut Monumenta Serica, 2012) is the notable exception to this generalization.

2 Evelyn S. Rawski, "Elementary Education in the Mission Enterprise," in *Christianity in China: Early Protestant Missionary Writings*, ed. Suzanne Wilson Barnett and John K. Fairbank (Cambridge, Mass.: Harvard University Press, 1985), 135–51, esp. 136.

3 Lai, *Negotiating Religious Gaps,* 60.

4 Jane Kate Leonard, "W. H. Medhurst: Rewriting the Missionary Message," in Barnett and Fairbank, *Christianity in China*, 47–59.

5 Patrick Hanan, "The Bible as Chinese Literature: Medhurst, Wang Tao, and the Delegates' Version," *Harvard Journal of Asiatic Studies* 63, no. 1 (2003): 197–239, esp. 208.

6 Walter Medhurst, *China: Its State and Prospects with Especial Reference to the Spread of the Gospel* (Boston: Crocker & Brewster, 1838), 269.

7 Other Christian *Sanzijings* include the *Sanzijing* of the Welsh Christian missionary, Griffith John (杨格非, Yang Gefei zhu, 1831–1912) titled *Yesu sheng jiao sanzijing* (耶穌聖教三字經) (http://nla.gov.au/nla.gen-vn1774941) and the *Sanzijing* of Hong Xiuquan (Franz Michael, "Trimetrical Classic," in *The Taiping Rebellion: History and Documents*, 3 vols. [Seattle: University of Washington Press, 1966–1971], 2:151–62).

8 Ryan Dunch, "Christianizing Confucian Didacticism: Protestant Publications for Women, 1832–1911," *Nan Nü: Men Women and Gender in Early and Imperial China* 11, no. 1 (2009): 65–101, esp. 66.

9 Robert Morrison, *Horae Sinicae: Translations from the Popular Literature of the Chinese* (London: Black & Parry, 1812), 2; Morrison even produced an English translation of it (*Horae Sinicae*, 1–20).

10 The contents of the remaining sections of the *Sanzijing* are as follows: part 2 (三[54-85]), an overview of the Confucian classics studied in school; part 3 (三[87-137]), a summary of the dynastic history of China; part 4 (三[138-74]), a summary of exemplary Confucian behavior; part 5 (三[175-86]), an exhortation to study with diligence.

11 Morrison and Milne's translation, titled *Shentian shengshu* (神天聖書, The Heavenly God Sacred Book) (1823), was based on the *Textus Receptus* of the Greek New Testament and on the English translation of the *Authorized Version* (1611); Robert Morrrison, William Milne, *Shentian shengshu* [神天聖書] (Malacca: Anglo-Chinese College, 1823); cf. Jost Oliver Zetzsche, *The Bible in China: The History of the Union Version or the Culmination of Protestant Missionary Bible Translation in China* (Sankt Augustin: Monumenta Serica Institute, 1999), 38 (available at http://www.streetpreaching.com/morrison/morrison_chinese_bible_1823.htm).

12 Patrick Hanan, "The Bible as Chinese Literature: Medhurst, Wang Tao, and the Delegates' Version," *Harvard Journal of Asiatic Studies* 63, no. 1 (2003): 197–239, esp. 200.

13 Hanan, "Bible as Chinese Literature," 210.

14 Hanan, "Bible as Chinese Literature," 207.

15 G. F. Fitch commenting on the Delegates Version in "On a New Version of the Scriptures in Wen-li," *Chinese Recorder*, August 1885, 298.

16 Medhurst produced this translation with Karl Friedrich August Gützlaff (1803–1851) and Elijah Coleman Bridgman (1801–1861).

17 Hanan, "Bible as Chinese Literature," 200–201.

18 Rawski, "Elementary Education in the Mission Enterprise," in Barnett and Fairbank, *Christianity in China*, 142–43.

19 Alexander Wylie, *Memorials of Protestant Missionaries to the Chinese: Giving a List of Their Publications, and Obituary Notices of the Deceased* (Taipei: Ch'eng-Wen Publishing, 1967), 27, 185.

20 A *Sanzijing* was later published with commentary; cf. Rawski, "Elementary Education in the Mission Enterprise," in Barnett and Fairbank, *Christianity in China*, 146.

21 Available online at http://nla.gov.au/nla.gen-vn1935673.

22 In 1856 Medhurst departed for London owing to health problems, where he died two days after his arrival.

23 M[1, 12, 22, 51, 75, 101, 111, 150, 159].

24 Lauren F. Pfister summarizes James Legge's analysis in his article "Some New Dimensions in the Study of the Works of James Legge (1815–1897)" (in two parts), *Sino-Western Cultural Relations Journal* 12 (1990): 29–50; and 13 (1991): 33–48; see esp. part 1, 48–49; for Medhurst's own view on this subject, see W. H. Medhurst, *A Dissertation on the Theology of the Chinese* (Shanghai: Mission Press, 1934).

25 S. C. Malan, *Who Is God in China, Shin or Shang-Te? Remarks on the Etymology of Theos and Elohim and the Rendering of Those Terms into Chinese* (London, 1855), 33, 38, 286–87.

26 S[11, 25, 27, 36, 41, 44, 51, 59, 63, 67, 71, 106, 113, 118, 120, 121, 123, 125, 127, 129, 133, 136, 137, 164, 168, 178, 200]. Though, perhaps in a nod to her brother-in-law, she does employ the term Shangdi once (S[108]).

27 Irene Eber, "The Interminable Term Question," in *The Bible in Modern China: The Literary and Intellectual Impact*, ed. Irene Eber, Knut Walf, and Sze-kar Wan (Sankt Augustin: Institut Monumenta Serica, 1999), 135–61, esp. 139–42.

28 Hanan, "Bible as Chinese Literature," 213–15.

29 The decision in favor of *Shen* did not have long-lasting consequences, for when Medhurst later organized a new translation project in 1843, culminating in *The Delegates' Version* (involving Medhurst, Bridgman, Milne, and others), the term *Shangdi* was used; cf. Delegates' Version: *Xinyue quanshu* [新舊约聖書, The Holy Bible] (Shanghai: BFBS, 1858; repr., Taipei: BST, 2006).

30 Paul Ricoeur, *On Translation*, trans. Eileen Brennan (London: Routledge, 2006), 4, 18–19, 33; Leovino Ma. Garcia, "On Paul Ricoeur and the Translation-Interpretation of Cultures," *Thesis Eleven* 94 (2008): 73, 77.

31 Ricoeur, *On Translation*, 4.

32 Ricoeur, *On Translation*, 4–5, 21–22.

33 Morrison's translation (which would have been familiar to Medhurst and Martin) is as follows: "In the beginning of man, his nature is good. The operation of his nature is immediate; of custom remote. If not instructed, nature becomes changed. In learning the path of virtue, excellence consists in devoted application of mind." Morrison, *Horae Sinicae*, 5.

34 無不 is unattested in *Sanzijing*.

35 三[29 (bis), 31 (bis), 33, 35, 41 (bis), 77 (bis)].

36 Cf. 1 Thess 4:13–5:11; 1 Cor 15.

37 A minor point of contention arose in the LMS over the correct Chinese word for *baptizo/baptisma* (to baptize/baptism) in Mark 1:9-11 (Matt 3:13-17/Luke 3:21-22). Though the traditional usage was *xi* (洗, to wash), another ancient usage, *rutang* (入湯), which implies baptism by immersion, was preferred by Morrison and Milne. But Medhurst goes his own way, using the compound term *shixi* (施洗, M[120]); cf. Toshikazu S. Foley, *Biblical Translation in Chinese and Greek: Verbal Aspect in Theory and Practice* (Leiden: Brill, 2009), 25–26.

38 "Another scroll was opened, which is the book of life. The dead were judged according to what they had done as recorded in the books."

39 "Then I heard the number of those who were sealed: 144,000 from all the tribes of Israel."

40 Cf. Wylie, *Memorials of Protestant Missionaries*, 40; David K. Y. Chng, "The *Yuenan Youji*: A Rare Book Published in Singapore (1888)," *Archipel* (1992): 43, 131–38, esp. 132.

41 While in Singapore, Sophia Martin married a "Dr. Little" and thereafter was known as Sophia Martin Little. But according to David K. Y. Chng, his name was actually "Whittle" ("Note on Sophia"); cf. David K. Y. Chng, "A Note on Sophia Martin Whittle's *Trimetrical Classic to Instruct Girls*," *Singapore Book World* 17, pt. 1 (1986): 40–42; cf. Sī Jiā, "司佳. 基督教女性三字经体布道文本初探 —以《训女三字经》为例" [A Preliminary Study on Christian Missionary Pamphlets in Trimetrical Chinese: Sophia Martin's *Three-Character Classic for Girls*], 《関西大学文化交渉学教育研究拠点》 [Journal of East Asian Cultural Interaction Studies] 4 (2011): 243–52.

42 According to John Lai, reception to the gospel was better among lower social strata persons and especially among women and girls. Indeed, girls made up a sizable group within the Christian mission schools; cf. Lai, *Negotiating Religious Gaps,* 26.

43 One of these texts was written by Empress Xu (徐后; her imperial title was Empress Renxiao, 仁孝皇后). She was the wife of the Yongle Emperor (永樂), 1403–1424.

44 The first of these texts was written by the daughter of Li Zongbai (李宗白), and the second by Miss Li (李氏), the wife of Yin Gongbi (尹公弼).

45 Tienchi Martin-Liao, "Traditional Handbooks of Women's Education," in *Women and Literature in China*, ed. Anna Gerstlacher, Ruth Keen, Wolfgang Kubin, Margit Miosga, and Jenny Schon (Bochum: Studienverlag Brockmeyer, 1985), 165–89.

46 Perhaps Martin is following Morrison here, whose translation ends "so the man who does not learn, never knows fully the noble exercise of *reason*." Morrison, *Horae Sinicae*, 6. Strangely, Morrison translates 三[13] as follows: "As the rough diamond not cut, never assumes the form of any jewel" (6).

47 Morrison, *Horae Sinicae*, 8.

48 Cf. Marianne Moyaert, "Oneself as Another: The Frailty of Religious Commitments and Its Impact on Interreligious Dialogue," *Ephemerides Theologicae Lovanienses* 86 (2010): 62, 359; Garcia, "On Paul Ricoeur," 73.

49 Jung Chang, *Empress Dowager Cixi: The Concubine Who Launched Modern China* (Toronto: Random House Canada, 2013), 57.

50 "And there is no creature hidden from his sight, but all things are open and laid bare to the eyes of him with whom we have to do" (cf. Ps 139:7).

51 This section closely articulates some of the key ideas of Heb 4:12-13: "For the word of God is living and active and sharper than any two-edged sword, and piercing as far as the division of soul and spirit, of both joints and marrow, and able to judge the thoughts and intentions of the heart."

52 愛: S[21, 35, 73, 90, 96, 100, 102, 111, 133, 134, 137, 170, 173]; 惡: S[8, 9, 54, 62, 74, 77, 82, 86, 90, 92, 98, 104, 170, 173, 176, 188, 195]. In contrast, Medhurst's tract mentions neither.

53 There are other allusions to Scripture in Martin's tract. In the statement "To people comes the Holy divine Spirit. It comes and presses a seal into the center of the heart" (S[67-70]), we find an allusion to either 2 Cor 1:22 ("putting his seal on his, giving us the Spirit in our hearts") or Eph 1:13-14 ("you were marked with the seal of the promised Holy Spirit").

54 富: S[85, 89, 103, 109, 140, 150, 160, 166, 168]; cf. *cai* (財, wealth), S[89], M[36]; *huocai* (貨財), M[36]. In contrast, Medhurst uses the term *fu* (富) only twice (M[58, 71]).

55 貧: S[85, 86, 87, 93, 97, 105, 111, 125, 144, 156]. In contrast, Medhurst uses the term 貧 (poor) only once (M[71]). In contrast, the term *pin* (貧, poor) occurs only once in the *Sanzijing* (*pinqiong*, 貧窮), where it states that one student was so "poor" that he could not afford candles and instead obtained adequate reading light by putting fireflies in a bag and by using the glare from the snow for light, which allowed him to "study unceasingly" (學不輟) (三[151]).

56 While both the *Sanzijing* and Medhurst employ the classical word for "dog," which is *quan* (犬) (M[43]), Martin employs the colloquial term *gou* (狗), which is more appropriate for a story about a beggar. In S[156], Martin translates the Greek term "lick" (*epeleichon*, Luke 16:21) by the term *shi* (舐, lick), while Morrison and the Union Version both prefer *tian* (餂).

57 The system for transliterating Greek terms in this article is explained in B. H. McLean, *New Testament Greek: An Introduction* (New York: Cambridge University Press, 2011), 17–26.

58 *Yuli chao chuan jing shi* (http://nla.gov.au/nla.gen-vn372910); cf. G. W. Clark, "*Yuli* or Precious Records," *Journal of the China Branch of the Royal Asiatic Society* 28 (1893–1894): 233–400; Theodore Hamberg, *The Visions of Hung-sui-tsuen, and Origin of the Kwang-si Insurrection* (Hong Kong, 1854); Mengyuan Rong, "Yan Luo he Yuli" [King Yan Luo and the Jade Record], in *Taiping Tianguo xuekan* 1 (1983): 189–200; Léon Wieger, *Moral Tenets and Customs in China*, trans. L. Davrout (Ho-Kien-fu: Catholic Mission Press, 1913), esp. 119, 347–49, 363–67, 391; Jonathan Spence, *God's Chinese Son: The Taiping Heavenly Kingdom of Hong Xiuquan* (New York: W. W. Norton, 1996), 38–39.

59 Of course, there are also differences between the Buddhist and Christian doctrines of hell. According to the Buddhist version, those who pass through the ten

courts of hell then proceed through the goddess Meng's "Tower of Forgetting," where they are made to forget their previous lives before they are reincarnated back in the world.

60 Moyaert, "Oneself as Another," 356.

61 George Hunter McNeur, *China's First Preacher: Liang A-fa, 1789–1855* (Shanghai: Kwang Hsueh Publishing House, 1934); P. Richard Bohre, "Liang Fa's Quest for Moral Power," in Barnett and Fairbank, *Christianity in China*, 35–46. A translation of Liang Afa's spiritual biography (tract VI) is available in Pei-kai Cheng and Michael Lestz, with Jonathan D. Spence, *The Search for Modern China: A Documentary Collection* (New York: W. W. Norton, 1999), 132–36.

62 Liang Afa, *Quan shi liang yan* [勸世良言, Good Words to Exhort the Age: Nine Miscellaneous Christian Tracts] (Canton: London Missionary Society, 1832; repr., Taiwan, 1965); a summary of the contents of the tract can be found in Ralph R. Covell, *Confucius, Buddha, and Christ: A History of the Gospel in Chinese* (Maryknoll, N.Y.: Orbis, 1986), 115–17.

63 This tract fatefully fell into the hands of Hong Xiuquan, through the efforts of Edwin Stevens. Hong went on to become the leader of the Taiping rebellion, in which 20 million people were killed; cf. Hamberg, *Visions of Hung-Siu-tschuen*, 14–25; Eugene Powers Boardman, *Christian Influence upon the Ideology of the Taiping Rebellion (1851–1864)* (New York: Octagon Books, 1972), 52–105; Vincent Y. C. Shih, *The Taiping Ideology: Its Sources, Interpretations, and Influences* (Tokyo: University of Tokyo Press, 1967), 147–64.

64 Ricoeur, *On Translation*, 4.

65 Moyaert, "Oneself as Another," 376–77.

66 Hans-Georg Gadamer, "The Universality of the Hermeneutic Problem" [1966], in *The Hermeneutic Tradition from Ast to Ricoeur*, ed. Gayle L. Ormiston and Alan D. Schrift (Albany: State University of New York Press, 1990), 147–58, esp. 105.

APPENDIX 1

1 As revised and reprinted in 1857 by *Mohai shuguan* [墨海書館, London Missionary Society Press], Shanghai; obtained from National Library of Australia (nla.gov.au/nla.gen-vn1935673). Printed with permission.

APPENDIX 2

1 Obtained from the Harvard-Yenching Library. Printed with permission.

7. JAY: THE "ISHMAEL" OF SINOLOGY

1 Henry James, "Paris Revisited," in *Parisian Sketches* (London: Rupert Hart-Davis, 1958), 5.

2 Charles Aylmer, "The Memoirs of H. A. Giles," *East Asian History* 13 and 14 (1997): 27.

3 H. A. Giles, *The Civilization of China* (London: Williams & Northgate, 1911), Preface, 9–10, 13–14.

4 E. M. Forster, *Aspects of the Novel* (1927; Harmondsworth: Penguin Books, 1971), 16.

5 The earliest dating of *Beowulf* places it in the eighth century AD, the latest sometime in the eleventh.

6 H. A. Giles, *A History of Chinese Literature* (New York: D. Appleton, 1901), 158.

7 *The Letters of Matthew Arnold*, ed. Cecil Y. Lang, 6 vols. (Charlottesville: University of Virginia Press, 1996–2001), 1:282.

8 Giles produced the interesting concept of "the illiterate reader" to characterize the illiterate Chinese who nevertheless benefitted from "wall literature." Giles, *History of Chinese Literature*, 426.

9 H. A. Giles, *Some Truths about Opium* (Cambridge: W. Heffer & Sons, 1923), 39.

10 Giles, *Civilization of China*, 74–77.

11 For his wife's short story collection, see Aylmer, "Memoirs," 27.

12 First published in 1819. Giles was probably offered the Shanghai edition of 1865.

13 Aylmer, "Memoirs," 8.

14 *Yü-yen Tzŭ-erh Chi: A Progressive Source Designed to Assist the Student of Colloquial Chinese as Spoken in the Capital and the Metropolitan Department* (London: Trübner, 1867).

15 Aylmer, "Memoirs," 8.

16 Within the text of Aylmer, "Memoirs."

17 The Charterhouse Registers, March 1859–May 1863. The website for the school (which is still active) is www.charterhouse.org.uk.

18 Aylmer, "Memoirs," 9–10.

19 Aylmer, "Memoirs," 11. Catherine Giles died in 1882, having given birth to nine children, six of whom survived.

20 Giles' memoirs recounted the occasion when Sir Thomas Wade had sent him an official rebuke for the mistranslation of a Chinese term, in which he had allegedly confused the words for the "captain" of a man-of-war and the "master" of a merchant ship. "I was able by the stroke of a pen to show that Sir. T. Wade had completely misread the Chinese, and in accusing me had made a bad mistake of his own." This exchange was apparently weeded from the Foreign Office file. Aylmer, "Memoirs," 12.

21 See "James Legge," *Oxford Dictionary of National Biography* (Oxford: Oxford University Press, 2004).

22 W. W. Cassels, "Wang: A Chinese Christian," in *China's Millions* (1894), 131–33.

23 M. Broomhall, *W. W. Cassels: First Bishop in Western China* (London: China Inland Mission, 1926), 52–58.

24 By all accounts my grandfather was an extraordinarily charismatic man, who was twice appointed chairman of that mecca of the international evangelical tribes, the Keswick Convention, but it would be safe to surmise that it was his clerical skills, acquired as an articled land surveyor, that originally commended him to Bishop Cassels as his right-hand man.

25 Andrew MacBeath, *W. H. Aldis* (London: Marchall, Morgan & Scott, 1949), 22.

26 MacBeath, *Aldis*, 27.

27 Broomhall, *Cassels*, 42–43.

28 James Legge, *The Life and Teachings of Confucius* (London: Trübner, 1867), 110–11.

29 L. Hidous, *Chinese Recorder* (1914): 371.
30 MacBeath, *Aldis*, 14–18.
31 MacBeath, *Aldis*, 27–28.
32 Kate Aldis died in Paoning on March 8, 1912.
33 MacBeath, *Aldis*, 29.
34 Information from Maria Berl Lee, "Rev. William H. Aldis Memorial Fellowship" (Overseas Missionary Fellowship publication). The fellowship was established by Dr. Yen to commemorate "one of the greatest missionaries England ever sent to China."
35 Stacey Bieler, entry for Yan Yangchu (Y. C. James Yen; 1893–1990), *Biographical Dictionary of Chinese Christianity*, http://www.bdcconline.net/en/stories/y/yan-yangchu.php, accessed April 22, 2015. However, Aldis was prepared to send his own oldest son at age six nearly two thousand kilometers to the CIM school in Chefoo (Yantai), from which he returned only once in four years.
36 He received an honorary degree from St. John's University in Shanghai as early as 1929 and further honorary degrees from Syracuse University, University of Maine, Temple University, and University of Louisville. At Carnegie Hall in New York City, in May 1943, Yan received a Copernican award with nine other "modern revolutionaries," including Albert Einstein, Orville Wright, Walt Disney, Henry Ford, and John Dewey.
37 Lee, "Aldis Memorial Fellowship."
38 Aylmer, "Memoirs," 27.
39 For the first two years the appointment was unsalaried, and for the following thirty-five years he was paid only £200 per annum.
40 David Jasper, "Two Nineteenth-Century English Translations of *The Travels of Fa-Hsien (399–414 AD)*," ch. 8 in this volume.
41 Elise Giles [Lise Boehm], "Of the Noble Army," in *Chinese Coast Tales*, 2 vols. (Shanghai: Kelly & Walsh, 1897–1899), 1:73–132, 96.
42 H. A. Giles, "Confucianism in the Nineteenth Century," in *Great Religions of the World*, by H. A. Giles et al. (New York: Harper & Brothers, 1901), 3–30, 12.
43 Lauren Pfister, *Striving for "The Whole Duty of Man": James Legge and the Scottish Protestant Encounter with China* (Frankfurt am Main: Peter Lang, 2004), 97.
44 I infer this from the style of Giles' own translations and from his remarks (*History of Chinese Literature*, 54) excusing the irregular meter and rhymes in the Chinese poetry between the death of Confucius and the second century BC.
45 E.g., "The Chinese will read almost anything, provided it is set in a faultless frame." Giles, *History of Chinese Literature*, 429.
46 Geng Youzhuang, "Poetically Translating Chinese Texts into the West," ch. 9 in this volume.
47 David E. Pollard, "H. A. Giles and His Translations," in *Europe Studies China*, ed. M. Wilson and J. Cayley (London: Han-Shan Tang, 1995), 492–511.
48 Giles, *History of Chinese Literature*, 23. The French orientalist Albert Étienne Jean Baptiste Terrien de Lacouperie had died in 1894.
49 Aylmer, "Memoirs," 13.
50 The information about Herbert Giles' father and his second father-in-law is derived from their *Oxford Dictionary of National Biography* (2004) entries.

51 Edersheim spent a year in Romania as a missionary to the Jews in the early 1840s, before turning to scholarship, becoming by turn a minister in the Scottish Free Church, then an Anglican clergyman, before being appointed to an Old Testament lectureship at Oxford.
52 Aylmer, "Memoirs," 65.
53 E. Giles, "Of the Noble Army," 1:105.
54 Aylmer, "Memoirs," 65.
55 Aylmer, "Memoirs," 23
56 Trevor Hart, "Revisiting the Missionary Stance," ch. 4 in this volume.
57 T. H. Barrett, "Chinese Religion in English Guise: The History of an Illusion," *Modern Asian Studies* 39, no. 3 (2005): 509–33.
58 E. Giles, "Of the Noble Army," 1:78–79.
59 Giles, "Confucianism," 20, 30, and 23.
60 Giles, "Confucianism," 32.
61 Giles, "Confucianism," 19.
62 Giles, "Religion and Superstition," in *Civilization of China*, 55–79, 55.
63 Giles, *Some Truths about Opium*, 36. Giles may, like Legge, have been an abstainer. He certainly seems disapproving in his *History of Chinese Literature* of the way in which many poets over the ages referred to alcohol as an essential part of their *daemon*. It never seems to have occurred to Giles that this may have become a poetic trope for an inspiration beyond the poet's control. A contemporary review, by a Japanese sinologist, of Giles' *History of Chinese Literature*, suggests that "the drinking habit" adopted by the "drunkard-poet-hermits," spurned by their imperial masters, "seems to have left a permanent effect on the rhymers of succeeding generations. . . . [P]oets, even if sober by nature, as a rule pretend to be drunkards." Teitaro Suzuki, "Discussions," *Monist* 12 (1901): 116–22, https://archive.org/details/jstor-27899288.
64 Ironically, given Giles' admiration for the good consequences of this facet of Chinese tradition, his Wikipedia entry claims that he was on speaking terms, at his death, with only one of the six sons he and his first wife conceived.
65 Giles, "Confucianism," 25.
66 Aylmer, "Memoirs," 29.
67 Aylmer, "Memoirs," 31.
68 E.g., Giles, *History of Chinese Literature*, 57; and his textual animadversions on Griffith John's translation of the Bible into Chinese (p. 29).
69 Giles, *History of Chinese Literature*, 96–97.
70 Giles, *History of Chinese Literature*, 73.

8. JASPER: TWO NINETEENTH-CENTURY ENGLISH TRANSLATIONS OF *THE TRAVELS OF FA-HSIEN (399–414 AD)*

1 Quoted in Helen Edith Legge, *James Legge: Missionary and Scholar* (London: Religious Tract Society, 1905), 205. In 1882 the former diplomat and acknowledged expert in Chinese Buddhism T. W. Rhys Davids was appointed to the nonstipendiary professorship of Pali in the University of London. Legge admitted that he was much indebted to Rhys Davids for his work on Fa-hsien.

2 Norman J. Girardot, *The Victorian Translation of China: James Legge's Oriental Pilgrimage* (Berkeley: University of California Press, 2002), 495.

3 Fa-hsien is Herbert Giles' spelling and will be used as the form of reference in this essay. Legge used the form Fa-hien. The usual modern rendering is Faxian.

4 Xiaofei Tian, "From the Eastern Jin through the Early Tang (317–649)," in *The Cambridge History of Chinese Literature*, ed. Kang-I Sun Chang and Stephen Owen, vol. 1, *To 1375* (Cambridge: Cambridge University Press, 2010), 226.

5 Earlier volumes in the series had covered the literatures of ancient Greece, France, England (modern), Italy, Spain, Japan, Bohemia, Russia, and Sanskrit.

6 H. A. Giles, *A History of Chinese Literature* (London: William Heinemann, 1901), 111.

7 Lauren F. Pfister, *Striving for "The Whole Duty of Man": James Legge and the Scottish Protestant Encounter with China* (Frankfurt am Main: Peter Lang, 2004), 2:117.

8 Giles, *History of Chinese Literature*, 110.

9 Girardot, *Victorian Translation of China*, 531.

10 Legge, who was much exercised by the arguments of the so-called term question regarding the Chinese term for God, was convinced of a fundamental monotheism in the Chinese Ruist tradition. The idea that China was a religionless civilization was a later "myth" arising from the newer scholarship of sinologists like Herbert Giles.

11 James Legge, Introduction to *A Record of Buddhistic Kingdoms* (1886; repr., Teddington, U.K.: Echo Library, 2006), vii.

12 Pfister, *Whole Duty of Man*, 2:222.

13 See further, Girardot, *Victorian Translation of China*, 408–9.

14 E. H. Parker, "M. Terrien de Lacouperie as a Sinologist," *China Review* 13 (1884): 301–5.

15 The Davis Chinese Scholarship in Oxford was established in 1876 by Sir John Davis to encourage greater academic interest in the rather remote study of Chinese literature and language. For some two decades Legge faithfully lectured in Oxford, his audience rarely rising above five people. Max Müller had been, to his intense fury, passed over for the Boden professorship of Sanskrit in Oxford in 1861.

16 Legge, Preface to *Record of Buddhistic Kingdoms*, i.

17 H. A. Giles, bibliographical note to *The Travels of Fa-hsien (399–414 AD)*, trans. H. A. Giles (Cambridge: Cambridge University Press, 1923), xiii. Cambridge University Press republished this edition in 2011.

18 T. H. Barrett, *Singular Listlessness: A Short History of Chinese Books and Scholars* (London: Wellsweep, 1989), 75–76.

19 Barrett, *Singular Listlessness*, 75–76.

20 Legge, Preface to *Record of Buddhistic Kingdoms*, i.

21 Giles, bibliographical note to *Travels of Fa-hsien*, xiii.

22 Giles, bibliographical note to *Travels of Fa-hsien*, xiv.

23 Legge, Preface to *Record of Buddhistic Kingdoms*, ii.

24 Legge, Preface to *Record of Buddhistic Kingdoms*, ii.

25 Ernst J. Eitel, *Handbook for the Student of Chinese Buddhism* (1870).

26 Legge, *Record of Buddhistic Kingdoms*, 24.

27 Legge, *Record of Buddhistic Kingdoms*, 57n270.

28 Herbert Giles, review of Legge's *A Record of Buddhistic Kingdoms,* in *Journal of the North China Branch of the Royal Asiatic Society* (1886): 319.
29 Anonymous review in *Saturday Review,* February 19, 1887, 270–71.
30 Girardot, *Victorian Translation of China,* 415.
31 Giles, Introduction to *Travels of Fa-hsien,* v (emphasis added).
32 Giles, Introduction to *Travels of Fa-hsien,* xvi.
33 Giles, *Travels of Fa-hsien,* 92.
34 Legge, Introduction to *Record of Buddhistic Kingdoms,* ix.
35 James Legge, translator's Preface to *Book of Changes* (*I Ching*) (1882; repr., New York: Bantam, 1969), xcv.
36 Giles, Introduction to *Travels of Fa-hsien,* v.
37 Giles, Introduction to *Travels of Fa-hsien,* vii.
38 Giles, Introduction to *Travels of Fa-hsien,* viii.
39 Giles, Introduction to *Travels of Fa-hsien,* ix.
40 The Ten Commandments of Buddhism, as laid out by Giles (and of which laypeople are bound only by the first five), have considerable overlap with the Ten Commandments of Exodus. But the last five apply solely to monks and include such injunctions as not sitting on a grand couch, not wearing ornamental dress, not wearing jewels, and eating at fixed hours only.
41 Legge, Introduction to *Record of Buddhistic Kingdoms,* vii.
42 Giles, Introduction to *Travels of Fa-hsien,* vi.
43 Legge, *A Record of Buddhistic Kingdoms,* 92–93.
44 *The Religions of China* has its origins in lectures given to the Presbyterian Church in London. Commenting that he himself is not a Presbyterian, Legge states, with ecumenical magnanimity, at the beginning of the book that "he longs to see a frequent interchange of services among ministers of different churches, who are in cordial sympathy in the faith and love of their common Lord." Legge concludes his book with a wish that the mission of the English Presbyterian Church in China may enjoy success, commenting that if the Christian missions to China had not met with enormous success, "we must blame ourselves: the inconsistencies and unrighteousnesses of professors; the selfishness and greed of our commerce; the ambitious and selfish policy of so-called Christian nations." Legge, *The Religions of China, Confucianism and Taoism Described and Compared with Christianity* (London: Hodder & Stoughton, 1880), 310.
45 E.g., John Chalmers of the London Missionary Society (old friend of Legge) and Frederic Henry Balfour.
46 Herbert A. Giles, "The Remains of Lao Tzu Retranslated," *China Review* 14 (1885–1886): 231–81.
47 Legge, Preface to *Record of Buddhistic Kingdoms,* ii.
48 T. S. Eliot, "Religion and Literature," in *Selected Essays,* 3rd ed. (London: Faber & Faber, 1951), 388–401.

9. GENG: POETICALLY TRANSLATING CHINESE TEXTS INTO THE WEST

1 Ernest Fenollosa and Ezra Pound, *"Noh," or, Accomplishment: A Study of the Classical Stage of Japan* (London: Macmillan, 1916), v.

2 "The blossoms of the apricot" is here a metaphor for Confucianism, since it is said that Confucian gave lectures to his pupils in an apricot pavilion, which is meant to be the place of teaching by a master in later China.
3 Ezra Pound, *The Cantos of Ezra Pound* (London: Faber & Faber, 1975), 60.
4 John Dryden, "Preface to the Translation of Ovid's Epistles," in *Essays of John Dryden*, ed. W. P. Ker (Oxford: Clarendon, 1900), 1:241.
5 T. S. Eliot, "Introduction to Ezra Pound," in *Selected Poems* by Ezra Pound (London: Faber & Gwyer, 1928), 15.
6 Ezra Pound, *Cathay* (London: Elkin Mathews, 1915), 7.
7 Pound, *Cathay*, 11.
8 Witter Bynner and Kiang Kang-Hu, *The Jade Mountain: A Chinese Anthology, Being Three Hundred Poems of the T'ang Dynasty, 618–906* (New York: Knopf, 1929), 62.
9 Barry Ahearn, "*Cathay*: What Sort of Translation?" in *Ezra Pound and China*, ed. Zhaoming Qian (Ann Arbor: University of Michigan Press, 2003), 43.
10 Ahearn, "What Sort of Translation?" in Qian, *Ezra Pound and China*, 46.
11 Christine Froula, "The Beauties of Mistranslation: On Pound's English after *Cathay*," in Qian, *Ezra Pound and China*, 50.
12 Froula, "Beauties of Mistranslation," in Qian, *Ezra Pound and China*, 51.
13 Qian Zhongshu, *A Collection of Qian Zhongshu's English Essays* (Beijing: Foreign Language Teaching and Research Press, 2006), 283.
14 Jonathan Stalling, *Poetics of Emptiness: Transformations of Asian Thought in American Poetry* (New York: Fordham University Press, 2001), 129.
15 See Zhaoming Qian, ed., *Ezra Pound's Chinese Friends: Stories in Letters* (Oxford: Oxford University Press, 2008), xv.
16 Ira B. Nadel, "Introduction: Understanding Pound," in *Cambridge Companion to Ezra Pound*, ed. Ira B. Nadel (Cambridge: Cambridge University Press, 1999), 17–18.
17 Hugh Kenner, *The Pound Era* (Berkeley: University of California Press, 1971), 197.
18 Zhaoming Qian, *Orientalism and Modernism: The Legacy of China in Pound and Williams* (Durham, N.C.: Duke University Press, 1995), 41.
19 Pound, *Cantos*, 494.
20 Ezra Pound, *Confucius: The Great Digest, the Unwobbling Pivot, the Analects* (New York: New Directions, 1951), 20.
21 Ming Xie, "Pound as Translator," in Nadel, *Cambridge Companion*, 204.
22 Xie, "Pound as Translator," in Nadel, *Cambridge Companion*, 211.
23 James Legge, *The Chinese Classics* (Shanghai: East China Normal University Press, 2011), 1:387.
24 Pound, *Confucius*, 105.
25 Wu Qiyao, *Ezra Pound and the Chinese Culture* (Shanghai: Shanghai Foreign Language and Education Press, 2006), 206.
26 Yang Lian, as quoted in Froula, "Beauties of Mistranslation," in Qian, *Ezra Pound and China*, 49.
27 Wai-Lim Yip, *Pound and the Eight Views of Xiao Xiang* (Taipei: Taiwan University Press, 2008), 132.

28 As quoted in John J. Nolde, *Ezra Pound and China* (Orono: University of Maine, 1996), 62.
29 As quoted in Nolde, *Ezra Pound and China*, 60.
30 Pound, *Cantos*, 245.
31 Zhaoming Qian, "Painting into Poetry: Pound's Seven Lakes Canto," in Qian, *Ezra Pound and China*, 91.
32 Pound, *Cantos*, 265.
33 Pound, *Confucius*, 209–10.
34 Legge, *Chinese Classics*, 1:174–75.
35 Pound, *Cantos*, 58.
36 Pound, *Cantos*, 495.
37 Pound, *Cantos*, 454.
38 Pound, *Cantos*, 802.
39 Pound, *Cantos*; as quoted in K. K. Ruthven, *Ezra Pound as Literary Critic* (London: Routledge, 2002), 133.
40 Pound, *Cantos*, 435. The "process" is Pound's translation of Dao or Way, the other translation of it by him is "footprints." And this process is meant to refer not to the Dao in Daoism but rather to the Way in Confucianism.

10. WANG: THE POWER OF POWERLESSNESS

1 XLIII, 98, 99.
2 Chapter 1, "Free and Easy Wandering."
3 Maurice Blanchot, *Political Writing, 1953–1993*, trans. Zakir Paul (New York: Fordham University Press, 2010), 88–89.
4 *Han Feizi* 45:2. See *Han Feizi quanyi*, ed. and annotated by Zhang Jue (Guiyang: Guizhou Renmin Chubanshe, 1992), 947.
5 *Han Feizi* 51:5. See *Han Feizi quanyi*, 1095.
6 *Han Feizi* 51:5. See *Han Feizi quanyi*, 1095.
7 Sima Qian, "Chapter 63: Laozi Hanfei liezhuan disan," in *Shiji* (Beijing: Zhonghua Shuju, 1999), 1713.
8 Sima, "Chapter 63," 1704.
9 "After the sixth year of the Jianyuan of Emperor Wu of Han (135 BC), Confucianism would gradually become the center of Chinese intellectual life, and would permeate common people's mind and their everyday life." Ge Zhaoguang, *Zhongguo sixiangshi* [An Intellectual History of China] (Shanghai: Fudan University Press, 2010), 270.
10 See Li Zehou, *Mei de licheng* [The Path of Beauty] (Beijing: Wenwu Chubanshe, 1982), 49. Mou Zhongjian, "A General Survey of Philosophical Daoism," in *Daojiao tonglun—jianlun Daojia xueshuo* [A Comprehensive Research on Religious and Philosophical Daoism], ed. Mou Zhongjian et al. (Jinan: Qilu Chubanshe, 1991), 100.
11 See "On Contradiction," in *Selected Works of Mao Tse-tung*, 1937, http://www.marxists.org/reference/archive/mao/selected-works/volume-1/mswv1_17.htm.
12 Mou, "General Survey," in Mou et al., *Daojiao tongiun*, 92.
13 Ge, *Zhongguo sixiangshi*, 234, 252.

14 See Liu Xiaofeng, *Zhengjiu yu xiaoyao* [Salvation and Wandering] (Shanghai: Shanghai Sanlian Chubanshe, 2001).

15 Michel Foucault, *The Thought from Outside*, trans. Brian Massumi (New York: Zone Books, 1987).

16 Thomas Carl Wall, *Radical Passivity: Levinas, Blanchot, and Agamben* (Albany: State University of New York Press, 1999).

17 The English translation is from *Tao Te Ching*, trans. D. C. Lau (Hong Kong: Chinese University Press, 2001).

18 Wing-tsit Chan, *A Source Book in Chinese Philosophy* (Princeton, N.J.: Princeton University Press, 1963), 136.

19 Edward Slingerland, "Effortless Action: The Chinese Spiritual Ideal of Wu-wei," *Journal of the American Academy of Religion* 68, no. 2 (2000): 302.

20 Tzvetan Todorov, "Reflections on Literature in Contemporary France," *New Literary History* 10, no. 3 (1979): 514.

21 Maurice Blanchot, *The Infinite Conversation*, trans. Susan Hanson (Minneapolis: University of Minnesota Press, 1993), 6.

22 Roland Barthes, "Lecture in Inauguration of the Chair of Literary Semiology,, Collège de France, January 7, 1977," trans. Richard Howard, *October* 8 (1977): 5.

23 Lao Tzu, *Tao Te Ching*, trans. D.C. Lau (Hong Kong: Chinese University Press, 2001).

24 See Georges Bataille, *The Unfinished System of Nonknowledge*, trans. Michelle Kendall and Stuart Kendall (Minneapolis: University of Minnesota Press, 2001); Michel Foucault, *Maurice Blanchot: The Thought from Outside*, trans. Brian Massumi (New York: Zone Books, 1987).

25 Alexandre Kojève, *Introduction to the Reading of Hegel* (Ithaca, N.Y.: Cornell University Press, 1969), 4.

26 Blanchot, *Infinite Conversation*, 205.

27 Liu Xiaogan, "Laozi zhi ziran yu wuwei gainian xinquan" [A New Interpretation of Ziran and Wuwei in *Laozi*], *Zhongguo shehui kexue* [Social Sciences in China] 6 (1996): 143.

28 Barthes, "Lecture in Inauguration," 4.

29 See *Zhuangzi jinzhu jinyi*, rev. ed., ed. and annotated by Chen Guying (Beijing: Shangwu Yinshuguan, 2014), 20.

30 Chen, *Zhuangzi jinzhu jinyi*, 43. The English translation is from *The Complete Works of Chuang Tzu*, trans. Burton Watson (New York: Comlumbia University Press, 1968), 35–36.

31 Chen, *Zhuangzi jinzhu jinyi*, 43.

32 *The Tao Teh King, or The Tao and Its Characteristics* [ebook], trans. James Legge, ch. 1, para. 1, Project Gutenberg, http://www.gutenberg.org/ebooks/216, accessed November 18, 2014.

33 Chen, *Zhuangzi jinzhu jinyi*, 37–38. The English translation is from *Complete Works of Chuang Tzu*, 31–32.

11. YANG: WHAT IS LOST IN THE CHINESE TRANSLATIONS?

1 William Shakespeare, *A Midsummer's Night's Dream*, Act III, Scene I, in *The Complete Works of William Shakespeare* (Hertfordshire, U.K.: Wordsworth Editions, 1996), 288.

2 In Chinese, it was translated as "changed a form" or "changed into another form." See William Shakespeare, *A Midsummer Night's Dream*, in *The New Complete Works of William Shakespeare*, ed. and trans. Fang Ping (Shijiazhuang: Hebei Education Press, 2000), 2:65–66.

3 Nevill Coghill, "The Basis of Shakespearean Comedy: A Study in Medieval Affinities," *Essays and Studies* 3 (1950): 1–28.

4 Barbara K. Lewalski, "Allegory in *The Merchant of Venice*," in *Shakespeare's Christian Dimension: An Anthology of Commentary*, ed. Roy Battenhouse (Bloomington: Indiana University Press, 1994), 79.

5 Nevill Coghill, "The Basis of Shakespearian Comedy," in Battenhouse, *Shakespeare's Christian Dimension*, 29.

6 Coghill, "Basis of Shakespearian Comedy," in Battenhouse, *Shakespeare's Christian Dimension*,30–31.

7 Roy Battenhouse, "The Merchant of Venice: Comment and Bibliography," in Battenhouse, *Shakespeare's Christian Dimension*, 68.

8 John R. Cooper, "Shylock's Humanity," in Battenhouse, *Shakespeare's Christian Dimension*, 84–85.

9 We have to point out that the famous Chinese translator Zhu Shenghao spent almost all of his adult life translating Shakespeare's works (from 1935 until 1944 when he died at age 32 of an illness). Another famous writer and translator Liang Shiqiu finished the translation of *The Complete Works of Shakespeare* from 1936 to 1969. In 2000 Fang Ping edited the new translation of the complete works of Shakespeare, in which he himself translated *The Merchant of Venice*.

10 Laura M. White's translation was categorized as "novel" when it was published in *Nü Duo bao*. The quotation here can be found in *Nü Duo bao*, September 1914–November 1915, collected by Shanghai Library.

11 Shakespeare, *Merchant of Venice*, Act I, Scene I. The original words are: "Your mind is tossing on the ocean, / There where your argosies with portly sail, / Like signiors and rich burghers on the flood, / Or, as it were, the pageants of the sea, / Do overpeer the petty traffickers, / That curtsy to them, do them reverence, / As they fly by them with their woven wings."

12 Shakespeare, *Complete Works*, 389.

13 Shakespeare, *Merchant of Venice*, in *New Complete Works*, 393.

15 Shakespeare, *Complete Works*, 388.

16 Shakespeare, *Complete Works*, 389.

17 Shakespeare, *Complete Works*, 402.

18 Shakespeare, *Complete Works*, 392.

19 Shakespeare, *Complete Works*, 411.

20 Shakespeare, *Complete Works*, 390.

21 Act IV; Shakespeare, *Complete Works*, 402–3.

22 Shakespeare, *Merchant of Venice*, in Fang, *New Complete Works*, 2:239.

23 Lewalski, "Allegory," in Battenhouse, *Shakespeare's Christian Dimension*, 78.
24 Shakespeare, *Complete Works*, 406.
25 Act IV, Scene I. Shakespeare, *Complete Works*, 410.
26 Act IV, Scene I. Shakespeare, *Complete Works*, 405.
27 Shakespeare, *Complete Works*, 410.
28 Act III, Scene II. Shakespeare, *Complete Works*, 410.
29 Shakespeare, *Merchant of Venice*, in Fang, *New Complete Works*, 271–72.
30 Georg Hegel, *Aesthetics*, vol. 3, trans. Zhu Guangqian (Beijing: Commercial Press, 1979), 331–34.
31 Coghill, "Basis of Shakespearian Comedy," in Battenhouse, *Shakespeare's Christian Dimension*, 27–29.
32 Lin Shu, "Preface to *Yin bian yan yu*," in Charles Lamb and Mary Lamb, *Yin bian xu yu* [Tales from Shakespeare], trans. Lin Shu and Wei Yi (Beijing: Commercial Press, 1981).
33 John Dryden, "An Essay of Dramatic Poesy," in *Literary Criticism: Plato to Dryden*, ed. Allan H. Gilbert (Detroit: Wayne State University Press, 1962), 639.

12. HASS: TRANSLATION AS TRANS-LITERAL

1 Plato, *Timaeus*, 50e, trans. Donald J. Zeyl, in *Plato: Complete Works*, ed. John M. Cooper (Indianapolis: Hackett, 1997), 1253 (emphasis added).
2 That this term takes multiple forms—and there are others (contronym, antagonym, self-antonym, antilogy, Janus word, enantiodrome)—already shows us the paradoxical nature of this term, which harbors synonyms and antonyms simultaneously within itself as homograph.
3 The OED claims this introduction occurs around 1775: "*bore* [as a past participle] (common in Addison, Swift, Thomson) was abandoned, *borne* was reinstated, and now used as the ordinary form, and *born* was restricted to a specific sense. Thus, *borne* is now the only pa. pple., active or passive, in senses 1–42 (he has *borne* a burden, the tree has *borne* fruit, the testimony *borne* by him); it is also used in sense 43 [giving birth to] in the active always, and in the passive with *by* and name of the mother, that is when it has the literal sense of 'brought forth.' *Born* is used only in sense 43, and there only in the passive, when not followed by *by* and the mother; it has rather a neuter signification = 'come into existence, sprung' without explicit reference to maternal action; hence it is the form used adjectively, and figuratively. Cf. 'She had *borne* several children, the children *borne* to him by this woman, *born* of the Virgin Mary, *born* in a stable, her first-*born* son, a lady *born*, new-*born* zeal, a flower *born* to blush unseen.'" http://www.oed.com.ezproxy.stir.ac.uk/view/Entry/16543?rskey=civgJo&result=7&isAdvanced=false#eid25253390, accessed July 18, 2014. Is it merely by coincidence that this period is precisely the period where, in philosophy, a radical shift was taking place in how we perceive the nature of knowledge and ontology (and the knowledge of ontology), and how they are born(e)? Jaspers writes, "The Kantian philosophy was born in the years from 1766 to 1781 (when the *Critique of Pure Reason* appeared). It was then [in that period] that he [Kant] published virtually nothing." Karl Jaspers,

Kant, trans. Ralph Manheim, ed. Hannah Arendt (New York: Harcourt Brace, 1962), 12.

4 Walter Benjamin, "The Task of the Translator," in *Illuminations*, ed. H. Arendt, trans. H. Zohn (New York: Schocken Books, 1968).

5 This is a point Paul de Man, among others, singles out in his interpretation of Benjamin's essay: "Conclusions: Walter Benjamin's 'The Task of the Translator,'" in *The Resistance to Theory* (Manchester: Manchester University Press, 1986), 73–105, 80.

6 The idea of an original "movement" Benjamin had introduced in an earlier essay: "On Language as Such and on the Language of Man," in *Reflections: Essays, Aphorisms Autobiographical Writings*, trans. Edmund Jephcott (New York: Harcourt Brace Jovanovich, 1978), 314–32, 332.

7 Benjamin, "On Language as Such," 315. More precisely, Benjamin had written: "The view that the mental essence of a thing consists precisely in its language—this view, taken as a hypothesis, is the great abyss into which all linguistic theory threatens to fall, and to survive precisely suspended over this abyss is its task." (*Die Ansicht, daß das geistige Wesen eines Dinges eben in seiner Sprache besteht, diese Ansicht als Hypothesis verstanden, is der große Abgrund, dem alle Sprachtheorie zu fallen droht, und über, gerade über ihm sich schwebend zu erhalten ist ihre Aufgabe.*) "Über Sprache überhaupt und über die Sprache des Menschen," in *Gesammelte Schriften*, vol. II-1 (Frankfurt am Main: Suhrkamp, 1977), 141.

8 William Franke, "Benjamin," in *On What Cannot Be Said*, vol. 2, *Modern and Contemporary Transformations*, ed. William Franke (Notre Dame: University of Notre Dame, 2007), 123.

9 Benjamin, "Task of the Translator," 80.

10 Benjamin, "Task of the Translator," 82.

11 Derrida understood this early on: the textual gap that figured in the early chapter "Tympan" in his 1972 *Marges de la philosophie* (Eng.: *Margins of Philosophy*, trans. Alan Bass [New York: Harvester Wheatsheaf, 1982]), which was but a prelude to the more radical, more central, gap in his 1974 tour de force on Hegel, *Glas* (trans. John P. Leavey Jr. and Richard Rand [Lincoln: University of Nebraska Press, 1986]). See Andrew W. Hass, *Hegel and the Art of Negation* (London: I. B. Tauris, 2014), 97–112.

12 Benjamin, "On Language as Such," 314, 317, 321–23.

13 See especially Martin Heidegger, *Poetry, Language, Thought*, trans. Albert Hofstadter (New York: Harper & Row, 1971).

14 E.g., "Translation is so far removed from being the sterile equation of two dead languages that of all literary forms it is the one charged with the special mission of watching over the maturing process of the original language and the birth pangs of its own." Benjamin, "Task of the Translator," 74. Or, "Thus translation, ironically, transplants the original into a more definitive linguistic realm since it can no longer be displaced by a secondary rendering. The original can only be raised there anew" (76).

15 As referenced by Lothar Ledderose, "Chinese Influence on European Art, Sixteenth to Eighteenth Centuries," in *China and Europe: Images and Influences in*

Sixteenth to Eighteenth Centuries, ed. Thomas H. C. Lee (Hong Kong: Chinese University of Hong Kong, 1991), 228.

16 See, e.g., Michael Sullivan, *The Meeting of Eastern and Western Art* (Berkeley: University of California Press, 1989).

17 The standard reference here remains Susan Bush, *The Chinese Literati on Painting: Su Shih (1037–1101) to Tung Ch'i-ch'ang (1555–1636)* (Cambridge, Mass.: Harvard University Press, 1971; repr., Hong Kong: Hong Kong University Press, 2013).

18 Sherman E. Lee, *A History of Far Eastern Art*, rev. ed. (Englewood Cliffs, N.J.: Prentice Hall, 1973), 254. Cf. James Cahill, "The Six Laws and How to Read Them," *Ars Orientalis* 4 (1961): 132–63.

19 See, e.g., Albert C. Barnes and Violette de Mazia, *The Art of Henri Mattisse* (Merion, Pa.: Barnes Foundation, 1933), 64–66.

20 *Kunst gibt nicht das Sichtbare wieder, sondern macht sichtbar*, from "Schöpferische Konfession" (orig. 1920), in *Kunst-Lehre* (Leipzig: Reclam, 1987), 60. Quoted by Sullivan, *Meeting of Eastern and Western Art*, 259, with a slightly different translation: "Art does not render the visible, rather it makes visible." An even more simplified form is Daniel W. Smith's translation of Gilles Deleuze's use of the quote in *Francis Bacon: The Logic of Sensation* (London: Continuum, 2003): "Not to render the visible, but to render visible," which Deleuze paraphrases as, "In art, and in painting as in music, it is not a matter of reproducing or inventing forms, but of capturing forces" (56).

21 Sullivan, *Meeting of Eastern and Western Art*, 259.

22 Friedrich Nietzsche, "On Truth and Lies in a Nonmoral Sense," in *Philosophy and Truth: Selections from Nietzsche's Notebooks of the Early 1870's*, ed. and trans. Daniel Breazeale (Amherst, N.Y.: Humanity Books, 1979), 84.

23 Nietzsche, "On Truth and Lies," 92.

24 See, e.g., James McFarland, *Constellations: Friedrich Nietzsche and Walter Benjamin in the Now-time of History* (New York: Fordham University Press, 2013). Of Benjamin's understanding of the discipline of philology, McFarland writes, "To imagine that the relative permanence of an enduring artwork—its material content—is genuinely eternal is to succumb to mythic duplicity. It is to imagine that philology grants direct access to truth. But philology grants direct access merely to the *claim* of permanence, and truth emerges only when that claim is recognised for what it is: deceptive appearance" (74).

25 Benjamin, "On Language as Such," 325.

26 As translated by Stephen Addiss and Stanley Lombardo: Lao Tzu, *Tao Te Ching* (Indianapolis: Hackett, 1993), §1. This is a significant volume, since it is accompanied by Stephen Addiss' bold ink paintings throughout. James Legge translates the opening line as "The *Tao* that can be trodden is not the enduring and unchanging *Tao*." Legge, *Sacred Books of the East*, vol. 39 (1891). Paul Carus famously translates the "Tao" as "reason," magnifying the divide between Eastern and Western conceptual traditions: "The reason that can be reasoned is not eternal Reason." *The Tao Te Ching*, trans. Paul Carus (London: Rider, 1913; rev. ed., 1999), §1, p. 30.

27 Carus, *Tao Te Ching*, §1, p. 30.

28 "TAO's presence in this world / Is like valley streams / Flowing into rivers and seas." Addiss and Lombardo, *Tao Te Ching*, §32.

29 Addiss and Lombardo, *Tao Te Ching*, §30.

30 This, at least, is Hegel's influential idea: "It is an advantage when a language possesses an abundance of logical expressions, that is, specific and separate expressions for the thought determinations themselves; many prepositions and articles denote relationships based on thought; the Chinese language is supposed not to have developed to this stage or only to an inadequate manner." Preface to the 2nd ed. of *Science of Logic*, trans. A. V. Miller (Amherst, N.Y.: Humanity Books, 1969), 32. Derrida, of course, will challenge this deeply held bias.

31 I am indebted to the Metropolitan Museum of Art in New York for curating an exhibition titled "Ink Art: Past as Present in Contemporary China" (December 11, 2013–April 6, 2014), in which I encountered Gu's work, and other Chinese artists featured below, for the first time.

32 Wenda Gu, interview with Melissa Chu, January 4, 2002, New York, as transcribed at http://wendagu.com/publications/wenda-gu-interiews/melissa-chu.html.

33 Figs. 1, 2, 5, 6, 7, 8, and 9 are the author's photographs.

34 Maxwell K. Hearn, ed., *Ink Art: Past as Present in Contemporary China* (New York: Metropolitan Museum of Art, 2013), 56.

35 Hearn, *Ink Art*.

36 Deleuze, *Francis Bacon*, 62–63.

37 Interview with Wenda Gu, November 9, 2009, Brooklyn, New York, for the Asia Art Archive at http://www.china1980s.org/en/interview_detail.aspx?interview_id=39; as transcribed in Hearn, *Ink Art*, 40.

38 Hearn, *Ink Art*, 40.

39 Interview with Wenda Gu for Asia Art Archive.

40 Fig. 12.4, *Christ of St. John on the Cross*, by Salvador Dalí, is on display at the Kelvingrove Art Gallery and Museum, Glasgow. Photograph by Howard Stanbury Photography, stanbury.org.

41 Interview with Wenda Gu for Asia Art Archive.

42 Interview with Wenda Gu for Asia Art Archive.

43 Deleuze, *Francis Bacon*, 34. "Sensation has one face turned toward the subject (the nervous system, vital movement, 'instinct,' 'temperament' . . .) and one face turned toward the object (the 'fact,' the place, the event). Or rather, it has no faces at all, it is both things indissolubly, it is Being-in-the-World, as the phenomenologists say: at one and the same time I *become* in the sensation and something *happens* through the sensation, one through the other, one in the other" (34–35).

44 Hearn, *Ink Art*, 45. The original title for the installation was *Mirror to Analyze the World: The Century's Final Volume*, a "last word" on the state of affairs in post-Revolution China (45).

45 That Bing's 2010 Phoenix Project, consisting of two large exotic birds built from construction site material and debris, has been transplanted into the nave of the Cathedral of St. John the Divine in New York (America's largest cathedral) suggests that whatever political message one may draw from Bing's work, spiritual dimensions are ever-present.

46 The art or manner of meaning, or the "mode of intention." Benjamin, "Task of the Translator," 74. See also S. Brent Plate, *Walter Benjamin, Religion, and Aesthetics: Rethinking Religion through the Arts* (New York: Routledge, 2005).

47 Hearn, *Ink Art*, 52.

48 Jean-Luc Nancy, *Hegel: The Restlessness of the Negative*, trans. Jason Smith and Steven Miller (Minneapolis: University of Minnesota Press, 2002), 50. See the entire chapter "Sense," 46–54.

49 Benjamin, "Task of the Translator," 71.

50 Cf. Jacques Derrida, "Les Tour des Babel," trans. Joseph F. Graham, as reprinted in *Acts of Religion*, ed. Gil Anidjar (New York: Routledge, 2002), where, in the context of a reading of Benjamin's translation essay, Derrida writes, "The work does not simply live longer, it lives more and better, beyond the means of its author" (114).

CONTRIBUTORS

GENG Youzhuang is a professor in the School of Liberal Arts, Renmin University of China. His most recent book is *Listening: The Perception Paradigm in the Post-metaphysical Era* (Peking University Press, 2013).

Trevor Hart is a professor of divinity at St. Andrews University, Scotland, and a parish priest in the Scottish Episcopal Church. His most recent book is *Between the Image and the Word* (2013).

Andrew W. Hass is a reader in religious studies at the University of Stirling, Scotland. He received his Ph.D. in literature and theology from the University of Glasgow. His most recent books are *Hegel and the Art of Negation* (2013) and *Auden's O: The Loss of One's Sovereignty in the Making of Nothing* (2014).

David Jasper is a professor of literature and theology at the University of Glasgow and a distinguished overseas professor at Renmin University of China. He holds degrees from the universities of Cambridge, Oxford, and Durham, and an honorary doctorate from the University of Uppsala, Sweden. His most recent books include *The Sacred Desert* (2004), *The Sacred Body* (2009), and *The Sacred Community* (2012).

Elisabeth Jay is a professor emerita at Oxford Brookes University. She has published widely on nineteenth-century British literature. Her other major interest is reflected in her coeditorship of the *Oxford Handbook of English Literature and Theology* (2009).

David Lyle Jeffrey is a distinguished professor of literature and the humanities at Baylor University and guest professor at Peking University. Among his recent publications are a theological commentary on Luke (2012) and an edited collection, *The King James Bible and the World It Made* (2011).

John T. P. LAI is an associate professor in the Department of Cultural and Religious Studies, Chinese University of Hong Kong. His research and teaching revolve around the interdisciplinary study of religion, literature, and translation. He has published two monographs, *Negotiating Religious Gaps: The Enterprise of Translating Christian Tracts by Protestant Missionaries in Nineteenth-Century China* (2012) and *The Afterlife of a Classic: A Critical Study of the Late-Qing Chinese Translations of* The Pilgrim's Progress (in Chinese) (2012).

B. H. McLean is a professor of New Testament language and literature at Knox College, University of Toronto. His recent publications include *Biblical Interpretation and Philosophical Hermeneutics.*

WANG Hai is a lecturer in the School of Liberal Arts, Renmin University of China. His research and teaching mainly include continental thought, Western literary theory, Taoism, and interdisciplinary study of theology and literature. His most recent book, published in Chinese, is *Action: From the Praxis of Body to the* Wu-wei *of Literature* (Peking University Press, 2013).

YANG Huilin is a professor of comparative literature and religious studies at the School of Liberal Arts, Renmin University of China. His most recent book is *China, Christianity, and the Question of Culture* (Baylor University Press, 2014).

ZHAO Jing was recently awarded his doctoral degree at Renmin University of China and is now a postdoctoral scholar at the University of Chicago. He recently spent a year researching at Sapienza University of Rome. His most recent book, published in Chinese, is *Animality: The Origin of Human Nature between Tradition and Modernity* (Peking University Press, 2013).

Eric Ziolkowski is the Helen H. P. Manson Professor of Bible at Lafayette College, Easton, Pennsylvania. His recent publications include the editorship of *Literature, Religion and East/West Comparison: Essays in Honor of Anthony C. Yu* (2005) and the monograph *The Literary Kierkegaard* (2011).

CREDITS

Chapter 3: "Pilgrimage to Heaven" was previously published as "Translating Buddhism: Timothy Richard's Christian Interpretation of *The Journey to the West*," *Cowrie: A Journal of Comparative Literature and Culture* 12, no. 2 (2014): 126–54, and is included by permission of Shanghai Normal University.

Chapter 5: The English translation, "A Study on the 'Preface' and 'Introduction' to James Legge's *Texts of Taoism*" is included by permission of Renmin University. This chapter was originally published in *Journal for the Study of Christian Culture* 26 (2011): 50–81.

Chapter 6: The transcription of the text of Sophia Martin's *Xunnü sanzijing* (Three-character classics for the instruction of girls) (Singapore, 1831) is included with the permission of the the Harvard-Yenching Library. The transcription of Walter Medhurst's *Sanzi jing* (Three-character classic) is included with the permission of the National Library of Australia.

Chapter 8: "Two Nineteenth-Century English Translations of *The Travels of Fa-Hsien (399–414 AD)*: An Episode in the Translation of China in England" was previously published as "The Translation of China in England: Two 19th-Century English Translations of the *Travels of*

Fa-Hsien (399–414 AD)," *Literature and Theology* 28, no. 2 (2014): 186–200, and is included by permission of Oxford University Press.

Chapter 11: Adapted from Yang Huilin, "Addition and Subtraction in the Trajectory of the Classics: A Case Study of the Chinese Translation of *The Merchant of Venice*," *Journal for the Study of Christian Culture* 32 (2014): 10–28, and is included by permission of Renmin University. It has also been published as "Christian Implication and Non-Christian Translation: A Case Study of *The Merchant of Venice* in the Chinese Context," *Studies in Chinese Religions* 1, no. 1 (2015): 82–90.

INDEX